Production

Versus

Plunder

By Paul Rosenberg

2nd Edition

Copyright Notice:

Cover art by Cecilia Castillo

With gratitude to

Hannah Arendt, Carroll Quigley and Alvin Toffler

for the illumination they provided.

Table of Contents

Preface To The 2nd Edition

The first edition of *Production Versus Plunder* came into being because history never made sense to me. As a schoolboy in the 1960s and 1970s, I could understand how math worked; I could verify it, test it and use it. It was the same with science: I might have to work at it, but once I did, I could understand how the various materials and forces interacted; it made sense.

History, however, was a jumble of disconnected facts and quasi-theories. When I left school, I intended on ignoring it, but somehow it remained with me and weighed upon me. And so for decades I read all sorts of history books (good ones, bad ones, wildly misguided ones), trying to make sense of the subject. I spent a lot of time in museums and I absorbed a lot of data, but I still had no depth of understanding.

Finally, in the autumn of 2008, I had my breakthrough. The pieces finally came together and most of this book was written, at white heat, over a three week period.

For the past nine years I've been very fortunate to have spent a large portion of my time studying and engaging in analysis. As a result, I've produced nearly 90 issues of *Free-Man's Perspective* as well as *The Breaking Dawn.* It's time for a revision of *Production Versus Plunder.*

The difficulty I faced in undertaking this revision was whether or not I should expand the book; after all, I've produced several hundred pages of carefully researched history over the past nine years, and I think that work is important. Nonetheless, I decided to keep *Production Versus Plunder* at about its initial length. I think it's more valuable as an overview than as much more detailed book.

That said, I've added a number of footnotes that point to specific issues of *Free-Man's Perspective* (which I've abbreviated as "FMP"). For those areas where you'd like in-depth information, you'll be able to find it in those issues.

As I did in the preface to the first edition, I will add here that this book does not attempt to cover the history of the entire world. Rather, it covers the West, from the ice age to the current day.

I will also repeat that I never intended this book to make dramatic claims. For example, it was a surprise to me when I first understood that Athens, rather than creating the Golden Age of the Greeks, ruined it. But the truth is what it is, and I have done my best to express it clearly.

I was likewise surprised by the great conclusion of the second half of this book: That Western Civilization is facing a major crisis – that it will either fail or reformulate itself into something better. Having been convinced of this, my purpose in publishing this book became clear: To clarify the historical record, thereby promoting a renewal of Western Civilization.

Paul Rosenberg

July, 2017

1

Who Are We?

What is man, that thou art mindful of him? and the son of man, that thou visitest him? For thou hast made him a little lower than the angels, and hast crowned him with glory and honor.
-- Psalms 8:4-5

It is an arrogance of modern man to think himself superior to his dim-witted and unimaginative ancestors. He is not. We are not. There have been no significant changes to the human species in 30,000 years, and perhaps not in 100,000 years. Our images of grunting cavemen are self-flattering nonsense. We are them; they were us.

Yes, our current style of living is far more advanced than that of our distant ancestors, but only because they – slowly and with great difficulty – were able to create our current mode of living, and to pass it down successfully to us. Hundreds of generations of men and women labored and suffered to bring us to where we are now. It wasn't magic and it was't because we deserved it; it was wholly their benefaction. They lived in dark times, fighting toward whatever bits of light they could find – opposed by other men nearly the entire time – and they scratched through enough thorns, weeds and underbrush to bring humanity to where we now find ourselves. We have no right to insult them and devalue them; it is cheap, and it is false.

An Ancient Superiority

Though we presently lead far more advanced lives than any of the ancients, there is one aspect of ancient existence that was superior to ours, and that is self-image. The core of this is captured in one of our older texts, the book of Genesis. A passage in the second chapter reads:

> The man gave names to all cattle, and to the birds of
> the air, and to every beast of the field; but among them
> there was not found a helper suitable for him.

This passage points out the most obvious conclusion of men who live in direct contact with nature: That they stand apart from it.

A great number of contemporary men, insulated from the world of nature, suffer with highly-cultivated senses of inferiority and self-doubt. Our early ancestors bore fewer of these burdens. Early man was immersed in nature, and he knew there was absolutely nothing in nature that was his equal. Our ancestors knew for certain that they were superior to the animals. Some of the beasts were friendly enough, some were useful and some were dangerous, but none was remotely man's equal.

This acknowledgement of superiority is largely a lost trait, and when it does appear, it is generally in a corrupted form, featuring a thirst for domination. This original form of acknowledged superiority seems to have been universal (living in daily contact with nature, it couldn't be avoided) and it seems not to have been destructive. In fact, it probably empowered a good deal of human progress.

The Impenetrable Past

For the last half-million years, our planet has experienced a string of at least four ice ages. In each of them, a large portion of the earth has been covered with ice and snow, and the rest of the planet was colder and dryer than it is now. And in each case, the surface of the earth was substantially changed, wiping out most evidence of human life before the ice came. We simply don't know what happened before the end of the last ice age in any detail. We don't know what humans built and we know little of how they lived.

It has been suggested[1] that evolution and migrations through these four ice ages separated the races of men. This may well be true, but the theory has little support from evidence at the current time, and, given that glaciers, runoff and hundreds of millennia are not kind to artifacts, not much may be forthcoming.

The surprising thing about the ice ages is that they were very, very long. Warm periods, such as the one we now live in, are the exception. Most of the time, earth is half-frozen[2]. Look at the following graph of temperatures and ice volume and consider that the world is in its current state only at the peaks

---

[1] See *The Evolution of Civilizations*, by Carroll Quigley.

[2] At the height of the last ice age, what are now Indianapolis and St. Louis were covered with glaciers.

on the graph. These warm peaks, called "interglacials" have generally lasted in the range of 10,000-12,000 years, meaning that we may be approaching the end of a warm period and closing in on a new – and very long – glacial period.

The last ice age on earth ended at about 9000 B.C. In the centuries surrounding that date, whatever humans that had survived the ice age began to spread out over the earth. We have little information on what these people did during the ice age. Since humans now and then are basically the same, we can imagine ourselves in such a situation and guess how they would have behaved, but evidence is lacking.

The traditional view of early man is that he lived, almost universally, as a hunter-gatherer, and while it is certain that many groups of humans lived that way (a few still do), that may not be a fair generalization. Some of this idea's popularity comes from the fact that it is a simple explanation and fits with our self-flattering opinion that we are different and better than our distant ancestors. It may be that men lived as hunter-gatherers (*foragers*, in more scientific terminology) for a hundred thousand years before they learned agriculture, but we are by no means certain of that – the ice age wiped out a lot of evidence.

Nonetheless, we do find evidence of foragers previous to the end of the ice age and we haven't yet found much evidence of agriculture. So, we'll stay with that model for now.

Human foragers generally organize themselves in small clan groups, in the range of 20-50 people. This is a functional type of grouping and has something of an instinctive base as well, since humans are very comfortable keeping fifty individuals clearly in mind, along with all of their abilities, needs and personal traits.

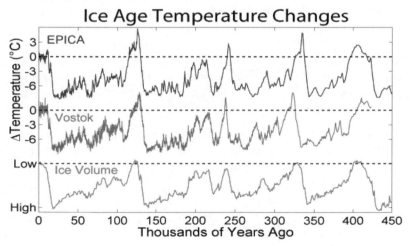

Courtesy Wikimedia Commons

Inside such groups, decisions are generally made by informal consent, and cooperation with other friendly groups form loose tribal associations. Such groups have also interacted violently with unfriendly clans. These were not mass wars as we know them, but they were violent and deadly, generally being fought with stone axes, arrows and spears.

The Minds of The Foragers

The foragers thought the same thoughts we would think, if we were in the same situation they found themselves in, and if we found ourselves with the same small knowledge base they had. These people concerned themselves with the same things humans always have: How to escape fear, pain, and sorrow; how to increase security, pleasure, and joy; how to realize their dreams of something better. Beyond this, they needed to find some way to make peace with the hard areas of life:

1. Sickness and death
2. Existence itself
3. Shame
4. Fear
5. Helplessness

These factors led to the first philosophies and religions. Because these people didn't have a great deal of knowledge, their philosophies would have included a lot of conjecture on things they couldn't explain. Having the faculty of imagination, they would have exercised it at some length, seeking clever answers to their questions. And, over time, the best and most entertaining of those imaginings turned into what we call myths.

These early religious myths tended to focus on imaginary beings and powers that lay behind nature. This could have begun in ways as modern as saying "The principle of the sun, which we do not yet understand," rather than saying "the Sun God," but the simplest ideas tend to be the ones that stick, and the Sun God would have displaced more scientific explanations.

Their Dispersion

There were very few humans on the planet at the end of the last ice age, and the available areas for living were as large as they are now. This meant that groups of humans were generally isolated from one another. This made the transfer of information slow.

The US Census Bureau produces a report called *Historical Estimates of World Population* (see figures below). According to this document, there were only about five million human beings on earth at the end of the last ice age. That is less than one thousandth of the current world population, spread over the same area. (And the earth is mostly empty space even now.) Imagine every human being on the earth wiped out, save only those in the city of Baghdad, and then scattering these survivors all over the earth. That was the condition at the end of the ice age. Humans were very few and widely scattered.

Aside from speech, which is not especially accurate over time, functional methods of transferring information barely existed. If you wanted information to last, you carved it into stone. So, not a lot of information was retained and shared.

YEAR	POPULATION (millions)
10,000 BC	5
8,000 BC	5
5,000 BC	8
4,000 BC	10
2,000 BC	27
1,000 BC	50
500 BC	100
200 AD	230
600 AD	200
1000 AD	300
1600 AD	500
1800 AD	1,000
2000 AD	5,000+

The result of an exceptionally low population density was not only that information traveled slowly, but that groups of humans were generally unopposed by other groups. So, once a group of humans found a way of life that worked for them, they could develop it with little exterior pressure. Bear in mind that the greatest obstacle for productive men has always been other men. That was much less the case at a time when there was almost no one else around. This allowed ideas to develop without what we might call "natural enemies."

The Invention of Cooperation and Harmony

It is not entirely natural for humans to get along. We tend to be more comfortable with those to whom we're most closely related and we've usually existed in conditions of scarcity, which has often-enough led to competition. Imagine two separate groups of foragers, attempting to gather food from the same forest: They would – based solely upon animal-level instincts – dispute whose food it was, which would lead to aggressive and perhaps violent behavior. In such conditions, human instincts are very similar to those of animals, and they push us to act as animals do – to defend, to attempt dominance, to claim status, and so on.

However, we are not mere animals, and we can override instinctive impulses. Specifically, we can imagine better ways of handling problems or remember how they were handled in the past – in ways that don't lead to injury and death, possibly in large numbers[3].

Most importantly, we can override our instincts. We can control them.

We have learned to recognize when impulses strike us and to restrain them before thoughtless actions are taken. We interrupt instinct and engage better, more rational courses of action. Our ancestors knew, just as we do, that envy, greed, fear, and impulsive actions can cause great harm. They learned to monitor their thoughts and to maintain harmony, against some of their instincts.

In other words, humans invented harmony – we were not born into it in some mythical past.

It's important to add, however, that not all humans chose cooperation as a primary way of life. A minority has always chosen to live at the expense of others. Franz Oppenheimer, in his book *The State*, explained it this way:

> There are two fundamentally opposed means whereby man, requiring sustenance, is impelled to obtain the necessary means for satisfying his desires. These are work and robbery, one's own labor and the forcible appropriation of the labor of others.

Oppenheimer missed a crucial factor is this – that appropriating the labor of others is better accomplished with trickery than with violence – but his principle stands. One may produce or one may plunder; aside from a few gray areas, these are the two modes of life that have always stood before humanity.

Three Groups Form

We have only partial information on how humans migrated at the end of the ice age, but one thing we do know is that three general groups formed in the greater Middle East. The figure below shows the general distribution of these groups. This particular distribution is from a later time, but it shows the same pattern.

---

[3] Killing unprotected humans is not particularly difficult. In ancient times it was generally accomplished with a stone ax or a mace. Almost any healthy post-adolescent can kill with a mace-blow to the head and even a non-lethal blow could kill in the days before antiseptics.

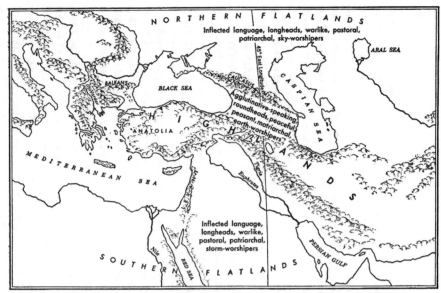

Inside the map:

NORTHERN FLATLANDS
Inflected language, longheads, warlike, pastoral, patriarchal, sky-worshipers

ARAL SEA

BLACK SEA

CAUCASUS

45° East Longitude

CASPIAN SEA

BALKANS

Agglutinative-speaking, roundheads, peasant, peaceful, matriarchal, earth-worshipers

ANATOLIA

HIGHLANDS

MEDITERRANEAN SEA

Euphrates

Inflected language, longheads, warlike, pastoral, patriarchal, storm-worshipers

SOUTHERN FLATLANDS

Nile

RED SEA

PERSIAN GULF

Sandwich distribution of peoples, languages, and cultures along 45th meridian East about 3000 B.C.

Courtesy Liberty Fund

Following the end of the ice age[4], there were several thousand years of quiet time: Not many humans and relatively little interaction between them. During such times, groups of humans tend to build specific characteristics. We tend to call these groups-with-characteristics "societies" or "cultures."

Over time, three early groups developed their own cultures – cultures that informed their ways not only of daily life, but of looking at the world. These groups produced distinct societal structures, including structures of cooperation and beliefs.

These three groups were of two primary types: Farmers and nomads.

Over time, different styles of living teach different lessons to men. In particular, farming tends more toward a cooperative model of thinking and living, while nomadic hunting and herding tend more to a warfare and domination model of living and thinking.

Farming is a modification of nature intended to reduce scarcity; that is, to intelligently produce. As a result, farmers generally learn to help and rely upon their neighbors. They build each other's barns, share tools, lend their expertise for repairing equipment, and so on. They also respect each other's property lines. Since farming involves human effort bring food out of the

---

[4] I am discussing the ice age as if it ended quickly, which is not true; the ice receded for several thousand years, then stopped receding at about 10,000 years before the present time. So, there is a certain amount of simplification built into this discourse.

ground, and since cooperation yields improved results in such a condition, there are long histories of mutual help and respect for property.

Herdsmen, on the other hand, often live in static environments. As a result, they tend to mistrust their neighbors and to hide information from them. When the nomadic herdsman finds good grazing land, he does not share that knowledge with another herdsman. If he finds a hidden water hole, he does not disclose the location. So, the overall balance is more toward *not* helping a neighbor.

What we see in these cases are two different sets of assumptions about the world. The farmers developed more of what economists call a *positive-sum* view of existence and the nomads developed more of a *zero-sum* understanding of existence.

Briefly, a *zero-sum* assumption is that there is a fixed pool of any specific good, and that in order for you to have more, someone else has to accept less. This is the essence of the common slogan, "there are only so many pieces of pie." If you want an extra slice, someone else will get one less. A *positive-sum* assumption, on the other hand, assumes that the pool of assets can be expanded. In other words, if there are not enough slices of pie for your liking, you can make a new pie.

The important thing about zero-sum and positive-sum assumptions is that they form mental patterns; analysis routines in our brains. Such routines form through repetition in human minds, and if not vetted, color wide areas of thought. People take these basic views of the world as givens: things they don't need to waste time examining. This built differences into the thoughts of the farmers and the nomads.[5]

> Young nomads were instructed to *take*, from a world of limited resources.
>
> Young farmers were instructed to use the world intelligently and to *create* food.

These early farmers, for the first time we know of, discovered a post-parasitic way of living on earth. They did not feed off of what already exists, as do parasites. Instead, they became actors in cooperation with the earth, and made it produce food for them.

Of course, animal husbandry does ride the line between the parasitic and the creative, but it was the farmers who crossed the line firmly and permanently.

---

[5] Again, I am simplifying. There were certainly individuals in each group that differed from the descriptions I am attaching to them. Furthermore, such characteristics among groups of humans are constantly varying. So, while I believe what I write here is accurate, it is only a general statement and certainly varied among individuals and sub-groups.

The Northern and Southern Nomads

The northern nomads lived in the flatlands above the Black and Caspian Seas, in what are now southwestern Russia, Ukraine, and western Kazakhstan. They tended to be taller and with longer heads. They were pastoral, war-like, patriarchal, and worshiped sky gods.

The southern nomads lived in the flatlands of Arabia. They tended to be slight-boned, had long heads, were pastoral, war-like, patriarchic, and worshipped storm gods.

It is difficult for modern westerners to understand the structure and incentives of such societies. Westerners expect cooperation in life. Most of the time, the store-keeper does not try to cheat us, we don't steal metal exposed on the sides of buildings, and so on. In short, we expect people to "play nice" because of the content of their character, not because they are forced to do so. We complain bitterly about the few criminals who do arise.

This assumption of cooperation within these groups was limited in its reach. We westerners derive (more or less) from farmers who presumed cooperation and creativity. These nomads assumed far more dominance and scarcity.

The nomadic culture featured a plunder model, placed on top of a clan model. At the base was the family clan. In these small groupings, there would have been a good deal of sharing and cooperative decision-making, but the final and large decisions would have been made by the senior male. And for these clans to form a larger group, a central dominator was required.

What these people saw as "normal" was a dominator in charge, with a clan structure below him. Each clan, of course, would have a protected place within that structure, along with certain privileges and allowances.

To change one of these structures, however, could result in hatreds that endured for centuries. When an outside group forcibly alters one of these societal hierarchies, the occupants live with tilted floors, so to speak, until the structure is righted.

The rigidity of this structure derives from the fact that it is a collection of clans, and the clans nearly always remain for centuries. Added to this, clans tend to constantly compare themselves with the other clans, and oppose any changes in status between them[6]. Because of these enduring bonds, the structure is not permitted to change. Thus, an altered hierarchy results in persistent humiliation.

Nikolay N. Kradin, in his paper, *Nomadism, Evolution and World-Systems: Pastoral Societies in Theories of Historical Development*, explains that the

---

[6] Again, this status consciousness is related to a zero-sum understanding of life. If what one wants is scarce, it must be grasped firmly, and re-taken if ever removed. A human with a positive-sum view of life might rather mourn the loss briefly, then go out to replace it.

nomadic empire is organized on the military-hierarchical principle, and survives by exploiting the nearby territories. He goes on to say:

> The most interesting and novel feature of the steppe empires was their dual structure. From outside they appeared to be despotic aggressive state-like societies because they were formed to extract surplus product from outside the steppe. But from within, the nomadic empires remained based on the tribal relations without the establishment of taxation and exploitation.

So, this structure is based upon clan relations at the base, and biased toward plunder in the overall.

The Central Farmers

The central farmers tended to be shorter, stocky, with round heads, short hair, no beards, and revered a fertility goddess. This group appeared in the highland area of what is traditionally Armenia, extending into what is now eastern Turkey[7]. Several sites date to 10,000 B.C., before the ice age had fully ended.

The most likely structure of their "society" would have been a decentralized farming structure, similar to later farming groups that functioned beyond the edges of state control. The natural clan group certainly would have formed some sort of base for these people, but since farming scatters and moves people across landscapes, this clan structure would have been dispersed[8], reducing its strength and effects.

It seems likely that these farming groups kept an older forager tradition to gather in much larger groups for a few weeks every year. At these gatherings, they would conduct ceremonies and festivals, make marriage arrangements and trade goods. A standing monolith and building, dated to approximately 8400 B.C. at Nevali Cori in western Armenia, may have been one of these ancient meeting places, located only three kilometers from the Euphrates river.

These gatherings would have been very much like the religious camp meetings of strict sects such as Methodists in the 18th and 19th Centuries or of various Pentecostal groups in more recent times. Obviously the pretext for such modern gatherings differs from ancient tribal meetings, but many aspects, such as ceremonies and marriage arrangements would have been almost the same. Again, these people were that same as us, only with less information. We should expect their behavior to resemble that of modern people.

---

[7] See FMP #73 and FMP #68.

[8] As we will examine in the next chapter, these farmers had not yet invented crop rotation, and were required to abandon their fields every several years and move to the next fertile area.

Male and Female Gods

As mentioned earlier, these early humans had a very limited knowledge of the forces that shaped the natural world. But they did have powerful minds and creative imaginations. So, they tried to imagine what made the world work, just as we would in the same situation. Over centuries, ideas such as these tend to shape themselves into forms that are easily repeated. This is no less a problem in our time than it was at the end of the ice age.

For example: Our common story of Adam and Eve's fall from paradise is supposedly based upon the Bible, but the ubiquitous form of this story – eating an apple – is nowhere to be found in the Bible. Yet the story is repeated endlessly, merely because it is easy to depict and because everyone else seems to do it. Precisely the same thing happened to the myths of the ancients.

The gods of the ancients tell us a great deal about the central assumptions they made about the world. The nomads, as mentioned above, saw the world as a place of scarcity and struggle against other men. They developed war gods and domination structures.

The term "patriarchal" is often used to describe such ideas in our times, and often wrongly in my opinion. The issue is not maleness per se, but dominance and submission. The domination/patriarch problem arises when a strong person (admittedly usually a male) "improves" himself by taking from others[9].

The farmers, on the other hand, developed female gods and cooperative cultures. Again, this is not because there is some inherently superiority in being female, but because the principles of creation and productivity – the opposites of scarcity – are embodied in females: their bodies literally bring forth new human beings.

For reasons that we will explain later, modern gods tend to be of the dominator type. For this reason, female gods are seen by some moderns as a dominator with a female face. This is not what female gods were to the earliest farmers. The female god was not a dominator, she was a *catalyst* - not striking from above, but *working with*. She was a magic embodiment of the creative/productive principle.

Inanna may have been the first goddess (she was certainly very early from our perspective) and the name itself indicates that it may have originated in the pre-Sumerian language of the Armenian farmers. She was, as mentioned above, the personification of the creative principle. Accordingly, her male consort was characterized as the force in the grain and as her priestly lover.

---

[9] It should also be noted that females tended to reward such behavior. Scarcity tends to create poor characteristics in all humans.

We'll close this chapter with some passages from Inanna's myth-poetry. In them you will notice the glorification of creation and production in many forms: The production of the female body, the production of the grain in the fields and the production of the herds. You will note the erotic aspects as well, which are odd and even troubling to many modern people, but were entirely sensible and laudable to the most-ancient farmers. After all, they were fundamental to the magical process of creation. Sex made them partners with the gods. It was glorious, not shameful.

> Last night as I, the Queen of Heaven, was shining bright,
> As I was shining bright and dancing,
> Singing praises at the coming of the night.

> He met me - He met me!
> My lord Dumuzi met me.
> He put his hand into my hand.
> He pressed his neck close against mine.
> My High Priest is ready for the holy loins.
> My lord Dumuzi is ready for the holy loins.
> The plants and herbs in his field are ripe.

> O Dumuzi! Your fullness is my delight!

> I bathed for the Shepherd Dumuzi,
> I perfumed my sides with ointment,
> I coated my mouth with sweet-smelling amber,
> I painted my eyes with kohl.

> He shaped my loins with his fair hands,
> The Shepherd Dumuzi filled my lap with cream and milk,
> He stroked my pubic hair,
> He watered my womb.
> He laid his hands on my holy vulva,
> He smoothed my black boat with cream,
> He quickened my narrow boat with milk,
> He caressed me on the bed.

> Now I will caress my high priest on the bed,
> I will caress the faithful shepherd Dumuzi,
> I will caress his loins,
> I will decree a sweet fate for him.

> As the farmer, let him make the fields fertile,
> As the shepherd, let him make the sheepfolds multiply,
> Under his reign let there be vegetation,
> Under his reign let there be rich grain.

> The King went with lifted head to the holy loins.
> He went with lifted head to the loins of Inanna.

He went to the Queen with lifted head.
He opened wide his arms to the Holy Priestess of Heaven....

2

Civilization Created & Overrun

Man was born free, and everywhere he is in chains.
– Jean-Jacques Rousseau

Throughout this book we will generally assume that cultures are the natural order of humanity; the refuge and training-place of humanity. We will do this because the mass of humanity has indeed organized itself in this way and because it is far more convenient for our purpose of analysis. Nonetheless, it is important to be clear about the fact that culture is not simply a good or preferable thing; culture is also limitation.

Once a man or woman conceives of themselves as "an Armenian," as "a Jew," or any other flavor of cultural identity, they introduce a specific pattern into their minds and accept it as "Me." That is an inherently limiting thing. We humans are massively adaptable and creative beings; to limit ourselves to being Armenian, Jewish, Irish, or whatever, is a stupid thing to do – it limits our thought processes and our creative output as beings.

Culture, per se, is not a good thing. It has value only to the extent that it's the least impractical among the options at hand.

So for the rest of this book, we will accept culture as a given, but it is important to understand that it is not something noble, pure and sacred. Cultural expectations are transgressions against a fully whole, healthy being. Granted, there have never been many humans whom we could characterize as healthy and whole, but were they to emerge, culture would be a formidable barrier to them. They would find crossing it a struggle and would justly condemn it as a false god.

From Armenia to Sumer

As mentioned in the last chapter, the first group of seriously productive human beings on earth were, as far as we know, farmers who emerged from the last ice age in the area of what is now Armenia.

Because they had no knowledge of crop rotation, they were forced to move from one area to the next every several years, after they had depleted the soil in their fields. This would have seemed normal and sensible to them, as it would have matched other aspects of nature, such as women being fertile for a limited number of years. It is thus no surprise that they accepted soil losing its fertility as normal. As a result, crop rotation would not have been sought and indeed was not discovered for a long time.

The Path From Armenia to Mesopotamia

This, however, was not considered especially problematic, since there was no shortage of land. The earth was all but empty; if you wanted new land, you could simply take any piece you wanted.

The map above shows some of the earliest settlements of these people, as they slowly moved away from Armenia, seeking fertile new fields. Note that they followed the Tigris river into what was much later called Sumer (also, mistakenly, Sumeria), an area often referred to as Mesopotamia and currently contained within the state of Iraq.

Becoming Stationary

As these farmers moved slowly across the face of the earth, they happened upon places where they could become stationary and not have to move every few years. These were the river valleys of the old world that flooded every year. (Scientifically termed *alluvials* or *flood plains*.) The group of farmers we are following found such a place in the Tigris-Euphrates valley. The valley flooded every year and a new layer of topsoil was deposited. Irrigation systems could be built to extend this flood effect over a large additional area. This allowed the farmers to stay in one place, build permanent houses and avoid the strain of moving every few years.

Carroll Quigley, in his *The Evolution of Civilizations*, explains this as follows:

> At the risk of considerable oversimplification, we might say that these earliest agriculturalists appeared in the hilly terrain of western Asia, probably not far from Armenia, about nine thousand years ago. Because they knew nothing about replenishing the fertility of the soil, they practiced "shifting cultivation," moving to new fields when yields declined in their old fields. In consequence, they expanded steadily, reaching Denmark and Britain in the west and China in the east before 2000 B.C., that is to say, within five thousand years. In the course of this movement they found, in various alluvial valleys, sites adapted to permanent large-scale settlement because, in such valleys, the annual flood replenished the fertility of the soil by depositing a layer of fertile sediment; and, accordingly, the need for "shifting cultivation" ended and the possibility of permanent, eventually urban settlement was offered. This possibility was realized in four alluvial valleys of the Old World, in Mesopotamia during the sixth millennium B.C., in the valley of the Nile shortly afterward, in the valley of the Indus river early in the fourth millennium B.C., and in the Huang Ho Valley of China late in the third millennium B.C.

Life in these Pre-Sumerian settlements followed a routine based upon the rivers. During the flood season (which lasted for months) the farmlands were partly or fully flooded by the rivers. During this season, the farmers built, maintained and extended irrigation canals to bring water to adjacent areas. Animals were moved away from the flood zones to prevent them from drowning. As the waters receded, seeds were sown and crops were cultivated. Finally came the dry season when crops were harvested and stored. Then, the cycle repeated.

It would be difficult to over-state the value to these early farmers of being able to remain stationary. Food was plentiful, goods could be accumulated, and large communities could be formed. This led to immense variety and specialization. Music appeared in variety and with many new instruments. Metallurgy developed, basic engineering began, and much, much more. It was the birth of man's intellectual life. Prior to this moment, men and women had the same creative capacities, but their creations never left their small groups. Now, they inspired each other. Humans played off one another, helped one another and corrected one another in very specific ways. For example, if you had the fortune to be born with unusual musical talent, the odds of finding a kindred soul among forty or fifty others would be fairly low. But finding someone of complimentary talents among a thousand was possible and even likely. And once you found each other, utterly new worlds of exploration opened to you.

Farm communities created an undreamed level of prosperity and human growth. Humans had long been capable of such growth, but they lacked the interaction that made it possible. Now, ideas could be compared, experiments conducted, results distributed and the knowledge shared among thousands. Mankind began to flower. It may have been the most exiting time our race has ever seen: Humanity awoke and the world opened to them.

The Westward Farmers

As our first farming culture spread out from Armenia, only some found their way to the Tigris-Euphrates flood plain. Most of the others headed west, carrying crops, animals and knowledge all the way to Ireland.

These people created, in fact, the first European civilization. There were a few ice age survivors in Europe before these people came, but the genetic inheritance of those people accounts for only about 20% of European DNA. These farmers are responsible for the rest. They are responsible for Europe's agricultural roots and for it's cultural roots.

These first farmers arrived in what is now Greece by 6800 BC, Austria by 6500 BC, Bulgaria and Serbia by 6200 BC, and Moldova, Ukraine and Romania by 6000 BC. They deserve a book of their own.[10]

The First City

One of the early stopping points for these people was the first city to appear after the ice age. It looked approximately like this, but many times larger:

[10] See FMP #73.

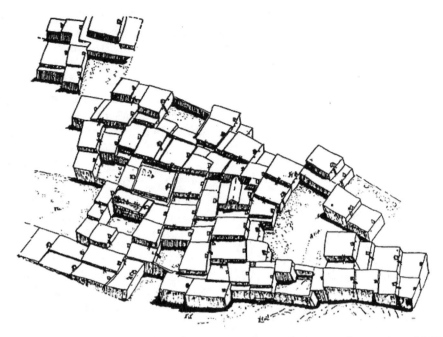

After James Mellaart, "Çatal Hüyük", Thames & Hudson Ltd., London, 1967

The site lies in Anatolia (now Southern Turkey) and has been excavated over the past few decades. This city, now called Çatalhüyük, thrived between 7400 BC and 5900 BC, and it was, to put it succinctly, a peaceful anarchy.[11] There was no courthouse, no tax collector, no central administration of any kind. As one of the archaeologists working the site wrote:

> It is hard to imagine that 10,000 people, minimally 2,000 families, were going out and doing their own thing, but that is what we see.

The people of Çatalhüyük were peaceful, cooperative, individualistic, and highly artistic. They were tender. They were clean, well dressed, well fed, and productive. Many were long-distance traders, and they may have used obsidian as a currency.

Violence and Immobility

> *No student takes seriously the seventeenth-century notion that states arose out of a "social contract" among individuals or between the people and the ruler.*
> – Will and Ariel Durant, *The Lessons of History*

Unfortunately there have always been people who will, given the right incentives, use violence to subdue others and empower themselves. And,

---

[11] See FMP #37.

tragically, the earliest Mesopotamian farmers were the first settled group to have this fact thrust upon them.

Professor Quigley[12] describes it this way:

> The chief event was the invention of agriculture, metallurgy, and civilized living by the Highland Zone peoples and the subsequent linguistic and cultural submergence of these peoples by inflective-speaking longheaded pastoralists who pushed in waves from the Flatlands by the two post-glacial dry periods. One of the chief results of this process, a result seen most clearly in Europe, was to create a political and social structure in which patriarchal, warlike, horse-loving, sky-worshiping, honor-seeking Indo-Europeans were established as a ruling class over peaceful, earth-loving, fertility-dominated, female-oriented peaceful peoples.

Farming created large stores of food, typically as grain, which did not rot if carefully stored. Following shortly were other imperishable goods, such as clothing, furs, tools, and so on. By ancient standards, these farmers were very rich. And while our farmers were happy living cooperative, productive lives, there were others who operated, not by a cooperation model, but by a plunder model. Our farmers were now immobile, and stationary targets are easy to hit. Furthermore, sedentary people are not well-suited for combat. They made easy victims.

The first plunderers were the nomadic hunters and herdsmen described previously. At some point they expanded into new areas and discovered that rich, stationary farmers were easy to rob. The consciences of these people were informed by sky gods who imposed power from above and by clan groupings that featured dominance, submission and structure. They were emotionally suited to plunder. Furthermore, these people had the necessary skills for rapid movement and killing; they hunted, captured and killed mammals regularly. They would also have resented the prosperity of the farmers, as it made them look second-rate, something that would not be permissible in their hierarchical, "we must be the head and not the tail" view of the world.

These nomads could easily remove the spoils of conquest, either to a safe place, or simply to the next settlement for the purposes of barter. And it is likely that their first actions against the farmers were simple looting missions.

In some places, these looters would have been so successful that they drove the farmers away, leaving them to look for new victims or return to their

---

12   Again, from *The Evolution of Civilizations*, published in 1960.

previous lives. Before long, however, the looters developed a third option: Steal only a limited amount, not enough to drive the farmers away. This way, you can work the same ground, as it were, for life. Thus the first rulers were born.

Governance began as persistent theft, with hierarchical nomad groups sustaining plunder at a level that was low enough for the productive farmers to accept their rulership with a limited level of resistance.[13]

On the farmer's side, giving a fifth of his crops to the thug every harvest was far less bad than facing death. And so he grimaced and paid, as do most modern men. To illustrate this point, here are the words of modern man in a similar situation: An exceedingly remote Tibetan nomad, commenting upon his first ruler[14]:

> The Panchen Llama owned areas and appointed officials to settle our disputes and collect taxes. He was our lord, although he never came here himself. Our taxes were heavy in those days, but we never went hungry.

This series of events could easily have been predicted in advance. The incentives the players faced led to precisely this situation: Stationary, peaceful farmers colliding with nomadic herding and hunting societies could hardly turn out any other way.

And God Changed

One way this "conquest of the productive by the plunderer" shows up in the archaeological record is in the mixing of the gods. We have said that the early farmers held to female gods based upon the productive principle. We have also said that the nomads held to male dominator gods.

Dianne Wolkstein and Samuel Noah Kramer[15], studying the development of the goddess Inanna, report the following:

> In the cycle of Inanna, we encounter aspects of the earlier Sumerian Dumuzi (her male companion) as well as the more politicized Akkadian Dumuzi. The Sumerian Dumuzi... is characterized as the force in the grain and as the priestly lover and attendant of the Fertility Goddess, Inanna. The Akkadian Dumuzi, coming from the northern nomadic peoples who emphasized the arbitrary will and power of the gods is characterized as the shepherd, the astral heavenly bull, and the king who has "godlike" powers.

---

[13] See FMP #24.

[14] National Geographic, June 1989

[15] In their book, *Inanna*

Whether imposed by force or accepted by intermingling over time, the dominator male gods of the nomadic plunderers were mixed with the productive female gods of the cooperative farmers. Again, this was sensible, since extracting plunder is an expensive process. (Violence is never cheap.) So, the sensible ruler would prefer to have his subjects give willingly, and because the gods were super-human, they were the obvious tool to use. Since the gods did not speak directly to men, their "true message" was a matter of interpretation and could be turned to the ruler's advantage.

Although the first instances of rulership were mostly naked impositions of force, an ethic was later created, saying that the commands of the gods, if followed, would assure safety and health. Furthermore, a priesthood was added to the equation. These first public intellectuals promoted a theology in which the king played an important role. Thus rebellion against the ruler became rebellion against the gods.

Under this new theocratic regime the female god – formerly the friendly catalyst of production – became an arbitrary withholder of prosperity.

Soon enough, the rulers began building temples and monuments under the rationale that these things would help them connect with now-arbitrary gods, who had been removed to somewhere above, not with them on earth. The gods became high and glorious, and the people became low and dirty. Only special men who were specially prepared could reach between the two worlds. By convincing people that special men, massive structures and dramatic statements were necessary to reach the gods, a larger share of crops and labor could be collected.

The first priesthood and state theologies were developed at these times. Related to this is the fact that many monuments of this era featured inscriptions regarding the importance of properly worshiping the gods. Such inscriptions had relatively little religious importance to the rulers. Rather, they were designed to encourage tax compliance. They were, in fact, the first propaganda campaigns.

Details varied from place to place and time to time, but since all the incentives of the time led directly to this line of development, it was, again, nearly inevitable. The subjects had acclimated to being ruled and the rulers wanted power and glory. The rest was obvious.

This more elaborate religious model mentioned above began forming in Mesopotamia at about 5400 B.C. and was present in Egypt before 3000 B.C.

The Horrifying History of Sumer

One sows, another reaps.
– Ancient Proverb

Our first farmers from Armenia suffered a fate common to a shocking number of the true innovators and benefactors of mankind: They were overtaken by aggressive and abusive outsiders who claimed the innovators' discoveries as their own. Worse, the names of the innovators – whose genius created human progress – were forgotten. Humanity's greatest benefactors have thus suffered the greatest injustice.

An annotated time line of human life in Sumer[16] shows this process:

Prior to 6000 BC

Early farmers travel down the Tigris River from Armenia into the land that will eventually be called Sumer. Stumbling upon the fact that they could create permanent settlements in the Tigris-Euphrates valley, they remain and create stationary agriculture. In effect, they create civilization. They become, as Samuel Kramer writes, the "first farmers, cattle-raisers, fishermen, weavers, leather workers, woodworkers, smiths, potters and masons." Nonetheless, we have no written record of these people, few artifacts and only traces of their language.

Shortly after the Tigris-Euphrates valley was settled, Semitic nomads from what are now Arabia and Syria begin to raid the agriculturalists. At some point thereafter, they invade and remain, setting themselves up as a dominant political group. In other words, they make themselves the first stationary rulers, collect a portion of the harvest every year and claim a monopoly on the right to dispense justice to the agriculturalists, all by force of arms.

6000-5400 BC

Some agricultural settlements continue under the coercive rule of the nomads, others are abandoned by inefficient rulers, some farmers hide their produce and others move down-river to escape.
Technologies and arts continue to develop, albeit more slowly.

5400-5000 BC

A new group of invaders arrive from the north and develop more efficient schemes of rulership. It is likely that they leave much of the previous ruling elite in place as middle-managers.

Eridu, the earliest city in southern Mesopotamia, is founded. Temples begin to appear and sacrifices are collected as religious obligations. A new myth is propagated, retelling the story of the goddess Inanna, and stating that she had to travel to Eridu in order to receive the gift

---

[16] This outline is partly upon Samuel Noah Kramer's essay, *Sumerian History, Culture and Literature*, which appears in the book *Inanna*, mentioned previously. Recent studies and findings were also used.

of civilization. Gods are used to create the moral legitimacy of the rulers and to decrease the difficulty of tax collections.

5000-3000 BC

City-state governments continually organize and control daily life. Technologies standardize while creativity declines. Groups of cities are built around temples, eventually almost within sight of one another.

3000 BC

A powerful ruler appears and organizes all of the city-states of the Tigris-Euphrates valley into a single empire. A list of kings calls this man Etana, and describes him as, "the shepherd, who ascended to heaven and consolidated all the foreign countries."

3000-2000 BC

A variety of kings and dynasties rule and fight for rulership of what is now properly (and finally) called the Sumerian civilization. They exercise great care in organizing and regulating human life. Creativity and production fall and the civilization degrades.

2000-1750 BC

The death throes of civilization in the Tigris-Euphrates valley. Overrun by the Babylonian empire of Hammurabi, the name Sumer ceases to be associated with any living group.

The Progressive Choking of Creativity

As illustrated by this time line, the great benefactors of humanity – the unnamed first farmers – experienced a stunning explosion of creativity and very shortly found themselves the effective prisoners of barbaric men who dominated and slowly ruined what they had created.

At first, the farmers simply gave up a portion of their harvest and tried their best to work around the rulers. It was only when a more clever set of rulers arrived that the more serious damage began. This, more serious damage, was two-fold:

1. Piece by piece, their actions were restricted and monitored. It is difficult enough to create useful things when a man is fully unopposed, but if, before he acts, he must also consider whether or not he will be punished, creativity is choked.

2. Their range of thought was restricted. The imposition of a dominating, arbitrary, punishing god upon men's thoughts is inherently intimidating, and intimidation destroys creative thought. When men fear that new thoughts will be punished, they allow few to pass through their minds, and admit to even fewer.

It is important to remember that the cities we are discussing here were small by modern standards. That meant that the ruler was never terribly far away and there was often no dark corner to hide in. The watcher was close and records were kept. Hiding was difficult.

As successive waves of rulership rolled over the Tigris-Euphrates valley, the structures of government and their associated theologies and punishments occupied more and more of men's minds and activities. During the city-state period (5400-3000 B.C.) temple complexes like the one shown below[17] were common.

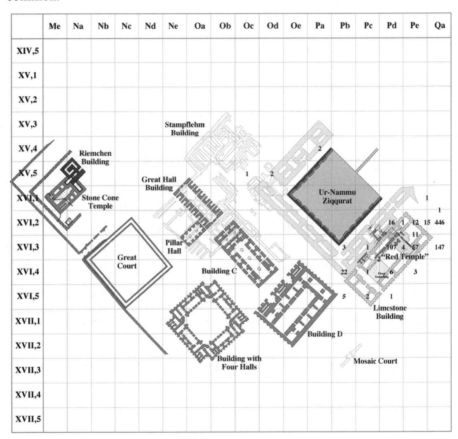

The Government Buildings of Uruk in 3400 B.C.

Image courtesy of R. K. Englund, UCLA

One of the primary features of these temple complexes was that they separated ordinary men from their rulers and, especially, from the holy places. Restricted passages, courtyards, and great stairways had to be traversed in order to reach the important places. This had multiple effects:

---

[17] This is an excavation grid from the city of Uruk, a major Mesopotamian city, which was constructed at about 3400 B.C.

- It instilled the idea that the rulers and priests were of a different class than the average men. They were literally above and figuratively above.

- When a man was given access to the special places, he felt as though an honor was bestowed upon him. He would now be considerably less likely to turn against the regime.

- The king, seeing that his subject was moved to be admitted to his presence, was confirmed in his own eyes as being of a higher class of humans and worthy of rule. The kings of old often considered themselves demi-gods, and this effect of reflected glory contributed to it.

- Occupying a position of power (able to call forth violence) and being associated with the gods made the ruler a powerful imposer of shame. That gave them a terrifying weapon for securing compliance.

Another function of the temple complex buildings and palace buildings were as halls of records. A love of control and order extended through the years after 5300 B.C. For example, an archive has been unearthed at a city called Ebla, dating from 2350 B.C. The room was ringed with shelves and held approximately 2100 clay tablets. On the tablets were administrative records of:

- Textile accounts
- Metal accounts
- Tax deliveries
- Temple offerings
- Letters
- State reports
- Scribal exercises
- Villages (hundreds)
- Large animal herds (thousands of animals)
- A wool industry
- Large quantities of gold and silver
- Tribute paid to a superior city named Mari

This is but one example of Sumerian record-keeping. Thousands of additional tablets have been found, recording things such as:

1. An appointment to a clerkship
2. The establishment of a Food Office
3. Legal documents in regard to slaves
4. Legal document in regard to an office
5. Agreements between parties
6. Deed of sale of palm grove

7. Deed of sale of a male slave
8. Receipt of purchase money for a pair of slaves
9. Documents in regard to loans of silver
10. Promissory notes
11. Acknowledgments of loans of grain
12. Acknowledgment of loan of dates
13. A bond
14. Receipt for silver
15. Receipts for grain
16. Receipts for vegetables of various kinds
17. Receipts for different kinds of beans
18. Receipt for dates
19. Receipts for figs
20. Receipts for straw
21. Accounts of the receipts for corn
22. Account of the receipts for bronze
23. Statement of silver, corn, oil, etc., received and at hand
24. Statements of shiploads of grain delivered
25. Statement of corn, wheat and vegetables delivered and at hand
26. Statement of garments at hand
27. Statement of chairs on hand
28. Storehouse accounts: corn, wheat, grain, vegetables, beans, dates, bronze
29. Accounts of the cost of the tilling of fields, as wages, feed of oxen,
30. Renting of fields to different persons
31. Account of fields, their measurements, condition
32. Enumeration of belongings, as implements, weapons, victuals, silver
33. Assignments of garments
34. Expenditure of sesame oil
35. Grain for the temple of En-lil
36. Grain for temple offerings
37. Flour and grain for temple offerings
38. Temple offerings and porphyry stone for couches for the deities
39. Lists of wages paid to officials, employees, artisans and laborers

A final and crucial area of importance was the general psychology of the people of Sumer. Enough records exist to reconstruct their general mind-set. Kramer writes[18]:

> A Sumerian tended to take a tragic view of his fate and destiny. They were convinced that man was fashioned from clay and created for one purpose only: to serve the gods by supplying them with food, drink and shelter so that they might have leisure for their divine activities.

---

[18] Again, from his essay *Sumerian History, Culture and Literature.*

You can see here the result of the long centuries of indoctrination. Holding a tragic view of life means that little action will be taken to change anything. By this point, these people had accepted a role that was little different than intelligent beasts of burden.

At about 2200 B.C., near the end of the Sumerian empire, a father writes this to his son:

> Do not talk too freely, watch what you say. Do not express your innermost thoughts even when you are alone. What you say in haste you may regret later. Exert yourself to restrain your speech.

> Worship your god every day. Sacrifice and pious utterance are the proper accompaniment of incense. Have a freewill offering for your god, for this is proper toward a god.

Note the caution and the fear of being impious. This is what control, regulation and fear breed. It created a mass of people who were easy to rule but unable to adapt, arise or create. Thus Sumer, the place of an explosion of progress, descended into uselessness and was overrun.

By the time of the death of the Sumerian empire, rulers the world over were trying to conquer city after city and string them into empires. This lasted for more than five hundred years, during which time there were Egyptian, Babylonian, Hittite, Assyrian, Kassite and Elamite empires.

The Invasions of 1200 B.C.

The historical world that most of us know and understand actually begins in the aftermath of the Great Catastrophe of 1200 B.C. This event marks the dawn of time to the the the Greeks, the Romans and to many others. They all claimed origins *after* this event, not before. As for the event itself: within forty or fifty years on either side of 1200 B.C., almost every significant city or palace in the eastern Mediterranean was destroyed, many never to be occupied again.

In effect, the decades surrounding 1200 B.C. erased the previous civilizations. Sumer had ruined itself and its replacements were not its equal. Egypt, which just barely survived the Great Catastrophe, became a shadow of its former self.

These civilizations had denuded themselves. In maximizing the technologies of rulership, they created processes which could not adapt. Further, they weakened the men and women upon whom all their actions ultimately depended. Kings, after all, do not till the soil and do not spin wool themselves – their subjects do all such things. And, in these cases, having restrained, unmotivated subjects ultimately ruined them. The "Sea Peoples" who attacked in 1200 B.C. were not listless, dull subjects – they were men on a mission – and they wiped out most of the ancient world in a moment.

Military Adaptation

The military adaptations that gave the invaders their advantage over the old empires were not works of genius. They were simple trial and error adaptations, along the lines of, "Gee, I wonder how it might work if we did this." But, regardless of the simplicity, the Sea Peoples[19] *did* think this way, while people of the old empires did not... or were forbidden to act upon it if they did.

Late Bronze Age kingdoms (that is, at just this moment in time), both large and small, depended on armies that featured a chariot corp. A king's military might was measured in horses and chariots, and a kingdom with a thousand chariots was many times stronger than a kingdom with only a hundred chariots. These chariots were often dispatched to scattered settlements to collect taxes and to defeat competitors. (The competitors were always called "invaders.") And when the chariots were off collecting taxes, the cities were left unprotected.

We do have written records of precisely this from the period: One clay tablet was found (in a city named Ugarit, in what is now Syria) abandoned in an oven, possibly from the eve of the destruction of the city, just a few years after 1200 B.C. In the text, a man named Ydn writes to "the king, his master," that they are being attacked and requests the king to equip and send 150 ships. In an earlier tablet from the same place, the king of Ugarit writes to the king of Alashia, saying:

> The enemy's ships came here; my cities were burned and they did evil things in my country. Does not my father know that all my troops and chariots are in the land of Lycia? … Thus, the country is abandoned to itself. May my father know it: the seven ships of the enemy that came here have inflicted much damage upon us.

The ship-borne infantries that defeated great chariot armies during the Catastrophe used weapons and tactics that were characteristic of barbarian hill people but had never been tried en masse in the plains and against the centers of the Late Bronze Age kingdoms. It seems not to have occurred to people that infantrymen armed with javelins could defeat a force of chariots. But once that lesson was learned, power shifted very rapidly from the existing kingdoms to collections of infantry warriors, many or most of whom seemed to arrive on boats, probably from the north end of the Mediterranean.

---

[19] Precisely who these people were is hotly debated.

A chariot was essentially a mobile platform for an archer. Groups of charioteers would ride in circles around infantrymen – at a safe distance – and inflict damage until the infantry fled. Chariot versus chariot warfare was more hazardous, but neither side had any great advantage, so great conquests were uncommon. Chariots had been built in Mesopotamia since 3000 B.C.

The new military model of the Sea Peoples of 1200 B.C. consisted of three primary weapons:

- Javelins. These were thin metal rods, less than an inch across and averaging about three feet long. When thrown by a trained man, they were deadly at about 30 meters and sometimes up to 50 meters. They were cheap and easy to make. These javelins were not generally thrown at the charioteers themselves, but at their horses. A horse, being a large target, was easy to hit. Then, once the horse was down, the charioteer was ill-suited to face the infantryman.

- Light armor. This consisted of light body armor and round shields. The body armor was only enough to stop arrows at a distance. Several varieties from the period have been found, some better than others, but most featured metal plates and all were intended to protect the soldier from arrows. The round shield, though not very large (a few feet across) was well-balanced and could be moved quickly and accurately. Again, a good defense against arrows.

- Long swords. Charioteers were generally equipped with shorter, thrusting swords and large shields. An infantryman with a long sword was very effective slashing the legs of a charioteer on foot. The infantryman could bring down the charioteer before the charioteer could get close enough to thrust his sword.

With these simple weapons, the Sea Peoples assaulted, plundered and razed the richest palaces and cities of the previous order.

It is highly significant that the old empires showed no signs of adaptation in the face of the onslaught. While evidence is thin, this is almost certainly related to the usual problem of hierarchies: Processes become fixed and the people who profit from them defend them. In this case, the chariot maker's guild (or some similar group) would have defended any change in the state's model of warfare. Likewise the guild of the bow-makers and arrow-makers. Likewise the suppliers of other military goods. They further would have influenced the king's advisors and the state's intellectual class. Adaptation fails badly in such conditions.

It is further telling to note that chariot warfare begins to disappear from the Earth at this time.

The Devastation

Dozens of destroyed sites show a thick ash layer, indicating destruction by fire. In general, it seems that the smallest settlements were abandoned and that the larger settlements were looted and burned. Afterward, however, a large number of the major settlements were rebuilt. We may presume that the invaders made themselves rulers, but evidence sufficient to establish this or any other hypothesis seems to be lacking. Some of the more illustrative findings have been the following:

- One city in Southeastern Cyprus, Kokkinokremos, was abandoned suddenly. The bronze-smith hid copper ingots and tools in a pit in the courtyard, the silversmith hid two silver ingots and some scrap metal between two stones of a bench, and the goldsmith carefully buried all his jewelry and sheets of gold in a pit. Obviously, they hoped to return and recover their goods. They never did; the archaeologists found them. The smiths were almost certainly killed or enslaved.

- Another site on Cyprus was burned, but rebuilt and occupied for about a generation after the destruction, then abandoned permanently.

- After about 1180 B.C, Crete suddenly changes over to larger settlements in remote and protected places. In particular, the people fled to the mountains and rebuilt there. We may also imply that their organizational structure changed. This was certainly true in Crete.

The Resultant Dark Age

After this devastation followed a period of several hundred years called the *Greek Dark Age*, the *Dark Age of The Ancient Middle East* or the *Collapse of The Bronze Age*. All descriptions begin at about 1200 B.C. and all last three hundred to four hundred years. During this period, humans reverted to a simple farming existence. Power devolved to the level of family groups. Few innovations are noted. Actually, the similarities of this period and the much later "Dark Ages" period of European history are striking:

- In both cases, a long-established, hierarchical, bureaucratic, old order failed.

- Life prior to the collapses featured peaks in the control of the state over the human lives.

- The remaining social structure, having been previously legitimized by the state, was left with no inherent legitimacy or prestige. Things that were previously considered by all "right-thinking men" to be the god-ordained order of the world, were suddenly made valueless.

- The previous religions – tied directly to the state – were left without moral legitimacy and were slowly abandoned.

- Hundreds of years were required for humans to fully adjust.

At the root of these prolonged periods was human psychology, and in particular the ripping apart of their expectations when the state/church establishment.

All states of all periods share a common foundation: A group of subjects who accept rulership. Without the minds of the subjects being willing to serve, no strong state has ever existed, or indeed could exist. All states work to keep their subjects willing and to identify with the state. This applies to democratic regimes, socialist regimes, republics, monarchies, theocracies or any other ruling arrangements. Rulership requires that most people accept you as legitimate in one way or another. Fear and terror *can* work, but not for long. If the people are unwilling, the state will fail soon enough.

Previous to the collapse of 1200 B.C., the minds of the subjects were strongly affected state/church ideology and their thoughts were kept within the boundaries of the broader state culture. Rather than developing as individuals, these people had ceded decision-making responsibilities to their rulers. But when their intellectual and emotional partner failed these people were lost, and remained so for generations.

When a respected and established order is somehow removed, the people who lived under it wish for it back, and if they can, they will fight to restore it. This occurred in the wake of the Great Pestilence of 1348 A.D. (the Black Plague). The circumstances between peasants and lords were irrevocably altered by the death of half the populace, giving the remaining peasants a stellar opportunity to improve their positions. But in actual fact, many of them did not want a new situation and fought its development. The peasants wanted the old ways back. The external reason for this was that they had rights and privileges guaranteed under the old system, and they didn't want to give them up. The internal reason, however, was that they had lost a center of reference for their thoughts and felt unsafe without it.

Another way of understanding the cause of Dark Ages is with the concept of Higher Powers. A Higher Power is a non-physical entity to whom people attribute some special power or value. Gods and states are the two most common forms. People very commonly imagine how deities or states would expect them to think or behave rather than making direct judgments. Thus Higher Powers are deeply involved in the daily thought patterns of many, many people. So, when his or her Higher Power is removed, the individual experiences a shock of aloneness. They are likely to pretend that the higher power still exists or will soon return.

The development of an independent identity is an arduous process; most men are all too happy to take shortcuts. This suits rulers perfectly. With a bit of pomp, impressive buildings, elaborate ceremonies and some nicely-spun national myths, they can give their subjects a fast, easy way to fill their developmental voids. When this trick fails, however, people are left grasping at nothing and recovery is slow.

The Great Trade

Between roughly 5400 and 3400 B.C., a great trade took shape; a trade between great numbers of humans and the hierarchical states that ruled them. This was a trade, not of money and goods, but a psychological trade. And being an internal issue meant that it was difficult to identify.

It is highly unlikely that this trade was purposely developed. Rather, it arose as several factors came into play in the same place and time:

- The painful conflicts built into human character.

- Rulers trying to convince their subjects to comply.

- A populace whose actions were constrained by regulations.

- A populace whose thoughts were constrained by fear of punishment.

The first point above is of great importance. Humans are *internally conflicted* beings. This is inherent in human nature, we are born to it. We see and value hard work, honest dealing and loyalty. Yet, we feel impulses that would drive us to grab what is available, whether it be honest or not, and so on.

This set of conflicts can certainly be trained and controlled (in fact, most of us do control ourselves quite well most of the time), but it takes considerable time and effort, and thus remains a universal problem.

The crucial factor here is simply that most men and women *do* feel conflicted, insecure and confused, and that they lack the time, skill or desire to fix the problem. So, they find ways to work around it, most notably to seek belonging in a group, with the half-conscious thought that by being merely one of many, blame and shame will not attach to them.

The Great Trade was and is this:

> *The state and/or church presents themselves to men as a superior entity – higher than man. To be joined to them provides sanction from a higher source than that of their internal conflicts.*

In our times we often hear this expressed as: *People need to belong to something larger than themselves.* They need to diffuse their confusion and conflicts into a higher entity.

In effect, the man or woman's internal conflicts become less important than the entity to which they are joined. It is the great assurance from the great adult, and it's easy to accept when you are surrounded by others who accept it.

Note that blame for this trade does not lie entirely with the state. Frankly speaking, the rulers weren't smart enough to have designed it. They merely watched as it developed and learned how to take advantage of it. The majority of blame lies with the people who flocked to the deal. Again, it was simply easier than making peace with one's self.

This trade is the hidden secret of politics and of rulership. People *wanted* the Divine Right of Kings. Rulers and politicians have merely played their roles as public theater.

You can also see from this why political science is so seldom scientific: the central ingredient buried in it is anything but, and may not be explicitly named without calling millions of comfort-transactions into question.

Analyzing The Characters of The Subjects

We have now been analyzing the charters of subjects at some length, and before we leave the subject, it is important to explain why such discussions have validity. After all, making grand pronouncements about millions of greatly-varying individuals is beyond the scope of normal human ability. In some very important ways, however, it is easier to analyze many than it is one, so long as we realize that any individual may vary from our conclusions. This is actually the same technique that is used in the analysis of gasses:

Trying to analyze the motions of each individual molecule of a gas is a practical impossibility. They push against each other randomly, impart momentum back and forth, and travel at constantly varying rates of speed. To measure each one, chart each one and determine from a study of 10×10^{24} individual molecules what will happen from compressing them would be a ridiculous waste of time and energy, presuming that we had the capacity to do it. But we *can* tell – almost perfectly – what a volume of gas will do, if we take it as a whole. Compress it and it heats, decompress it and it cools. This we can determine with great precision.

In the same way, we are often more accurate in analyzing the character of a mass of humans than we are when trying to analyze just one.

The Character of The Rulers

Another important area of exploration is the mind of the ruler. Rulers and subjects face very different sets of incentives, which greatly affect not only their actions, but their attitudes.

A first fact to establish, however, is that the rulers of this era were generally from a different cultural background than that of their subjects. And as mentioned earlier, the consciences of these people were informed by sky gods who imposed power from above and by clan groupings that featured dominance and structure. They were emotionally suited to plunder.[20] To rule

---

[20] See FMP #61.

over others was far easier for them than it would have been for the average farmer.

Perhaps the primary incentive for these rulers was simply to stay in power. One reason for this is that humans experience increased levels of pleasurable hormones[21] when in positions of power. It literally feels good. Another was that being deposed could mean death. Yet another is that many of these rulers were sociopaths, meaning that they had no sense of empathy and felt entitled to use humans as mere tools[22].

Adding to these things that related perks of status and wealth, we can see why rulers didn't walk away from power.

The incentives above, however, are common to rulers of every era. What set this era's rulers apart was the need for ferocity. Whether (early) to get farmers to capitulate, or (late) to keep sub-rulers in obedience while they were away, the low population density made extending power difficult. Ruling one settlement could be done fairly well if you remained there. But if you wished to rule another three or four settlements, you needed to extend your power. And since soldiers are expensive, other methods were required.

This difficulty was solved with terror. The rulers of this era were especially willing to boast of the horrible pain and punishments they inflicted upon anyone who rose against them or refused them. They wanted people to hear about these things and to fear disobedience.[23]

Here in a quotation from a ruler of this type (though later), the Assyrian, Ashurnasirpal II:

> I stormed the mountain peaks and took them. In the midst of the mighty mountain I slaughtered them, and, with their blood, dyed the mountain red like wool... I carried off their spoil and their possessions. The heads of their warriors I cut off, and I formed them into a pillar over against their city. Their young men and their maidens I burned in the fire... I flayed all the chief men who had revolted and I covered the pillar with their skins; some I walled up within the pillar; some I impaled upon the pillar on stakes... Many within the border of my own land I flayed, and I spread their skins upon the walls, and I cut off the limbs of the royal officers who had rebelled.

---

[21] Serotonin in particular.

[22] See FMP #59.

[23] It is of some interest that the first ruler of men mentioned in the Bible is also the first man with an impressive legend: Nimrod, the mighty hunter.

3

Classical Civilization

*Our love of what is beautiful does not lead to
extravagance; our love of the things of the mind
does not make us soft.*
– Pericles

Even though there was a long and dark period following the catastrophe of
1200 B.C., men did re-gather themselves and begin to move forward again.
But this was not a cold restart. Tremendous amounts of knowledge had been
assembled and passed on. Men knew what had been done and more or less
how to do it. They understood many things, such as:

- Farming.

- The calendar and seasons.

- Trade.

- Seafaring.

- Rudimentary navigation.

- Basic mathematics.

- The use of currency.

- Accounting.

- Reading and writing.

- Metallurgy. (Brass, copper, iron.)

- Military technologies.

The Greek Dark Age was long. The previous, warlike, Mycenaean civilization vanished at some point between 1200 and 1150 B.C., along with writing and many other things. Then, no visible progress appeared for almost four hundred years. As shown above, there was not an absolute lack of knowledge at this time, especially for the Greeks, whose lives were closely aligned with the sea. All through these dark years, there did remain a sea-faring culture that had not failed at 1200 B.C. – the Phoenicians[24]. This Semitic merchant culture was thriving in the Mediterranean during this time and they definitely had outposts where they interacted with Greeks. The later Greeks (after the roughly four hundred years of silence) borrowed heavily from the Phoenicians, who had long organized themselves into city-states and collaborated in leagues or alliances when threatened.

Power devolved throughout this period, until the fundamental unit of organization was the family. It seems to have been at this point that development restarted. and it is highly significant that these people emphatically rejected the idea of having a king[25].

The Rise of The Independent Myth-Maker

As the Greeks began to recover themselves, one of the first things they did was to create stories. There were not mere entertainments, they were stories with moral lessons as central elements. And, very importantly, these stories were not sponsored by, censored by or approved by state institutions. They evolved separately from imposed authority. Stories were accepted and writers rewarded solely upon merit. A good story teller would prosper and a bad one might not.

Homer seems to be the first great Greek poet to arise. He was, as is still commonly known, the author of *The Iliad* and *The Odyssey*, and seems to have lived and written in the late 9th Century B.C., close to four hundred years after the great Catastrophe. Herodotus says that Homer lived four hundred years before his own time, which would place him at around 850 B.C.[26]

Sappho was another famed and early Greek poet, living approximately between 620 B.C. and 570 B.C. In history and poetry texts, she is sometimes associated with the city of Mytilene on the island of Lesbos. Sapho's poetry was well-known and greatly admired throughout antiquity. Most was lost, but

---

[24] See FMP #81.

[25] We see this at the very beginning of the Roman republic. Under the consulship of Publius Valerius (circa 509 B.C.) it was decreed that any man trying to make himself king could be killed without a trial.

[26] Some modern scholars question Homer's actually existence, much as they do Shakespeare's. His stories, however, are evidence of his existence, as are the beliefs of all the ancients (including Herodotus). Added to this, there is no direct evidence that speaks otherwise.

her immense reputation has endured and is attested to by a few fragments of her works that have survived.

Many other poets flourished between the 5th and 7th Centuries B.C., creating all sorts of stories and songs, covering virtually all aspects of life and generally conveying some sort of message.

Recitations of poetry, especially Homer, were very popular at Greek festivals of the period. By the 5th Century, there were a great number of playwrights, such as Thespis, Aeschylus, Sophocles, Euripides and Aristophanes. Theater performances were extremely popular and were little-connected to the state. What we think of as entertainment began in Greece, and it was one of the ways in which the Greeks came out of their dark age.

It is very important to understand that the Greek myths were a radical departure from those of previous civilizations; they were written so that people could find meaning in them. The theologies of the empires addressed men's actions; the Greeks had stories that addressed men's souls. And there was something else: in the Greek myths, men were not small, insignificant and powerless before the gods. In the Greek myths, men challenged the gods and sometimes won! They beat the gods through superior thinking. This was a radically new intellectual development.

The Separation of Knowledge and State

During the long period prior to 1200 B.C., there were very strong ties between knowledge and state/church systems. The intellectuals of the era – the priests – were the keepers of the most important technical information of the time, astronomical knowledge. They spent considerable time studying the positions of the sun, moon and stars during the various seasons and their association with precipitation, freezes and floods. The obvious reason for this was to keep track of the right times to plant their crops. They learned to predict with some assurance when the last freeze or flood might be expected. This system was eventually replaced by the calendar, but the important issue is that this knowledge was strongly controlled by the ruling system, with the knowledge often mysticized. This was useful to the cause of rulership.

Mechanical and other types of knowledge prior to this time generally concerned technologies, not science per se. In other words, it concerned the end uses of things, not their operating principles. The Greeks, however, were about to change that forever, and the first of them to do so seems to have been a man named Thales.

Before Thales (624 B.C.-546 B.C., though these dates are uncertain), Greeks explained the origin and nature of the world through myths of gods and heroes. Phenomena such as lightning or earthquakes were attributed to actions of the gods. Thales attempted to find reasoned explanations of the world, without presuming the supernatural. In other words, he and others like him began to inquire not just about *how* things worked, but *why* they worked.

According to Herodotus, Thales used his knowledge to predict a solar eclipse [27]. This would have been a monumental thing in the ancient world, and it was certainly a story that was repeated often. Some of Thales' conclusions proved to be inaccurate, but his method of looking for reasons was a giant leap forward.

Thales was a moral teacher as well. A few of his principles were these:

> That for which we blame others, let us not do ourselves.

> Be rich, yes, for success is sweet. However, do not be rich badly.

> A happy man is one who is healthy in body, resourceful in soul and of a readily teachable nature.

It is with Pythagoras, however, that modern science begins to take shape. Pythagoras seems to have lived between 580 and 490 B.C., though, again, these dates are not certain. His pivotal discovery was that music was based on proportional intervals of the numbers one through four. He believed that this number system, and therefore the universe's system, was based on the sum of the numbers 1, 2, 3 and 4, which is 10. Pythagoreans swore by these numbers ("the Tetrachtys of the Decad"), rather than by the gods.

According to legend[28], Pythagoras discovered that musical notes could be translated into mathematical equations one day as he passed blacksmiths at work and thought that the sounds emanating from their anvils (when struck) were beautiful and harmonious. He decided that whatever scientific law caused this must be mathematical and could be applied to music. He spent time observing the blacksmiths to learn how this had happened. He examined their tools and discovered that it was because the anvils were simple ratios of each other. One was half the size of the first, another was 2/3 the size, and so on.

Thus Pythagoras discovered the numerical basis of musical harmony. He spent a great deal of time examining this subject and decided that all of the universe could be understood and predicted with numbers. It was one of the most important intellectual discoveries in history and almost all subsequent science has used this fundamental premise.

Pythagoras went on to discover the trigonometric theorem named after him, the square root, that the earth was round, that all planets have an axis, and that all the planets travel around one central point. He also went on to form a

---

[27] This seems to have been the eclipse of May 28, 585 B.C.

[28] And all we really have are legends, as none of his writings remain to our time.

complex cultic group around his teachings and became highly secretive. After this point Pythagoras, or at least his followers, seem to have become overly enamored with their own doctrines and ran boldly into grand pronouncements for which they had no evidence. The Pythagoreans developed a series of mystical beliefs that later affected Plato.

Language

One final issue of importance was the language that the Greeks spoke. Their Indo-European grammar, with its categories of gender, its sharp distinction of person and number, and its great emphasis on chronological tense, instilled in them (as it does in most every Indo-European speaker) a certain level of logical attitude toward life.

This is not a minor point, and the Indo-European languages differ in this way from others, such as the languages of the Far East which emphasize relative class levels. What people assume[29] in their speech has a powerful effect upon them.

Having This Mind In Them...

Because of the mountainous and irregular geography of Greece, city-states could not be strung together into an empire. A single organization was never able to dominate the entire civilization. Because of this they never developed a strong nationalistic priesthood that served the state. Their mythology became more a set of moralistic fables than what we would call a theology. Then, with an intellectual life separate from rulership or a central priesthood, these men and women examined human life in the light of reason, more or less independently from domination. It was from this base that the gifts of Greeks – geometry, fine arts, drama, comedy, philosophy – took shape.

Their practical organizational methods of city-states and temporary defense alliances also rested on this base.

Greek applications of democracy included such practical measures as random drawings for public duties and a mandate that an attempt was made at a private settlement before almost any case could be brought to court.[30]

The basic unit of politics in Ancient Greece was the *polis*, or city-state. Each city (and there were more than a thousand of them) was essentially independent. Some cities might be subordinate to others (a colony traditionally deferred to its mother city) and some might be dependent upon others, but the supreme power of each city was located within that city. This meant that when Greece went to war, it took the form of an alliance going to

---

[29] The important thing is that these things are learned in early childhood, when we have very little analytical ability. After that, they are assumed and rarely analyzed.

[30] See FMP #42.

war. It also allowed for wars within Greece, between different cities. (These were often an annual occurrence.)

The Greeks exhibited a vigorous intellectual life. Those wealthy enough to enjoy leisure went to the *gumnasion*, which was a place to exercise both mind and body. They flocked to watch Greek tragedy, a subtle and sophisticated artform. And, as evinced by their public art, they had a keen eye for technical as well as artistic excellence.

The well-rounded natures of the early Greeks were admirable (at least for their times), and their general situation lasted for a few hundred years, until Athens found itself in a position to lord it over the other cities... and did.

Athens Leads Greece Into The Way of All Empires

In the wake of the Persian Wars (491–479 B.C.), Greek city-states formed a voluntary alliance, "to exact vengeance by ravaging the Persian king's lands." This, as vengeance so often does, led them to their eventual downfall, as the alliance was converted into an Athenian empire.[31]

The alliance – called the Delian League because its treasury was on the island of Delos – was formed in 478 B.C. and led by Athens. Policy decisions were made at meetings on Delos, where all members had one vote. Athens calculated the states' annual contributions, which were made in either warships or in cash. The League was especially popular among Greek states along the western coast of Asia Minor (modern Turkey), being more exposed to Persians than anyone else.

At first things went well and membership of the League reached nearly 200 states. But signs of dissatisfaction with Athens began to appear. The islands of Naxos and Thasos tried to secede, the latter in a dispute with Athens over mining and trading rights. Athens forced them back. Around 454 B.C., the League treasury was moved from Delos to Athens. At about the same time, Athens started planting settlements of Athenians on "allied" territory. When cities began attempting secession later, Athenian overseers and garrison commanders took control.

Around 450 B.C. a final peace was made with Persia, but Athens saw to it that the League kept going. By this time, only three states contributed ships, and all the rest money. Athenian inscriptions relating to the League began to read: *The cities which the Athenians control.* Pericles (the renowned wise man of Athens) admitted that Athens had become "like a tyranny."

What had started as a free union of states pursuing mutual interests slowly turned into an empire run by Athenians pursuing their own interests. It would still be some time before Greece would reap the rewards of this moral devolution, but this was the turning point and no one went about to reverse it.

---

[31] It's highly ironic, but this story line would make an excellent Greek Tragedy.

Even Pericles acquiesced, saying that if it was dangerous to start it, "it would be worse to let it go."

In 405 B.C., the Spartan general Lysander virtually destroyed the Athenian fleet. Athens surrendered one year later, to end the Peloponnesian War, which left devastation in its wake. Many of the cities were unhappy with the Spartan dominance that followed, and this induced the Thebans to attack. They defeated Sparta at the Battle of Leuctra in 371 B.C., inaugurating a period of Theban dominance in Greece.

In 346 B.C., unable to prevail in its ten year war with Phocis, Thebes called upon Philip II of Macedon for aid, and he quickly conquered the exhausted cites of Greece. The basic unit of politics from that point on was the empire, and the golden age of Greece had fully ended. The conquests of Alexander did follow, but they were short-lived and contrary to what had once been considered 'Greek'. Within 150 years, Greece became an unremarkable province of Rome, and nothing more.

Reprise: The Wrong People Get The Credit

In this case, again, it can be seen that the wrong people have been given the credit for human advancement. The Athenians, who fell heir to the creations of earlier Greeks, have generally been heralded as the great developers and examples, when it was, in actual fact, they who ruined the operation.

This is a parallel to the situation we explained in the previous chapter, where the people who have been given the credit for creating the first civilization were not the ones who did it, but were rather the usurpers and destroyers of human progress. As we explained, the Sumerians were a much later group of people than the early creators, and they presided over the final decline of that civilization.

A few lines are in order to explain why this is:

1. The things that are easiest to repeat tend to be those that *are* most repeated. Instead of explaining the actual events, it's easier to say, "Sumerians and Athenians." This is incessantly repeated to school children and it tends to stick.

2. In both of these cases, creation was fairly quickly overrun by ruling structures and absorbed. Not only are those who take over diligent to claim credit, but the true creators seldom are. So, the only story passed down is that of the usurper.

3. The proliferation of goods does not take place at the moment of creation, but only after a period of time. New creations are almost always opposed at the beginning, are finally accepted, and only then begin to spread far and wide. (The idea, after all, survives the death of its creator.) As a practical matter, it took centuries for the

discoveries of the Armenian farmers and the early Greeks to spread and to produce mass results. Commentators are frequently unaware of this fact and give credit to the people who were in charge when the goods proliferated.

4. Museums and archaeologists have long been closely aligned with large institutions and have shared a 20th Century over-respect for things large; also, the 20th Century's over-regard for things centralized and hierarchical. In both of these cases, largeness and centralization came at the end of the development cycle.

But for whatever reasons, credit has gone to the usurpers and wasters of human progress. One sows, another reaps. Productivity is overrun by plunder. The following graph shows this process in a generalized form.

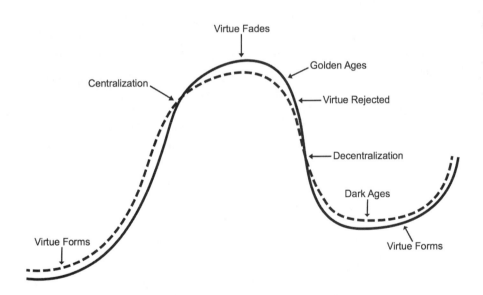

The General Cycle of Production and Plunder

This production/plunder cycle[32] plays itself out in the following way:

1. Virtues form after cycles have bottomed out.

2. Production follows virtue.

---

[32] Note that this graph shows the same relationships as those between parasite and host, and between predator and prey.

3. Centralization feeds upon production.

4. A Golden Age occurs when plunder is at a peak, and is characterized by monuments, public works and self-glorification.

5. Virtues are overrun by the forces of centralization. This leads to a loss of production, but not immediately. The lag period may be a century or more.

6. Centralization fails some years after production fails.

7. After a long period of decentralization and psychological reset, virtues appear again, beginning a new cycle[33].

Cometh Rome

Rome deviates from the cultural pattern we have been examining, in that their creativity was less home grown and yet they didn't simply overrun nearby creative peoples. Instead, they gathered to themselves the good ideas of distant peoples and made use of them, without trying to subjugate the creators. This may sound contrary, since Rome is known as a conquering state, but it should be stated, on Rome's behalf, that they didn't originally go about to conquer everything in sight, as Alexander had when he ruled Greece. Often they just conquered others who wanted to conquer them. Rome was an empire of city-states and not really a territorial empire.

Rome began, as best archaeologists can determine, in the 8th century B.C., comprised of people in two fortified settlements and another in the nearby woods. One group settled on the Palatine Hill (called *Rumi*) and another on Quirinal Hill (called *Titientes*). The people in the woods were called the *Luceres*. These were three of numerous Italic-speaking communities that had formed in *Latium*, a plain on the Italian peninsula, in the 1st millennium B.C. The origins of these people is not known, but their Indo-European languages migrated from the east in the years between 1500 B.C. and 1000 B.C.[34]

The group that most affected the early Romans were the Etruscans, who lived north of Rome in Etruria (modern Tuscany and northern Lazio). Their influence is shown by the Roman list of kings, in which early names were Etruscan. The gladiatorial displays that we think of as Roman actually evolved out of Etruscan funeral customs. The Romans learned to build temples from the Etruscans, and they may also have introduced the worship of a triad of gods, Juno, Minerva, and Jupiter, taken from the Etruscan gods, Uni, Menerva and Tinia.

---

[33] See FMP #18.

[34] Languages can be very effectively traced by specialists, and provide an excellent tool for tracking the movements of peoples. Since the people who became Romans came from the east in the time-frame of 1500-1000 B.C., it is quite likely that they fled the Catastrophe of 1200 B.C., then settled in Latium. Their legends also make this claim.

Roman religion was hallowed by tradition, centered on rituals carried out in the right way at the right time. At its heart was sacrifice (which meant, literally, "making sacred"). With luck, the god you honored with valuable goods (your sacrifices) would then answer your prayers, the most common of which were to be safe, prosperous, fertile and healthy.

When Romans found new gods in new cultures, they assimilated them into their pantheon. Minucius Felix, in the 3rd century A.D. said, "All nations have their own gods, but Rome welcomes the lot." Felix attributed Rome's success to this. Rome would rather absorb than conquer.

The questions of where the Etruscans came from has intrigued archaeologists for some time. The Greek historian Herodotus says that the Etruscans emigrated from Lydia, a region in western Turkey. Recent genetic studies[35] point to the conclusion that Etruscan culture was imported to Italy from somewhere in the Near East. Etruscan settlements were frequently built on a very steep hill and surrounded by thick walls, arguing for organizing principles that were informed by the great Catastrophe of 1200 B.C., which, presumably, they fled.

After about 650 B.C., the Etruscans expanded into north-central Italy. Expanding also to the south, the Etruscans came into direct contact with the Greeks. After initial success in conflicts with Greek colonists in southern Italy, Etruria went into a decline. Taking advantage of this, Rome rebelled and gained independence from the Etruscans in 507 B.C. Like the Greeks, the Romans strongly rejected monarchy, replacing it with a republican system.

The republic was a scalable form of democracy that had been tried in a few Phoenician and Greek cities. A republic added a layer of representatives on top of a democracy, moving the citizens one step further away from the actual use of power. Under city-state democracy, those who could vote did so directly; they decided and the decision was implemented. Those who could vote in a republic chose a politician to do their bidding; they, themselves, were removed from the process.

The Roman Republic, though highly complex, was based on a Senate, composed of the nobles of the city, along with popular assemblies which ensured political participation for most of the freeborn men and elected magistrates annually. The structure of the operation is shown below.

---

[35] See the New York Times, April 3, 2007.

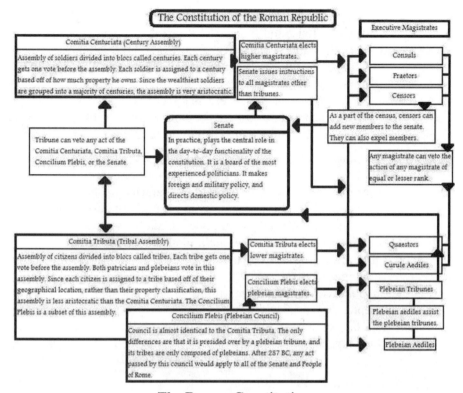

The Roman Constitution

The Constitution of the Roman Republic

Comitia Centuriata (Century Assembly)
Assembly of soldiers divided into blocs called centuries. Each century gets one vote before the assembly. Each soldier is assigned to a century based off of how much property he owns. Since the wealthiest soldiers are grouped into a majority of centuries, the assembly is very aristocratic.

Comitia Centuriata elects higher magistrates.

Senate issues instructions to all magistrates other than tribunes.

Executive Magistrates

Consuls

Praetors

Censors

As a part of the census, censors can add new members to the senate. They can also expel members.

Tribune can veto any act of the Comitia Centuriata, Comitia Tributa, Concilium Plebis, or the Senate.

Senate
In practice, plays the central role in the day-to-day functionality of the constitution. It is a board of the most experienced politicians. It makes foreign and military policy, and directs domestic policy.

Any magistrate can veto the action of any magistrate of equal or lesser rank.

Comitia Tributa (Tribal Assembly)
Assembly of citizens divided into blocs called tribes. Each tribe gets one vote before the assembly. Both patricians and plebeians vote in this assembly. Since each citizen is assigned to a tribe based off of their geographical location, rather than their property classification, this assembly is less aristocratic than the Comitia Centuriata. The Concilium Plebis is a subset of this assembly.

Comitia Tributa elects lower magistrates.

Concilium Plebis elects plebeian magistrates.

Quaestors

Curule Aediles

Plebeian Tribunes

Plebeian aediles assist the plebeian tribunes.

Plebeian Aediles

Concilium Plebis (Plebeian Council)
Council is almost identical to the Comitia Tributa. The only differences are that it is presided over by a plebeian tribune, and its tribes are only composed of plebeians. After 287 BC, any act passed by this council would apply to all of the Senate and People of Rome.

The Roman Constitution

Courtesy Wikimedia Commons

After 500 BC, Rome joined with other Latin cities to defend themselves from the nearby Sabines. Then, over the next hundred years, Rome incrementally expanded over the entire area of Latium.

In 387 B.C., however, Rome was sacked and burned by a group of Celts recently come from Gaul to eastern Italy, called the Senones. These Senones had also recently invaded Etruria. After this, Rome hastily rebuilt and went on the offensive, conquering the Etruscans and seizing territory from the Gauls in the north. By 290 BC, Rome controlled over half of the Italian peninsula and soon brought the Greek colonies in the south under its control as well.

At this time, the core ideals of Rome had been in place for some time, but there were none of the impressive buildings and monuments that we usually associate with it. The great monuments were produced later, under the Empire, once they could be financed by the movements of the people's surplus to the Emperor's storehouses.

By the 1st Century B.C. (beginning 100 B.C.) serious internal problems threatened the existence of the Republic. The Social War (between Rome and its allies) and the Servile Wars (slave uprisings), were very expensive conflicts, all within Italy, and forced the Romans to change their policy with regard to their allies and subjects. By then Rome had become an extensive power, with great wealth (tribute, food or slaves) taken from conquered peoples . Rome's allies, however, were unhappy. They had fought side by side with the Romans, yet they were not citizens and shared little in the rewards. So, to keep peace, by the beginning of the first century A.D. practically all of the free inhabitants of Italy were made Roman citizens.

Between the massive expansion of Roman power, the necessity of managing it, and a massive increase in the numbers and types of people who could now vote, new problems shook the Republic. In January of 49 B.C., following numerous crises, Julius Caesar marched his legions against Rome. Within a few years he had defeated all his opponents, and then ruled Rome for four years. After his subsequent assassination in 44 B.C., the Senate tried to reestablish the Republic, but its champions, Marcus Junius Brutus and Gaius Cassius Longinus were defeated by Caesar's lieutenant Mark Antony and Caesar's nephew, Octavian. After a long struggle, a final naval battle took place on September 2nd, 31 B.C. Octavian (soon to be called Augustus) was victorious, and became the sole ruler of Rome and its empire. On that day, the Republic ended and the *Principate*, the first phase of the Roman Empire, began.

The Democratization of Plunder

In the empires of the ancient world, plunder was reserved to kings and emperors (kings of kings). These rulers had the right to plunder and made war to assure that they had no competitors. Each city was a separate unit, and its surplus production went directly up the hierarchy to a local ruler, with a portion of it continuing to a ruler above that one. This surplus allowed the rulers to live lush lives and to build the great monuments of the old world: Pyramids, hanging gardens, ziggurats, colossal statues, and the like.

The Greeks and early Romans, however, rejected this arrangement and democratized the plunder. Their model involved each property holder owning a small number of slaves, whose work in the field he carefully supervised and often assisted personally. The surplus production of the slaves became the property of the land owner, which allowed capital to be used in productive endeavors.

But the improved use of surplus capital was not the only attribute to this new arrangement. It also turned thousands of people into small-scale plunderers. This had a range of effects, which are difficult to properly weigh at our current distance of over two thousand years. However, some of the major effects seem to have been these:

1. **A reduction in the respect for hierarchy and fear of the ruler.** The individual land-holder was not awed by the power of the ruler, who

was much less powerful than the rulers of the ancient era, and may not have been much of a ruler at all. In fact, during the earlier parts of the classical age, a ruler (if there was any) was chosen from among the land-holders and would likely return to them. He was not separate from the others in class, only in temporary function.

2. **Coarsening of the land-owners, stratification of humanity and the rise of fate.** Holding slaves, even when treating them "well," leads humans to devalue those who they own. Unless, of course, the slaves are seen as victims of chance. So, to accommodate the presumed necessity of slavery, the earlier Greeks and Romans developed the idea that slaves were slaves because of the acts of the gods, or by fate, or by cruel chance; and not by the slave-holder's actions. And in some cases this was almost true: There were then, as there are now, many people who would gladly trade their freedom for a position of entitlement. If they feel they'll be guaranteed a basic sustenance, be treated with a modicum of compassion, and have some promise of protection from abuse, they accept servitude. (Freedom has always been far more of an attractive slogan than a way of life to be pursued.)

3. **Citizen armies.** When power is distributed, military defense cannot be assigned to a class of experts, simply because such a class does not exist. So, an army of citizens is required. Since the workforce could be relied upon to function fairly well in the land-owner's absence, this was not an insurmountable obstacle. And, it must be said that the Greeks and early Romans acquitted themselves quite well in military endeavors.

Ancient Economics

It is important to understand the ways in which the economics of the classical world differed from the economics we're familiar with.

First of all, the ancient mechanism of economic growth was the social organization of slavery. During the centuries of the Republic this was not, as noted above, slave gangs on plantations. But, since the slaves could not be holders of property, the surplus they produced was taken over by the slave owner and became investment capital. This was then applied to productive uses. And, since the owner understood the agricultural process, he was usually an excellent judge of where investment was best applied. Rome became very rich.[36]

This system worked quite well during the Republic. The slaves were forcibly shortchanged in the bargain, but slaves were often valued, commonly freed or adopted, and could engage in independent activities. Nonetheless, their

---

[36] See FMP #32.

surplus production belonged to their owner. A Roman (or Greek) of the time would justify this as the only conceivable social organization that could produce progress.

Another great difference between the modern and classical world was the currency. Minted coin was the sole monetary instrument, and there were no systems for creating credit. (There were, of course, private loans.) There were no banks in our sense, and only two sources of wealth: agricultural and mineral, with the former being more important. This had multiple consequences.

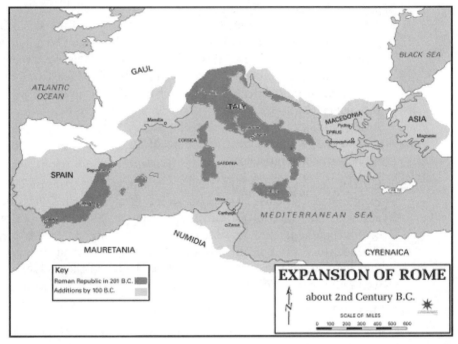

Courtesy Wikimedia Commons

One consequence was that funding military expeditions was difficult. (With fiat currency, war money can simply be created on demand.) For example, in 483 B.C. the Athenians had tense relations with the Persians, but hadn't done much about it. Then, the lead mines at Sounion suddenly revealed a fabulous seam of silver. Immediately, the leaders of Athens built a fleet and defeated the Persians at Salamis.

So, excess wealth could be pulled from the earth, erratically though dramatically, in the form of precious metals. Or, it could be produced regularly and predictably from a farming-slavery culture in the form of foodstuffs.

There was much concern in the ancient world over the storage and retention of gold and silver. One of the ancient laws of Rome (contained in their

Twelve Tables) stated that: *Gold, no matter in what form it may be present, shall, by all means, be removed from the corpse at the time of the funeral.* They did not allow gold to be wasted. (Though they did make exceptions for gold dentistry.)

At the same time, many problems we encounter, such as exchange rates, were complete non-issues. Gold was gold, no matter whose name was slapped on the coin, and all forms of gold or silver were of equal value. This aided commerce.

Another important factor was the Roman attitude toward wealth. Members of the classical civilizations tended to be moderate in their attitudes toward money. They frowned on the idea that either profit or power should be the goals of life, but rather tended to regard honor and the esteem of one's equals as at least as important as simple accumulation. The early Romans, being instructed by Greek mythology directed toward the inner man, were imbued with an appreciation for self-development. In this way at least, it was a more elegant time.

At a personal level, credit was provided in the form of transactions between friends, neighbors and relations. There were no securities, interest or even written agreements, which implied distrust. Aristocrats, for example, felt an obligation to take on the debts of friends. Cicero, the great jurist, distinguishes two categories of givers: those who squander their money on public banquets, food doles, gladiatorial shows and wild beast fights (to gain political credit), and those who take over friends' debts, help in providing dowries for their daughters or assisting them in acquiring property. Each man was, in effect, his own bank.

The Economic Fall of Rome

This slave economy was a crucial factor in the fall of Rome. Rome's reserves increased steadily through foreign conquests. (They quadrupled between 200 B.C and 70 B.C., for example, then doubled again in the 60s B.C.) Under the Empire, the city of Rome was highly subsidized, with roughly 15 to 25 percent of its grain supply being paid for by the central government. Julius Caesar found 320,000 beneficiaries in Rome; one in three. Claudius (41-54 A.D.) had 200,000 heads of families getting free wheat. Commerce and industry played small roles; the economy was based upon conquest and agriculture; other forms of commercial activity were looked down upon.

The nobility of Rome were excluded from commerce, by law. This kept a great deal of capital and talent out of the general marketplace and drove the nobles to build ever-larger farms if they wanted to increase their personal surplus. (The elegant monetary ethic of earlier times was overrun during the Empire.) This, of course, required a continual supply of new slaves. Obtaining more slaves, however, required more conquest. Rome was now dependent upon plunder to keep the system going. This was not sustainable, and those Romans who wished to know, knew. The others kept their eyes closed and pretended that all things would continue.

During the earlier years of the Empire (31 B.C. into the 3rd Century A.D.) Rome kept its citizens happy with plunder from the new provinces and with low taxation. But this could be maintained only so long as plunder from the provinces kept coming in. After centuries of expansion, Rome eventually reached its limit and further expansion cost more than it gained.

One surprising fact is that Rome was able to retain elements of its moral core for quite some time. It occupied a great deal of 'mental territory' among its subjects. The standard mode of conquest in those days was to lay siege to an opponent city, surrounding it and burning or invading it. Almost inevitably, someone would open the gates of the opposing city, usually for a bribe. No one ever opened the gates of Rome, even under terrific siege. The Roman symbol was the *fascio*, a bundle of sticks bound together into an unbreakable whole. This allegory had evidently taken deep root, and Romans bought into the idea that they, like the sticks, could remain together and become supremely strong. During those years, no one ever left the bundle to open the gates.

But, as was inevitable, once Rome could no longer extend its frontiers the operation rotted where it stood. It did not rot instantly, however. Economic problems began first, as the treasury ran low on funds and the Emperors began to mix base metals into their silver coins. This, as always, created inflation and led to economic difficulties.

Government efforts to overcome economic depression led to a much larger government bureaucracy and tax burden. This fell primarily upon the landlords who were, after all, stationary. Merchants could avoid the tax-gatherer, landowners could not. The landowners were clever people, however, and they develop a method of avoiding taxes, by saying that their tenants had moved along in search of better wages.[37] To counter, the Senate passed laws that tied the tenant farmers (called *coloni*) to their tenancies and made them hereditary. Thus the coloni and their children were tied to the land, and the landlord could no longer avoid taxation.

Because of this relationship, the coloni came to look to the landlords for protection and to settle their disputes. As the government became weaker and more distant, the landlords became more powerful. Laws were passed to stop this process, but they were not enforced. As the Empire withdrew, the landlords became the last vestige of government.

The Path To Centralized Power

As noted earlier, a great strength of the Roman Republic was that it was decentralized. Power and responsibilities were shared among many groups

---

[37] Their taxes were calculated by the number of tenants, more or less.

and no one of them could ruin the entire operation. The family was the core of Rome and the base of its decentralized structure. This went beyond the virtue of "having a stake in the game." They were bound by tradition, and the tradition was: *Work the land, fight for your country, go back to working the land. Expand your holdings. Make Rome wealthier. Your family will profit thereby.* This worked for three hundred years. If you owned property, you were a citizen, you had rights, and you served in the army when needed.

During these years, the army was comprised solely of Roman citizens. Then, as the Republic expanded, more soldiers were necessary and there simply weren't enough citizens. In 100 B.C., Marius opened membership to the masses (called the *capiti censi,* which literally meant "the headcount"). So, non-citizens enrolled in the Army, and they did so for future benefits, which was a radically different motivation from the self-sovereignty and responsibility that moved the Roman citizen. These new recruits trusted their General to secure benefits for them, and that was the end of the matter. The exchange wasn't dishonest, but it put power into the hands of officials and took it away from the citizens.

It must be added that this had a further degrading effect upon the idea of Rome itself. The citizens, like their fathers and grandfathers long before them, saw themselves as self-sovereigns, cooperating together in a sensible structure. But the masses, who were now users of force, had little understanding of Rome's roots, and cared little. Their loyalty extended only to the General who secured their benefits. They sought payouts, while the citizens prattled on about concepts that seemed outdated to them.

Another issue was that the army had political power. This gave non-citizens the power to enforce rules upon citizens, at least when acting in concert with other political groups. In other words, people with no stake in the game could now dictate policy. They could vote themselves favors that would be paid for by others, which, soon enough, they did. Again this took surplus away from the citizen families and put it under the control of the central state. Surplus began flowing away from the farms, where it could be used productively, and into the hands of the political class. This caused grave economic problems; the farmer who wanted to make improvements had no excess to spend on them.

After the Second Punic War of 218-201 B.C., rich Romans began taking over large properties (called *Latifundium*) in the conquered provinces. This was crucial or attaining status; the wealth of a Senator was measured in his land. When a Censor examined the Senate and expunged those who were not wealthy enough – as happened from time to time – it was based on the amount of land owned by the Senator's family. So, obtaining large tracts of land became important in retaining one's rank in the aristocracy. And obtaining lands from conquest required friends in the central structure of the state. Those who wished for status had nothing to gain from the noble, scattered farmers. And so they championed the state, and especially their friends within the state. And again power passed from the distributed farms to offices in the city of Rome.

The constitution of the Republic was built around a separation of powers and checks and balances, often taking the form of a struggle between the aristocracy and the average Roman. Over time, the laws that allowed the landed aristocracy to dominate the government were repealed, and the result was the emergence of a new aristocracy which depended on political allegiances to maintain dominance. Thus power was transferred from families into a centralized political state.

The collapse of the Roman Republic in the 1st Century B.C. was largely due to the naked power that people like Caesar and Pompey could wield by having private armies at their back. Cicero lamented in a letter to Brutus: "We are made a mockery by the whims of soldiers and arrogance of generals. Everyone demands as much political power as the army at his back can deliver. Reason, moderation, law, tradition, duty count for nothing." The reason, of course, was that moderation, law and tradition no longer had any bearing on the use of power. They may still have mattered to a many citizens, but they didn't matter to the ruling classes. And by this time, the citizens had lost much of their power. They were talked to far more than they were listened to.

Caesar was simply a realist who saw that only power really mattered. Tradition was for the workers in the fields, not for men of action. So, he consolidated military power, overcame the rest of Rome's armies, and made himself dictator[38]. Two centuries before, there would have been little power for Caesar to grab, but by the middle of the 1st century B.C. the central state had a huge amount of power, making it an irresistible target.

Upon Caesar's assassination in 44 B.C., his adopted son Octavian became his heir. Thirteen bloody years later, Octavian emerged as the first emperor, Augustus. With the Romans sick of internecine strife, he brilliantly maneuvered all power into his own hands, created a single army accountable only to the state and, because he kept institutions such as the consuls and Senate, he persuaded the Roman people that the traditional constitutional order had been restored. Many of the farmers wanted to believe that the old ways still mattered, and so they played along.

A Postmortem Analysis

Rome, in its own way, follows a pattern that we have seen in both ancient Mesopotamia and in the Greeks: Virtue, creation and production at the beginning, which is usurped by semi-plunderers or outright plunderers, who

---

[38] The actual events were more complex than are stated here.

end up getting credit for the entire enterprise. Note that very few people know anything of the Roman Republic, but they do know the Roman Empire with Julius Caesar, Nero fiddling while Rome burns, gladiators, stadiums and mass spectacles.

Initially, Romans organized themselves and adopted the best virtues that they could find, from whatever source they found them. They took freely from both Etruscans and Greeks, and from the Phoenicians as well. They made the virtues of these foreign peoples their own. This gave them useful views of reality and respect for technology. They used these in their own ways, to be sure (the Romans majored in engineering rather than science itself), but they used them vigorously.

Rome, from the origin, had a very short, practical set of laws, the Twelve Tables, which aided not only in basic governance, but was also a great boon to commerce, by making life relatively safe in every place to which the Roman model had come. Even though commerce was looked down upon by the agricultural Romans, the amount of trade was immense. As Professor Lionel Casson of New York University reports:

> The Roman man in the street ate bread baked with wheat
> grown in North Africa or Egypt, and fish that had been
> caught and dried near Gibraltar. He cooked with North
> African oil in pots and pans of copper mined in Spain, ate off
> dishes fired in French kilns, drank wine from Spain or
> France... The Roman of wealth dressed in garments of wool
> from Miletus or linen from Egypt; his wife wore silks from
> China, adorned herself with diamonds and pearls from India,
> and made up with cosmetics from South Arabia... He lived in
> a house whose walls were covered with colored marble
> veneer quarried in Asia Minor; his furniture was of Indian
> ebony or teak inlaid with African ivory...

This was a global economy. Trade has always been surprising in its range (traders being the unsung heroes of world history), but never like this. And along with traders came new ideas. For the first time, ideas passed from one end of the known world to the other in a relatively short period of time.

In a coastal town of northern England, there is a Roman funerary monument dedicated to a 30-year-old woman named Regina. It is dated to about 200 A.D., at the height of the Roman occupation of Britain. It tells us that she was originally a slave from a town near London, and was then freed by a man named Barates, from Palmyra in Syria, whom she then married. Barates, it should be noticed, was more than 4,000 miles from his home, and certainly conducting business of some sort. Note also that this trader was from a province and not the city of Rome or from Italy, where trade was ill-regarded.

Romans governed their provinces with a very small bureaucracy involving the local elite and generally continuing their ancient customs. Rome might demand its annual tax skim and the right to station legions, but apart from that they imposed no monetary system, no educational system, no rules and regulations, and, aside from basics, no laws either. Under the Empire, you could more or less do as you wished, so long as you paid the required taxes (generally low by modern standards) and didn't make trouble. Rome's arrival opened people to the massive economic network that was the Roman Empire. The map below shows the extent of the Empire at its greatest reach in the 2nd century A.D. (You will also see from this map why the Mediterranean was sometimes referred to as a "Roman Lake.")

The Roman Empire At Its Zenith

Courtesy Wikimedia Commons

But, again, early virtues gave way to later corruption. The Romans were proud of their original legal code, but lawmaking expanded endlessly, regardless of occasional attempts to cut it back By 533 A.D., when the eastern emperor Justinian published a Digest of Roman law, his men had to condense this new work from 2,000 volumes. As one of Rome's own historians, Tacitus, said, "The more corrupt the state, the more it legislates."

Likewise, Roman rulers began fairly well and ended very badly. The great example of Roman virtue was also one of the earliest: In 458 B.C., the highly regarded Cincinnatus was happily plowing his field as Rome fell into military danger. The Senate sent messengers and called upon him to assume absolute power in Rome and to save the city from assault. Grudgingly he agreed, and led a successful defense. But as soon as the danger was past, Cincinnatus went back to the Senate, resigned as Dictator, and returned to his field. This sort of relinquishing of power was rare in the ancient world, and Cincinnatus became Rome's shining example of virtue above power.

By the time of the Empire, this virtue was gone. Rome's "Five Good Emperors" were most definitely exceptions and it's not certain that they were as good as advertised.

An example of imperial conduct is this: The unclaimed property of those who died with no will became a great source of state income, along with the property of anyone who had been condemned on a criminal charge. So, when the emperor Tiberias faced a shortfall, he drummed up a charge against the richest man in Spain, Sextus Marius, accusing him of incest with his daughter. Consequently, Marius was thrown off the Tarpeian rock in Rome, leaving Tiberius to seize his extensive gold and copper mines.

From the start of the Empire in 27 B.C. until the end of the Western Empire in 476 A.D., there were 90 emperors. Of these nearly three in four were killed, usually by their own troops or by suicide. No one became or stayed emperor without blood on his hands. The fear of losing immunity upon becoming a private citizen played a part, as did the prospect of losing status and respect, however artificial respect for an emperor may have been.

Every emperor depended on the army's political power as well as its military power, and the army expected its kickback. At some point, the emperor's personal soldiers (the Praetorian Guard) realized that it was they who made the emperor, and not the emperor who made them. From that point on, the "idea of Rome" no longer played a significant role in the daily life of the emperor. All that really mattered was naked power.

The details regarding the end of the Empire are illuminating:

The Roman Empire exerted authority over its provinces because it had an army ready to punish anyone who stepped out of line. This army was paid out of the taxes that the provincials raised. If you consider this for a moment, you can see that this is the same slave economy writ large. The Romans didn't treat the provinces especially poorly (much as they did not usually mistreat their slaves), but they did siphon off their surplus production. And, like local slave production, it had limits. Once stretched beyond those limits, the economies failed.

The empire suffered serious financial setbacks in the 3rd century A.D. (called the *Crisis of the 3rd Century*), after limits were reached and the structure could no longer sustain itself. Rome's hold over its distant provinces weakened. In 376 A.D., a group from the east, the Huns, attacked the peoples on the borders of the Roman Empire and chased them into the Empire proper.

(They entered with permission.) Rome did not have the ability to reach out any further and deal with the Huns, and so the western empire was slowly flooded with Germanic peoples.

It must be remembered that by this time, all of the virtuous conduct and values that created Rome were long absent. And while many Romans were blind to that fact, the Germanics *could* see that the Roman ideal had no connection to reality, and they knew that they were beyond Rome's military effectiveness. They had no real inclination to obey and they were no longer afraid. Thus, they could not be ruled.

Very shortly, "barbarian"[39] kingdoms formed all along the periphery of the empire, even into Italy itself. Realizing their tentative positions, local Roman elites began colluding with these new kingdoms, against the Empire. As a consequence, tax revenue was creatively diverted and remained in the local kingdom. Without their resource supply, Rome was no longer able to raise armies and force the provinces back into obedience. Rome's borders weakened.

Roman central authority could now issue what orders it liked, but no one had any real need to obey, because they knew there would be no consequence. Rome had finally failed. In 476 A.D. the last Roman emperor, Romulus Augustulus, was quietly paid to go live in Campania by the barbarian Odoacer. The provinces allowed him to remain as the titular head of the Roman Empire, but he and his succesors had little power and could do little but watch as, once again, centralized power slowly devolved.

One thing that doomed the Romans was their fetish for stability and permanence. To the Romans, change implied failure. This left them psychologically unable to adapt and to choose another method of economy once their agricultural, slave and plunder economy reached its limits. All else was forbidden. They had staked their very identities to the *exemplum* of the past. Their basic concept of organization was rooted in the ideal of the initial Roman families of a bygone era: reliable, solid, held together by bonds of affection, the foundation of stable society. This in turn was tied to piety, which bonded gods and men and nourished them.

This is also why the early Christians were persecuted: they cast off these bonds, which Romans took as either an insult to their way of life (thus insulting all Romans, past and present) or, as a direct threat, by making the gods unhappy and undermining the spirit of Rome. (The Christians were thus referred to as "atheists.")

In this way, the Romans were no different from modern people who expect doom if proper conduct in not maintained by every person (or at least the overwhelming majority) in a society. Saying "God will judge us for our

---

[39] In the classical era, the term meant *foreigners* more than it implied bad conduct.

culture's immorality" is little different from what the Romans did, save that many fewer moderns resort to open violence[40].

---

[40] In fairness to the Romans, it must be said that the number of Christians who were actually killed in persecutions is far lower than is popularly thought, possibly as low as 10-20 thousand over a roughly 300 year period. Also, there is no evidence that any Christians were ever fed to lions in the Coliseum. It is certainly possible that a few died there in gladiatorial fights, but even this is speculation.

4

Plato's Empire

To Plato is given the praise of having perfected philosophy.
– Saint Augustine

Toward the middle of the classical era (about 380 B.C.) the Greek philosopher Plato developed a new mysticism of the state. This formulation was of little effect upon the classical civilizations of Greece and Rome (whose formative stages were behind them), but its effects upon future civilizations would be profound.

The religions of both the ancient world and the classical world are often categorized as *sympathetic magic*. The central exchange of sympathetic magic is that by performing an act that is somehow parallel to what you want, you influence the gods to act sympathetically, using their vastly superior power.

Sympathetic magic appealed to those who were desperate and to those who hoped for easy production: to get more than they had earned. Both are common human traits.

Among the Sumerians, for example, farmers would have some sort of fertility ritual, which they hoped would influence the gods to act along with them, and to keep the earth fertile. By the time of the Romans sacrifices became acts taken to appease the gods, but the pattern held.

Plato began to teach in about 400 B.C., as a student of Socrates. He had a strong affinity for governmental control. Here are three of his thoughts on the subject:

> Then first, we must set up a censorship over the fable-
> makers, and approve any good fable they make, and
> disapprove the bad; those which are approved we will

> persuade the mothers and nurses to tell the children, and to mold the souls of the children by the fables.

> The guardians must allow no innovations in gymnastics and music against the established order.

> Often the rulers have really to use falsehood and deceit for the benefit of the ruled; and we said all such things were useful as a kind of drugs.

You can see from these that Plato would have little in common with the early founders of Greece, Rome or the first agriculturalists – all of these people were innovators. He would, however, share a great deal of common interest with the rulers of Sumer in its later stages. And, of course, he has been much admired by ruling types ever since. It is true that Plato, being a very bright and thoughtful man, did develop some useful and even noble thoughts, but championing the lordship of the few over the masses remained a priority for him.

Another of Plato's primary teachings was that Earth is merely a shadow of a higher, better, unseen reality. According to Plato, men should not waste their time addressing earthly things, but they should seek to conform their lives, and the world in general, to a heavenly *pattern above*[41]. This, he promotes, will be the great catalyst that raises man to the heights of prosperity and enlightenment. He famously explains this in his book *The Republic*, which contains the following:

> But the true earth is pure and situated in the pure heaven... and it is the heaven which is commonly spoken by us as the ether... for if any man could arrive at the extreme limit ... he would acknowledge that this other world was the place of the true heaven and the true light and the true earth.

This idea of a heavenly world is very normal to us, but it was not so normal in the classical world. The Greeks, for example, described their gods as living high on an actual mountain named Olympus, not in a completely separate, higher realm. The idea of a separate world seems to have begun with the Egyptians, but regardless of the original source, it was Plato who originated the modern idea of Heaven[42].

---

[41] Specialists call this the Theory of Forms.

[42] Jesus never taught Plato's heaven and Christianity's first two centuries focused on resurrection, not heaven. See FMP #64.

Plato replaced the mythical gods of old with a mythic, ideal society. And this pattern of Plato's, as he spent a great deal of time explaining, was a city, a culture, the pure and perfect organization of human beings.

Plato replaced the gods with a perfect society – a heavenly society. He created an ideal that said this: *If you faithfully imitate the pattern above, you'll get the same benefits you sought from the gods.*

Plato describes this ideal state in *Phaedo*:

> Colors are brighter far and clearer than ours; there is a purple of wonderful luster, also the radiance of gold and the white which is whiter than any chalk or snow on the earth... and in this far region everything that grows - trees and flowers and fruits - are in a like degree fairer than any here. And there are hills, having stones ... more transparent, and fairer in color than our highly-valued emeralds and sardonyxes. The people have no disease, and live much longer than we do, and have sight, and hearing and smell ... in far greater perfection. They converse with the gods and see the sun, moon and stars as they truly are.

Plato's description, of course, was appealing. The clear implication was that by imitating the perfect pattern above, the conditions of the heavenly state above would begin to appear in your earthly state. You would magically receive benefits... more than you had actually earned.

But this was not merely implied by Plato. He gets specific, writing:

> The State, if once started well, moves with accumulating force like a wheel.

> Our State, if rightly ordered, is perfect.

> No State can be happy which is not designed by artists who imitate the heavenly pattern.

> What has been said about the State and the government is not a mere dream, and although difficult, not impossible.

So, from Plato's time on, people took comfort in thinking that if their government was run properly, they would get more out than they had put in. This line of thought remains with us, and we tend to call it *idealism*.

Idealism functions on the instinctive hook of getting something for nothing. (Pay for a little, get the rest for free.) It implies someone acting for you, so you don't have to be responsible. This is the political form of sympathetic magic, in which championing political ideas replaces sacrifice to the gods.

You can see how the formulations of the old gods and Plato's idealism are structurally the same:

Proper sacrifices gain sympathy from the gods and bring magic.

Right political positions cause harmony with the ideal and bring magic.

Following is a table, showing the relationships graphically:

	Action	**Mechanism**	**Result**
The Old Gods	Right sacrifices	The gods	Magic
Plato's Idealism	Right political positions	The heavenly ideal	Magic

No direct evidence was ever required for the old god formulation and none has been required of Plato.

Platonic societies have featured the belief that, by grouping together and conforming to the ideal, people get more than they could on their own. Accordingly, they labor long and hard to get others to join them in their political positions, in symbolic acts, and in sacrificing to the ideal. These are appeals to sympathetic magic.

So how different are we, really, from the ancients who made offerings to the gods of wind and rain?

Plato's Opportunity

Plato's writings were widely distributed during the time of the Roman Empire. But as mentioned previously, their ideas were not implemented on a large scale; there was an existing structure and no one was going to rip it down to attempt something new. The rotting and inevitable doom of Rome, however, provided them with an opportunity.

The crisis of the 3rd century marked the end of Rome's strength, and the collapse of their method of expansion. They had reached their limit and could no longer bring in masses of new slaves and make huge land grants to prominent families. Civil wars became almost constant and for the first time in centuries, Rome had to worry about invasions. They could no longer drive barbarians further and further away, and their economy was falling apart without new conquests.

A return to their early days was no longer practical. Power had long since left the virtuous farmers and had been siphoned away to a massive political center which would never agree to dismantle itself. The distributed power model of republican Rome was hopelessly lost.

In 273 A.D., Emperor Aurelian finished encircling the capital with a massive wall, making it clear that that the empire was vulnerable to attack. Rather than driving the Goths away, Rome would soon have to forge relationships with them and allow them to settle within the Empire.

Immoral emperors had made a mockery of Rome's virtues and there was no legitimacy left, only raw power... and that had faltered. The original mechanism of production had been eliminated and the new mechanism had failed. Rome was slowly collapsing.

Diocletian (who ruled from 284 to 305) enacted political reforms that made the city of Rome almost irrelevant. (This would have been unthinkable in earlier times.) Rome was stripped of its traditional role as the administrative capital of the Empire. The emperors, most of whom were now military men of foreign extraction, began to rule from Milan, or from Ravenna, or from cities in Gaul.

By the time of Constantine I (who ruled from 306 to 337) it wasn't terribly hard to see that the empire was headed for ruin. It was at this time that Constantine decided to re-constitute it.

As is widely known, Constantine consolidated all power beneath himself, made Christianity a legal religion in Rome, took pains to support it, and established a new capital at Constantinople. This was a major reworking of the Empire.

Precisely why Constantine chose Christianity as the new religion of Rome (others were available) has long been debated. When examined from the standpoint of an amoral ruler, however, the answer becomes somewhat more clear. So, it is to this question that we now turn.

Why Christianity?

Almost no one in the early 4th century believed in the moral legitimacy of the Roman Empire. People might have *feared* the Empire, or hoped to get rich from it, but they didn't respect it. The Roman aristocracy lauded their own greatness, but they didn't convince many people, and they certainly didn't convince the Goth, Gauls and Huns.

Once military force had failed, only legitimacy was left to support the state. Fear can keep taxpayers in compliance, or faith can keep them in compliance, but with neither they ignore the state and keep their money at home. And without tax revenues, no government can survive. So, Constantine had to pursue legitimacy.

Rome might have regained its security by dismantling the imperial structure, giving up the provinces and going back to the Republic as it was in 200 B.C., but this was certainly not something that the holders of power would consider. And so the restoration of legitimacy remained as Rome's primary option.

Constantine came face to face with this problem in his mid-30s, following a career that drew him through many parts of the Roman government. So, he understood the problem quite well. And the most pressing daily issue for him was money. (Military expenditures at this time were 40% to 70% of the state budget.) He needed gold to flow into his headquarters. Since Rome was now centralized, only cash flowing into the imperial treasury mattered.

There was, of course, the option of cutting back expenses, but that would have been ruinous. Everyone in power would have been diminished by this, and Constantine would almost certainly have been executed. In addition, the populace had become addicted to distractions and hand-outs.

In this difficult situation, Constantine chose Christianity[43] as his way out. It provided him both money and legitimacy. The entire empire wouldn't change religions all at once, of course, but this strategy provided what the empire needed and nothing else did.

So, Constantine embarked on his plan[44]. He and his two co-emperors ordered the end of Christian persecution in 311, a year and a half *before* the Battle of the Milvian Bridge, where he supposedly had a conversion to Christianity. In this *Edict of Toleration,* Constantine's co-emperor (Galerius) more or less admits that the persecution of Christians under Diocletion had failed.

The story of Constantine's conversion, of course, is that God promised him victory before the battle of Milvian Bridge on October 28, 312, after which he became the first Christian Emperor.[45] The facts of his life, however, do not support this story.

As we noted, Constantine stopped Christian persecutions about eighteen months earlier. And his victory procession after the Milvian bridge victory included no Christian symbols at all. He also continued his personal devotions to Mars and especially to Sol Invictus. These are not acts that a proper Christian would take once, much less repeat for decades. In addition, Constantine was as bloody as most other emperors. He broke a solemn oath and executed his brother-in-law, as well as other competitors. In 326, he ordered the execution of his oldest son, Crispus, who had not only been

---

[43] As historian Paul Johnson notes, "from the start, Constantine adopted Christianity as a spiritual and social aid to central government."

[44] We have no written record of Constantine's thinking aside from the conversion story.

[45] Constantine had the Chi-Rho symbol (along with others) on his army's shields and staffs considerably earlier.

appointed Caesar[46] and had served as consul, but had recently distinguished himself in a military campaign. In the same year, Constantine ordered the death of Fausta, the mother of three of his sons. So, any claim of Constantine's personal devotion to Christ must be rejected.

Solving The Legitimacy Problem

Near the end of chapter two, we described a Great Trade between humans and the higher powers who offer them shelter from their insecurities, and we stated that the trade was this:

> The state and/or church presents themselves to men as a superior entity – higher than man. To be joined to them provides sanction from a higher source than that of their internal conflicts.

Rome was no longer able to provide this. People had only to watch the emperors to understand that Roman virtues were a joke. The rulers were a group of corrupt men, and joining one's self to them could never impart any sort of absolution or cover one's inadequacies. Rome had no moral core and that fact was visible.

Christianity, however, had an astonishingly solid moral core (one that bloodshed didn't shake), which made it a perfect choice as a replacement. Unlike imperial Rome, Christianity *did* give people a reason to sublimate their insecurities into something higher than themselves. Christianity provided full remission of sins, paid for by an innocent. And not just this, but it was proven to be right, in that the great God raised this innocent from the dead. *That* is legitimacy, and it provided a powerful salve for the internal conflicts faced by humanity.

Now the emperor would regain his moral authority by joining himself with Christ. And, of course, he would need some special status within the Church structure[47], which was shortly arranged.

Constantine especially required legitimization because he and Diocletian and had removed the final connection between the state and its sovereign citizens.[48] When Augustus had created the Empire, more than three hundred years prior, he retained the form of the Republic, basing his legitimacy upon the sovereignty of the people. Having done away with all pretenses to this source of legitimacy, Constantine required something new. Further, one god among many would not do, since it would only legitimize him with a fraction

---

[46] The office of Caesar was akin to being the emperor designate – set to be the next emperor.

[47] It should be noted that the original "way" of Jesus and his students – before the term *Christianity* existed – was a non-hierarchical group of individuals and had limited resemblance to the Christianity of Constantine's time.

[48] With Diocletian begins the last, and openly despotic, period of the empire, usually called *the dominate*.

of the populace. And he had just learned that Christianity was not going to be defeated. So, the choice was clear: Christianity was in; the others would be pushed out.

Solving The Money Problem

It seems that Constantine and his followers gained a great deal of income in the transfer from pagan religion to a single version of Christianity. The state had long taken the estates of those who died *intestate* (without a will) and of those who were convicted criminals. By changing religions, the Empire created whole new classes of criminals, many of whom were restricted in their abilities to create wills. And since the state controlled the legal system, very few people could avoid their asset seizures.

And not only were the assets of the newly criminalized taken in this process, but the property and art of the pagan temples passed to the state as well. Either the pagan temples became churches – in which case the state had some claim upon them – or they were taken over in criminal proceedings. Constantine began the process by removing gold and silver treasures from the temples, starting in the East.

Here is a partial list of edicts issued (and the year in which they were issued) by Constantine and his successors, as they pursued this agenda:

313 – Any property which has been taken from the Christians in persecution is to be restored. This includes gardens, buildings, or any other property, and is to be done in haste.

321 – Every person shall have the right to leave property to the catholic church in his will.

322 – Heretical groups are forbidden to assemble. Their buildings must be surrendered to the catholic church.

333 – Christians shall not be forced into participating in pagan practices; anyone who forces a Christian into such an act shall be publicly beaten, unless he holds an honorable rank, in which case he will be fined and the money given to the state treasury.

333 – All works of Arius or Arians be burned, and that anyone hiding a work of Arius suffer capital punishment.

346 – Pagan temples are to be closed; access to them is denied, and violators face capital punishment. The property of a violator will be given to the state treasury. Governors who fail to carry out this punishment will be punished.

347 – Donatists are ordered to be reconciled with the catholic church in North Africa. Those who refused are to be exiled or killed.

352 – Persons who join Judaism from Christianity, if the accusation can be proven, shall have their property confiscated and given to the state treasury.

356 – Those guilty of idolatry or pagan sacrifices must suffer capital punishment.

377 – If a Manichaean should go underground and hold secret meetings, he is subjected to the law and must leave his goods to relatives or the government.

383 – Confirmed Christians who have turned to paganism may not issue a will to anyone.

389 – Manichaeans are to be expelled from Rome and banished from the empire. Their property is to be confiscated, and their wills are void.

392 – If heretical clergy are ordained, the property where the ordination occurred is to be seized by the government if the ordination occurred with the owner's permission. If it was done without his knowledge, he may be fined or beaten and deported, depending on his income. If it occurred in a public place, the procurator is to be fined.

396 – All heretical assembly places are to be confiscated, and heretics driven out of Constantinople. They are forbidden to enter the city for the purpose of gathering. If this occurs even in a private house, the penalty was a fine of 100 pounds of gold.

396 – Christians who became guilty of idolatry are not allowed to bequeath property in their wills to anyone other than parents, siblings, children, or grandchildren.

405 – Anyone who performs rebaptism will have his property confiscated, unless, for the sake of his children, he returns to the catholic church. Places where rebaptisms were performed will be confiscated. Re-baptizers may not make contracts or leave wills.

429 – Anyone who converts an orthodox Christian from the catholic church to another religion or heretical sect will have his property confiscated and be executed.

The Church Is Established

The changeover to Christianity was more difficult and divisive than Constantine had apparently planned. It seems that he was sincerely surprised by the divisions among Christians. It's certainly true that he worked long and hard to reconcile the various groups. He expended great effort to reconcile the Donatists and the catholics[49], for example, an effort that ultimately failed and required death sentences upon the Donatists.

Constantine worked to centralize Christianity, which was far from homogenous at that time. At the council of Nicea, in 325, he more or less forced the attendees to come up with a unified Christian creed. Several hundred bishops from all parts of the empire met in the imperial palace for a month to reach their agreement. Constantine then went forth to impose that creed upon the empire.

Here are some of the imperial edicts that unified Christianity as a single doctrine and established it as a single organization which was part of the Empire:

> 313 – Imperial subsidies to be given to the catholic priests of North Africa. In addition, those who are seducing the catholic Christians of North Africa need to be corrected.

> 313 – All catholic clergy are free from compulsory public service.

> 318 – Constantine gives Christians the right to take their cases before an ecclesiastical court rather than a secular court. The ruling of those bishops will carry the same authority as a secular court.

> 343 – Clergy and their servants shall not have to pay any taxes, or any new taxes in the future, nor shall they have to quarter strangers, and they shall be tax exempt if they start their own businesses.

> 349 – Clergy are exempted from all compulsory public services and municipal duties. Their sons should continue in the clergy unless obligated by service in the Senate.

> 355 – Bishops shall not have to appear before secular judges; accusations against them shall be brought before other bishops.

> 394 – Heretics are forbidden to teach their doctrines or appoint priests or other clergy. Judges and other officials must enforce this law.

> 395 – All pagan festival days are declared *non*-holidays. No one is permitted to perform a pagan sacrifice.

---

[49] Up to this time, "catholic" was only a descriptive term, meaning *universal*. This dominant group of Christians were also called "orthodox" at the time, which is not to be confused with the Orthodox (Eastern) Churches of modern times. Again, this was more of a descriptive term than a formal name.

395 – Anyone who disagrees with the Catholic Christian Church even on a minor point of doctrine is considered a heretic.

396 – Local leaders and officials are not to be selected from the Alexandrian craft-guildsmen unless they are Christians.

398 – Eunomians and Montanists (non-conformist Christians) are to be expelled from the cities, and if they reside in the country and hold assemblies, they are to be deported and the owners of the land punished. Heretical books are to be destroyed. Those who refuse to surrender such books are to suffer capital punishment on the charge of sorcery.

408 – Laws in place against Donatists, Manichaeans, and other non-conformist groups remain effective. Prosecution against them must continue vigorously.

409 – Only orthodox Christians may be appointed as defender of a city, with the bishop and clergy joining the distinguished citizens in making the appointment.

412 – Anyone who hides a Pelagian (non-conformists, again) will suffer the same penalties as a Pelagian. St. Augustine is authorized to publicize the penalties for Pelagians.

425 – No spectacles in honor of the emperor are to take precedence over worship of God.

It can be seen from this list that the emperors made great efforts to establish the church not only as a state religion, and as a *secular* power as well. (Secular means *pertaining to worldly things*.) This development was erratic but seems to have been finished with a good deal of violence.

This distribution of power to approved Christians created problems within Christianity by inducing leaders to fight for position. When proper doctrine is rewarded with money and power, that becomes the thing people fight over. Once such battles are underway, the only thing that can stop them is a central strongman who cannot be overcome. This was probably a driving force behind the papacy, which was not part of Christianity before this time.

Constantine's Second Move

Apparently seeing that the Western Empire might not be saved, even with Christianity, Constantine moved the capital to a new city at the east end of the Mediterranean in 330. The city was built around a small, old town called Byzantium, and it was renamed *Constantinople;* it was also called *New Rome*. This city was positioned astride the trade routes between East and West.

In his new capital, Constantine stabilized the coinage[50] and made changes to the structure of the army. This allowed the Empire to recover much of its military strength and to enjoy a period of stability and prosperity. It gave them breathing room.

This modified version of the Empire welcomed trade. It strictly regulated it, but allowed it to expand. The Empire, seeking to maintain control as all governments do, demanded a monopoly on the issuance of coins, controlled interest rates, and controlled the activities of guilds and corporations. There were price controls from time to time, especially on grain.

As in the West, surplus was removed from the farms and from individuals and passed to New Rome, where it was spent on the military, on free food distributions, or for public works.

It is important to understand that the people in the East did not have the old Roman foundation of distributed power and virtuous living. They were children of the Empire, and did not know the virtues of the now-ancient Republic. (The old agricultural virtues weren't critical for a trading empire.)

More importantly, the people of the east felt honored that they had been chosen as the new center of the Empire. In response they gladly amplified the glory of Rome. To praise Rome was now to praise themselves, and few men shrink from such opportunities.

As New Rome was established, part of the Roman aristocratic class left Italy and came to the new seat of power, followed by artists and craftsmen. The eastern, Greek half of the empire, based in Constantinople, was never the power that the original Rome had been, but it did survive, more or less and with small gaps, until 1453. Moderns refer to this as the *Byzantine Empire,* but they called themselves Rome.

Plato's Apostle

Once Constantine had moved his capital to the east, the Western Empire was left to its slow decline. Certainly there were emperors who wanted to restore the glory that had been Rome, but it was manifestly beyond restoration. The barbarians grew stronger and Rome weaker. Through many of these years, Rome was paying the barbarians hundreds of pounds of gold every year, in exchange for peace. The Western Empire became a vassal state of the barbarians.

Into this mix comes the man we know as St. Augustine. Born in 354, he obtained an extensive education and by the time he was twenty nine he was operating one of the best schools in Rome. By his thirtieth birthday (in 384), he was appointed the professor of rhetoric for the imperial court at Milan. This was the most important academic appointment in the Latin world (that

---

[50] Very likely with gold taken from the pagan temples of the East.

is, the Western world, as opposed to the Eastern, Greek world). It was also a powerful political position.

Two years later, Augustine went back to his home in Northern Africa and became a monastic Christian. His conversion came about after a long journey through multiple beliefs[51] and groups. Soon, Augustine was a renowned preacher and by about 396 he was a full bishop. Shortly thereafter, Augustine set out to remove the heresy of Donatism[52] from his territory. At first he pushed the Donatists to join the approved church, but when that failed, he called for government force to repress them.

In 410, the city of Rome was sacked by barbarians under the leadership of the Visigoth Alaric. As always, people sought someone to blame. Some said that their new Christian religion might be to blame for the disaster. The ruling class in particular complained that any religion that championed "turning the other cheek" and that held worldly empires in low esteem, was dangerous.

In response to this an imperial commissioner named Marcellinus, a friend of Augustine's, asked him to respond to the charges. Augustine quickly produced the first several chapters of his book, *The City of God*, which rather effectively quieted the complaints. (He continued the book over a number of years, until it was finally complete.)

It is important that Augustine was not merely a clergyman; by 419, he was personally acquainted with the emperors Honorius and Theodosius II, and was authorized by them to undertake the publicity of their edicts. It is also highly important that Augustine's teachings in *City of God* became the foundation of the Catholic Church's theology for approximately a thousand years, and are highly influential still. In short: *Augustine formed the theology of the Roman Catholic Church.*

It is almost without question that Augustine is still considered the greatest theologian of the Church. But, to buttress the point, here are quotations from Pope Benedict XVI:

> [Augustine is] the greatest Father of the Latin Church.
>
> It could be said that all the roads of Latin Christian literature led to Hippo, the place in North Africa where he [Augustine] was Bishop from AD 395 until his death in 430.

And, this was the case very early as well. At the Second Council of Constantinople in 553, only three Latin authorities[53] are quoted: Hilary, Ambrose, and Augustine.

---

[51] Christian, Manichean, ascetic and Neo-Platonist.

[52] The Donatists rejected any priesthood imposed upon them by the Emperor, especially priests they considered unrighteous.

Augustine's *City of God* presents human history as being a conflict between what Augustine calls the *City of Man* and the *City of God,* which strongly parallel's Plato's ideas on the *heavenly pattern* and the *ideal state.*

Augustine is not shy about his regard for Plato. In *City of God*, he gushes over him:

> Among the disciples of Socrates, Plato was the one who shone with a glory which far excelled that of the others, and who, not unjustly, eclipsed them all. By birth, an Athenian of honorable parentage, he far surpassed his fellow disciples in natural endowments, of which he was possessed in a wonderful degree. Yet, deeming himself and the Socratic discipline far from sufficient for bringing philosophy to perfection, he traveled as extensively as he was able, going to every place famed for the cultivation of any science of which he could make himself master.

Augustine sees Christianity as the ideal and perfect philosophy, but he hold's Plato's ideals in exceptionally high regard, saying: *It is evident that none come nearer to us than the Platonists.*

Roman Christianity, from Augustine's time onward, was a Platonic Christianity.

A New Kind of Empire

By the end of the 5th century (by 500 A.D.), the Church of Rome found itself in a unique position: Abandoned in the midst of a dying empire, with greatly reduced access to force[54], but in a strong position of legitimacy. It is from this unusual position that they began to build an unusual form of empire.

The Church found itself with a tremendous amount legitimacy, which they expanded to a near monopoly. If they proclaimed something to be approved by Christ, a large number of people would presume that the person or thing was deserving of support, and would act accordingly. And if the Church condemned something, it would be condemned by their followers. It became almost the sole provider of large-scale legitimacy in what had been the original Roman Empire.

This is not to say, however, that the Church had control at 500 A.D. In fact they had little control and their lines of communication to churches in small

---

[53] "Latin" authorities are those who wrote in the Latin language and came after the writers of the New Testament and the men of primitive Christianity, all of whom wrote in Greek.

[54] The Church had previously used state force to get rid of heretics. They complained of many fewer heresies after they lost access to power in the late 5th century... and not again till it was restored, centuries later.

towns were poor. Small churches and monasteries were on their own for a very long time. But still, the word of the Bishop of Rome carried weight.

In this situation, it became crucial for the Church to exploit its legitimacy. And so it developed dazzling ceremonies, dramatic fables, and inserted their images into the minds of Westerners in ever-improving ways. It sought to become the center of reference for every human mind in Europe. Beyond all else, this imperative guided the Church. And this odd empire was successful. They certainly proved that great masses of men and women can be controlled without weapons.

One of Plato's more important teachings was that philosophers should rule over men, instead of soldiers and old-style kings. For example, he says:

> Until philosophers are kings, or the kings and princes of this world have the spirit and power of philosophy, and political greatness and wisdom meet in one... cities will never have rest from their evils,-- nor the human race, as I believe,--and only then will this our State have a possibility of life and behold the light of day.

And, the same sentiment in a more direct form:

> Until philosophers bear rule, States and individuals will have no rest from evil.

The Church at Rome went about to rule as philosopher-kings. Beginning with very little military power – and unlikely to have much for some time – they worked long and hard on techniques of persuasion, guidance and manipulation.

Students of the Middle Ages have often commented on the oppressive nature of the Catholic Church upon the minds of men. This was often true, but it was not generally the goal of Church leaders to be cruel: it was to maintain power in conditions of limited force[55]. And the truth is that the greatest of all word-based motivations is the fear of shame.

For whatever reason, humans are grossly over-affected by shame and will cower before those who are able to impose it. Accordingly, the Church became expert at applying shame and fear. It was necessary if they were to maintain the difficult position of rulership without violence. This does not excuse their cruelty, but it goes a long way toward explaining it.

---

[55] To force people to obey at the end of a sword is one thing; to manipulate them into obedience with mere words is quite another, and requires much greater skill.

Attempts At Re-Conquest

The Church was not, however, willing to forgo military power. They knew its importance and wished to get it back. To do this, they would have to turn legitimacy into military power.

During the 5th and 6th centuries, military power withdrew from Europe, devolving to the level of local (and partial) rulers with mobile courts. Constantinople, in what is now Turkey, was being established and the eastern Empire was doing fairly well, but power slipped away in the west till there was almost none left. Even by the time of Pope Leo I (440-461), he was left as the senior imperial civilian official in the city of Rome.

The famous story of Pope Leo was that he went out of the city of Rome to meet Attila the Hun in 452. The dramatic story begins as Attila wreaks havoc throughout Italy and ultimately arrives at the gates of Rome. Then Leo, with two other civil functionaries, goes out to meet Attila and somehow convinces him to go away. Since this was highly contradictory to Attila's character, the Church proclaimed it a miracle and published the legend of Leo the Great far and wide.

According to numerous sources, the basic facts of the story are true: Attila did come to Rome, Leo did go to see him, and Attila did leave. From this point on, however, the stories begin to differ. Leo's contemporary, Priscus, opines that a large sum of gold may have been involved, or that logistical concerns may have been the true reason for Attila's withdrawal. The Hun army had dramatically stretched their supply lines and were overflowing with plunder; so, the Pope's plea for mercy may have served as an honorable reason for withdrawal. In any event, Leo was unable to prevent the Vandals from sacking Rome just three years later. But, this latter episode was forgotten. The Church championed their version of the first story because it was wonderful for their legitimacy. Miracles proved that they were associated with the great God. And the miracle of defeating the most fearsome army of the age was perfect for legitimizing the rule of philosophers above mere soldiers.[56]

This event was also crucial in allowing Leo to promote the Papacy as the one true voice of Christianity. This theme, of the "universal jurisdiction of the Roman bishop," is found in many of his letters and even in the record of his orations, ninety-six of which still exist.

The Church at this time was still in their period of expansion. By converting the barbarians to Christianity, they didn't immediately gain military power, but they greatly expanded the range of their legitimacy. The map below shows the spread of Christianity during the early years of the Church.

---

[56]Relics of saints became a major factor at this time, but that is a subject we will pass up.

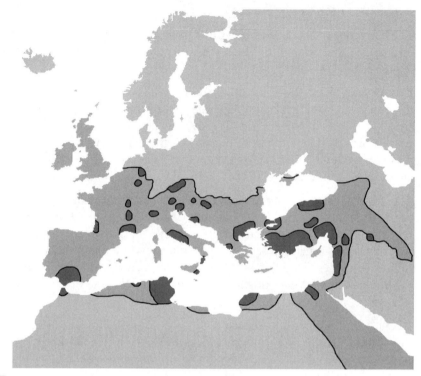

■ Spread of Christianity to 325 AD   ■ Spread of Christianity to 600 AD

Courtesy Wikimedia Commons

As traveling rulers were converted, the Roman Church supported them and they supported the Church. The Church had difficulty issuing direct orders to the kings and princes, but the rulers had to consider the effect of the Church's opinions upon their people. In a few famous incidents kings had to beg a Pope for forgiveness or else be ruined by excommunication.

The Church tried to gain secular power, of course, with limited success until their pacts with the Franks, and especially with Charlemagne. Their early efforts, however, resulted in some of the more entertaining passages in history. These involve forged documents and massive donations of land (and its governance) to the Church.

The first donation was a fairly mundane affair called the *Donation of Sutri*. This was simply an agreement between Liutprand, King of the Lombards and Pope Gregory II in 728.[57] At Sutri, the two reached an agreement by which the city and some hill towns were given to the Papacy, "as a gift to the

---

[57]This was just at the time when the Church had broken its last substantive ties to Constantinople and the power they could provide.

blessed Apostles Peter and Paul." The pact was only important in that it became a precedent[58] for the accumulation of Papal States.

The next episode, called the *Donation of Constantine*, was far more dramatic. In about 750, a letter was produced by the Church, supposedly written by Constantine I on his death bed. The *Donation* grants Pope Sylvester I and his successors, as inheritors of St. Peter, dominion over lands in Judea, Greece, Asia, Thrace, Africa, as well as the city of Rome, Italy and the entire Western Roman Empire, while Constantine would retain imperial authority in the Eastern Roman Empire from his new imperial capital of Constantinople.

The text of the *Donation* claims that it was Constantine's gift to Sylvester for instructing him in the Christian faith, baptizing him and miraculously curing him of leprosy. The Church did not immediately try to collect all of the lands that Constantine "donated" to them, but they kept their right to those lands very much in the minds of the men and women of Europe.

The most dramatic story of magic letters occurred just a few years later, in 754, when Pope Stephen II is reported to have received a letter from heaven, written in the hand of St. Peter, to the king of the franks, Pepin the Short. This letter, written in pure gold on the finest vellum, was widely considered legitimate during the Middle Ages. It is reported to have read as follows:

> Peter, elected Apostle by Jesus Christ, Son of the Living God. I, Peter, summoned to the apostolate by Christ, Son of the Living God, have received from the Divine Might the mission of enlightening the whole world.
>
> Wherefore, all those who, having heard my preaching, put it into practice, must believe absolutely that by God's order their sins are cleansed in this world and they shall enter stainless into everlasting life.
>
> Come ye to the aid of the Roman people, which has been entrusted to me by God. And I, on the day of Judgment, shall prepare for you a splendid dwelling place in the Kingdom of God.
>
> – Peter, Prince of the Apostles.

Previously, Pope Stephen had traveled to Paris to anoint both Pepin and his sons as a new line of kings, thereby supplanting the old Merovingian line.

Shortly after the letter was publicized, Pepin went to war with the Lombards who were taking Italy and heading toward Rome. After driving out the Lombards, Pepin gave the Pope the lands which the Lombards had taken

---

[58] This relies on an odd human weakness – that if something has been done before, it must be "okay."

from the Byzantine Empire. Thus the Church was handed a sizable piece of the Italian peninsula – lands that would be called the *Papal States* and which were the basis of the Papacy's secular power for a thousand years.

Pepin confirmed his Donation of land to the Church in 756, and in 774 his son Charlemagne confirmed the donation of his father.

In 800 Pope Leo III crowned Charlemagne as a Roman Emperor, establishing what became known as the *Holy Roman Empire*[59], and from that date onward the popes claimed the right to crown its emperor. This gave them a legitimacy above the kings of the earth – just the right position for an institution of philosopher-kings, whose rule would continue without a major interruption for another five and a half centuries. It also gave them a powerful army that they could call in an emergency.

Life In The New Empire

The Church's goal for daily life under their reign was stability, with the Church as the moral center of the universe, able to move the various secular rulers into paths that the Church chose, or at least into paths they could use with a backup plan.

The Church was never able to obtain full compliance, but they did succeed impressively. The Pope, to at least a significant degree, reigned over kings by maintaining a monopoly on legitimacy. (Though again, the situation was complicated.)

Europeans of the Middle Ages were taught that the order of their lives had been established by God and that to challenge that divine order was a horrible offense. They saw a world made up of three types of people:

1. *Latores.* The kings and lesser nobles, who protected everyone else.

2. *Oratores.* The clergy, who interceded with God for everyone else.

3. *Laboratores.* The peasants, who fed everyone else.

There were always people on the fringes, up to a third in some places. These included itinerant traders, Jews, runaway serfs, and assorted dispossessed people.[60] Nonetheless, these people were subject to violence if they attracted too much attention.

This was a horrible structure for production. Humans, after all, vary greatly in their talents, and any system that makes good use of human ability must allow people to operate where their personal talents are most effective. But if breaking out of your hereditary 'place' is a sin, your talents are a non-issue. It was God's will that you were born into a certain class, so that is where you

---

[59] Which was, as noted in a famous quip, "neither holy, nor Roman, nor an empire."

[60] The surprisingly large numbers of people who joined mass movements in the middle ages very often involved these groups.

had to stay. And, once again, this rigid structure was prescribed by Plato. He wrote:

> You are brothers, yet God has framed you differently. Some of you he has made like gold, who have the power of command, and also they have the greatest honor; others he has made of silver, to be auxiliaries; others again who are to be husbandmen and craftsmen he has composed of brass and iron; and the species will generally be preserved in the children. ... God proclaims as a first principle to the rulers, and above all else, that there is nothing which should so anxiously guard, or of which they are to be such good guardians, as of the purity of the race. ... If the son of a golden or silver parent has an admixture of brass and iron, then nature orders a transposition of ranks, and the eye of the ruler must not be pitiful towards the child because he has to descend in the scale and become a husbandman or artisan ... When a man of brass or iron guards the State, it will be destroyed.

A very interesting comment follows, after someone asks whether instilling this idea in the populace is a practical possibility. Plato continues:

> Not in the present generation... there is no way of accomplishing this; but their sons may be made to believe in the tale, and their sons' sons, and posterity after them.

This is precisely what was done in medieval Europe. The people were made to believe something that did not come naturally to them – and it affected their minds for a thousand years. And, to an extent, this idea remains; it has strongly contributed to the feeling of many mixed-race people that they are somehow inferior. The amount of suffering caused by this lie has been astronomical.

Gathering The Surplus

We have previously described methods by which civilizations expanded, and noted that they all involved surplus production. This is a critical mechanism, a defining characteristic of a civilization.

In the Mesopotamian civilization, surplus went directly upward from the people to a ruler. Then, as small centers of ruler-dominance were strung together into empires, portions went upward through middle layers to the top levels of kings-of-kings. All through this era, surplus was used to build armies and monuments, and very little went to productive uses, such as the improvement of agriculture, metallurgy or the like.

In classical civilization, surplus-gathering was decentralized. Surplus passed into the hands of a local farmer, who put it to work directly, and usually productively. In the early days of Greece and Rome, very little surplus left the places where it was generated, and the civilizations thrived. Only later was surplus diverted to central political centers, where, again, it was used for armies and monuments. And, again, the civilizations rotted.

During the time of this Platonic Empire, surplus was gathered by spiritual coercion far more than it was by direct force or even by political authority. Although production through this era was widely distributed, and it was consistently gathered by the Church in the form of tithes, alms and other donations. (The royals got better at taxing as the centuries passed.)

Probably the most effective method of surplus-gathering was bequests to the Church. A bequest to the Church assured that the deceased would have many Masses said for him, greatly reducing the unpleasant time he would otherwise have to spend in Purgatory. And so, by the time of the Protestant reformation, the Catholic Church owned a shockingly large number of properties in Europe. This may have exceeded a third of all the land that comprises modern France.

Once Again, Legitimacy Fails

In the film, *Ben Hur*, the Tribune Messala utters a memorable line, saying: *I'll tell you how to fight an idea - with another idea!* This is what happened to the Church of Rome.

The Church had worked to control knowledge, but they could never do away with it. For one thing, they needed to be the arbiters of Jesus, and Jesus' words had been written. They remained. The Church tried to keep them wrapped up (available only in Latin), but they also needed literacy in order to operate their empire. And that meant that a considerable number of people had to be literate. And that was risky; the Church losing control of Jesus' words would make alternate interpretations possible. This would bring them back to the days before Constantine's council of Nicea and a unified doctrine. If that happened, their legitimacy would be fractured. And with no monopoly on legitimacy, their rule would end.

There are anecdotal stories all though the rule of the Church, telling of non-conformists in the Alps who retained both the scriptures and their own interpretations of them. Additional stories tell of these people doing things like smuggling passages of scripture (in the local language) into schools. Although there is little confirmation for these stories in the first millennium, it is certain that such people, commonly called Waldensians, did exist by the

12th century (1101-1200)[61]. And, the Church, understanding the threat, made great efforts to eliminate them.

Learning broke out of Church control, however, in the 12th century.[62] While manuscripts of Aristotle had long existed in Latin, they didn't get much play. By by early 13th century however, Aristotle was very popular in the schools of Paris. As a result, a Papal legate in Paris forbade teachers to lecture on Aristotle in 1225. Deeming this insufficient, Pope Gregory IX formed a commission to edit out all objectionable passages of Aristotle's works in 1231. But there were, at this moment, another group of forgotten heroes in Paris – more of the true benefactors of our race, whose names are lost to history. These people were willing to face serious risks for what they believed, and they simply disobeyed the Pope, his emissaries and his orders. The seemingly omnipotence of the papacy was unable to stop them.

As a result, by 1260 Aristotle was taught in virtually every Christian school. The Church did its best to merge Aristotle with their teachings, but it was a difficult mix. The Church had been built upon Plato, and Aristotle wrote some of his works in refutation of Plato. Europe's "New Learning" began to emerge.

It is fairly well known that most early Christian reformers were clergy. These were literate people who had access to the New Testament, and reading Jesus' teachings led them to question the system they served. Ultimately, the bravest of them rejected the Roman Catholic system, which had become horribly corrupt over time... as structures of central power always do.

The first great reformer was John Wycliffe, and he undertook the work of condemning the Church for extra-biblical teachings and corruption with exceptional ability. Then, Wycliffe created an even greater irritation to the Church by publishing the New Testament in English. This was a serious threat to the Church's legitimacy. Once anyone could read the record of Jesus for himself, he could form his own opinions and the Church's monopoly on legitimacy would be wounded at the least.

The Church tried to stop John Wycliffe, but he was far from Rome and the processes of the day were ill-designed for this sort of threat. By the time they came for Wycliffe, he was already dead[63]. Worse, there was a decentralized group of followers called *Lollards* continuing his work. Over time, they influenced many more reformers, such as Hus and Luther, who put a final end to Rome's monopoly on legitimacy.

---

[61] There are stories tracing the line of the Waldensians back to Claude of Turin in the 9th Century, but I have yet to find evidence for them.

[62] We'll touch on this in chapter 6.

[63] They did dig up his body, burn it, and throw his ashes in a nearby river.

The Church struggled long and hard to reverse the situation, but by the year 1500 it was clear that the changes were unstoppable. Guttenberg's printing press not only made Protestantism's victory certain, but it greatly sped up the process. The official end of Plato's Empire came in 1638, when the Peace of Westphalia legally removed religious compulsion from rulership and gave Protestantism (in any number of forms) equal standing with the Church of Rome.

Certainly the Church of Rome continues, and certainly it continues to claim a special legitimacy, but its ability to maintain a monopoly on legitimacy is gone, and with it, its empire.

5

The Subversive Seed

*That which is highly esteemed among men
is abomination in the sight of God.*
– Jesus

I had no intention of writing about Jesus in this book. This was not because of any disregard I have for the man, I just didn't see how he played much of a role in the story. But as the text took shape, he kept appearing. Before long, I understood that he was a major figure in my analysis. I couldn't keep him out and still write an honest book.

None of this has anything to do with Jesus being the son of God or not. I am not dealing with beliefs here; I am concerned with the recorded teachings of Jesus and the effects they had upon the Western world. If the story of Jesus were nothing but a fable, it would make no difference to this analysis.

The Western civilization that follows Jesus is unique. It has gone through several rises and falls, yet it has never failed altogether. This is something that Professor Quigley noted nearly sixty years ago and that puzzled him. Why is it that this one civilization keeps resurrecting itself? I never worked on the question very directly, but it did remain in the back of my mind. Then, piece by piece, an answer began to form, and its threads kept leading back to Jesus. So be it.

The Insertion

Jesus' teachings enter history in a very advantageous spot. The place is the Roman Empire, where communication and travel are approaching a peak that was not re-attained for nearly two thousand years. Literacy is high by ancient standards. In the province when Jesus arises, literacy is definitely high and the inhabitants have their minds unusually open to ideas[64]. The moment is just after the Roman Republic has been replaced by the empire. The first emperor is in place, and the seeds of Rome's demise have been sown.

Jesus seems to have been a fairly secretive man, and one who even his closest students couldn't understand. Jesus himself wrote nothing that we are aware of. Yet within ten years of his death[65], his followers can be seen spreading far and wide, convincing foreigners with their message. Within forty years of his death, the vast majority of his now-many followers were forcibly removed from both the city of Rome (49 A.D.) and from their center in Jerusalem (66 A.D.) As they went, they spread Jesus' teachings through the cities of the empire; their usual adherents being the proletariate; that is, productive working people.

There were few restrictions on their travels and the empire was a surprisingly open place for new religious ideas. Pagans did not think their gods had to be the only gods. All in all, this was a good moment for the spreading of new concepts.

The Gift of The Hebrews

It is well-known that Jesus was a Jew and lived among Jews. Less understood is the fact that he (or, rather, his students) transferred Hebrew ideas to the non-Jewish world.

The Hebrews, at some point in the 3rd millennium BC, turned the collective religion of the Sumerians into a personal religion.[66] This was a crucial adaptation because it freed individual will from the claims of the group; it set a divine hedge around individuality.

Furthermore – and this is seen throughout the entire length of the Hebrew tradition – *the God of the Hebrews spoke to powerless people, not to the mighty*. This was a new and heretical adaptation, and a potent one. This revolutionary sentiment finds voice all through the Hebrew scriptures and a thoroughly equal voice in the Christian gospels. The God of the Hebrews and

---

[64] As usual for such situations, there were many ideas – both good and bad – flying around at the same time. But better this sort of confusion than the bleak periods when no one cares to think much at all.

[65] I am referring here to the spreading of Jesus' teachings throughout the Greek world, prior to the murder of James the son of Zebedee in about 44 A.D.

[66] See FMP #68.

the God of Jesus reached down to the humble and turned his back on the mighty.

Ben Hecht, an important 20ᵗʰ century writer, noted this in his *Guide for the Bedeviled*:

> The Jews... had demanded, to the consternation of Kings and Powers, that right and wrong, good and evil, be based on the needs and talents of the humble. The practicality of their requests had made them anarchists.

The Hebrews, not surprisingly, had no king from their beginnings until about 1000 BC. And even then, the prophet Samuel repeatedly warned them against taking a one. Likewise, the Hebrews had no priests from their origins until they were established in Canaan. And they abandoned that priesthood some 1,300 years later, as they left Canaan.

The Power of Monotheism

Monotheism was a more potent formulation than is commonly understood. A strong argument can be made that it has succeeded because of psychological advantages – primarily in that it harmonizes with human nature and legitimizes the more efficient modes of human reasoning.

The Hebrews may or may not have been the first monotheists; a few Egyptians and Persians seem to have come up with the idea independently. But it *is* fairly certain that the Hebrews created the first monotheistic culture.

An argument for the utility of monotheism consists of four primary points:

1. Humans are, by their inescapable structure, individuals. We feel only the pain produced in our own bodies and we are only aware of thought produced in our own minds. (Unless we communicate, of course.) Our use of energy and creativity are individual enterprises. We may cooperate, but we are fully individual entities, not corporate entities[67].

2. What people hold to as the highest and best has a profound effect on them. Images they hold as "high and great" are centers of reference. This colors their thoughts and decisions on a moment-by-moment basis.

3. Monotheism sets a distinct individual as the highest and greatest being that ever was or ever will be.

4. With this pattern in the minds of men, they are less afraid to think as individuals, which suits their nature. As a result, they tend to come up with marginally better ideas and to produce better results; not

---

[67] This is utterly obvious, but needs to be pointed-out because of pop-philosophies that champion imaginations of inherent unity.

because monotheism correctly describes any particular deity, but because it encourages humans to think as individuals and to develop self-reference.

The image of a single, perfect god not only gives men the courage to think for themselves but it makes it easier for men to compare themselves to the highest and the ultimate. By imagining how the ultimate being sees things, we can understand what it means to be high and great... and we can emulate it.

There could, of course, be many versions of monotheism. The Sikhs, for example, have a formulation that includes reincarnation. The Judeo-Christian version of monotheism, however, has these additional characteristics of interest:

> *Supreme Goodness.* The Judeo-Christian god is generally seen as qualitatively perfect. This gives believers something to strive toward. And since there is a prominent theme of the believers being associated with God, many attempt to embody these characteristics as well.

> *The Ethical Becomes the Eternal.* Judeo-Christian monotheism magnifies ethical choices. Acting charitably toward your neighbor doesn't just matter here and now, it creates an eternal reward. Thus, ethical choices become hyper-important, and believers tend to improve their conduct.

Who Is God?

In Chapter 2, we explained how gods became mixed in the ancient world as one group overran another and superimposed their god upon the previous god. Eliminating the old god was not practical for the goal of rulership, and so it was merely changed, with a new version becoming a partner in the enterprise. The particular case we covered was a female production-god being overrun by a male plunder-god. The gods of men have been mixed ever since.

So, who was god to be? Is he (or she) kind or vengeful? Does the god champion creative synthesis or lordly control? Does he save or does he punish? Who is this being, really?

Jesus sets out a new version of God, and one that is further from the plunder-god and closer to the production-god. It is true that elements of each come across in the recordings of Jesus' words, and it is likely that the versions we have are not identical to his actual teachings. Regardless, to a very significant extent, Jesus went about to unmix the gods. Whether Jesus thought of it this way or not, a good deal of his message addresses this issue, and in ways that are seldom appreciated.

First of all, Jesus separates his god from all previous gods, even the god of the Jews. At one point, he tells a group of religious Jews, "It is my Father that honors me; of whom you say, that he is your God: Yet you have not known him." His followers would maintain that Jesus was trying to bring the Jews back to the true god – and Jesus may well have said this himself – but the point remains, he describes a god who is *different in nature* from the one they are currently worshipping.

To begin with, Jesus' God is not an arbitrary judge above; he is Jesus' father. And, more than that, a loving father. And this father loves "his own" in the world. In fact, Jesus goes so far as to say that his father loves his followers as much as he loves Jesus.

Jesus further brings divine ability back down among men, much like the production-goddess did. When people are healed, he tells them: *Your faith has made you well.* He tries (to little avail[68]) to convince them that divine power is present among normal humans, not just in a special man like himself. *According to your faith, it is done unto you,* he tells them, advising his students that they'll be able to do everything he has done. And even though the message was apparently lost by these men, the record of his attempts remains.

Religious leaders of all types have usually preferred to make God very high and man very low, creating a great separation, making themselves necessary as intermediaries. Jesus, however, resolutely condemns the idea of a special class of priests and makes "the greatest" a servant.

This is a rich subject for believers and for theologians, but we will not spend great time on it here. The crucial issue is that Jesus made significant and persistent efforts to describe the true nature of god as much closer to the production goddess than the plundering ruler.

- The goddess was benevolent and loving: Jesus' father fiercely loved men.

- The goddess was not above, but among men: Jesus insists that the power of god is among men.

- The purpose of the goddess was to effect production: Jesus incessantly demands that his followers should "bear fruit." That is, to be productive.

- The goddess provided the magic spark of production to men: Jesus came *to serve, not to be served.*

---

[68] As in many other applications, it is easier to paint a man like Jesus as "the great one," justifying one's own lack of advancement, since "we are not special like him." Self-improvement is a difficult business, and one that many people evade.

Right Over Might

The cultures of the pre-Christian world, with the exception of the Hebrews, maintained fairly strongly that might made right. There were always individuals who knew that this concept was barbaric, but ruling cultures like Rome felt otherwise, and their opinions carried a long way. Christian Europe, however, explicitly reversed the model, believing that right made might.

The resurrection of Jesus was, and probably remains as, the most potent human image of right triumphing over might. And so it was in Christianity that right-over-might took root and became, among other things, a central factor in most subsequent dramatic stories. Typically this is called "the romantic ideal," and it is found wherever a hero faces off against overwhelming power and triumphs because of goodness and understanding, not by merely amassing more power.

A Code of Production

Within Jesus' teachings and those of his close friends, there is a code of production that has continually informed Western civilization. (We will come to Western civilization in the next chapter.) Whether Western civilization currently retains any belief in Christ matters little; Jesus' words (as recorded and passed-down) made the West what it is. It is this code of production that made the West cooperative and productive. Following are some of the ideas that form this code of production, with New Testament passages inset:

An Expectation of Reason

> Why, of your own selves, do you not know what is right?

> Examine yourselves... prove your own selves.

There are a few anti-reason passages in the New Testament, but the command to reason exists, and most emphatically from the mouth of Jesus himself. This gives a Christian full leave to use his or her mind.

> Be ready always to give an answer to any man who asks you a reason.

This makes the believer responsible for understanding. He or she must consider, understand, internalize the essential facts, and be able to assemble and present them to others.

Compassion for the Outsider

> If a man have an hundred sheep, and one of them be gone astray, does he not leave the ninety and nine, and go seek that which is gone astray?

> There shall be more joy in heaven over one sinner
> that repents, than over ninety-nine who need no
> repentance.

Considering that hatred of "the other" has caused enormous death tolls under many belief systems, this love for the outsider is a critical feature indeed.

Violence is Discouraged

> If a man strike you on one cheek, turn to him the
> other.

This discouragement of violence (sometimes considered a prohibition) has often kept human behavior far less bad than it might have been. Where use of force is reduced, freedom and prosperity are increased. Whether any particular group of Christians followed this admonition is not the issue; this primary message in the New Testament has been helpful.

Self-Reliance

> How is it that you go to law, one against another?

In modern terms, we might say, "Why are you suing each other in court? If you can't solve your own problems and are running to a government to do it for you, you're no examples of my teachings." The author of this line expected people to solve their own interpersonal problems. In effect, it says, "If you can't handle self-reliance, you're not much of a believer."

Co-Dominance

> Love your adversaries.

Let's say you're in the construction business; so are a dozen other people in your town; you compete against them every day. Can you still respect them and care about them as human beings? This is what Jesus demands of his followers.

Where co-dominance is absent, anger festers, compassion fails, grudges are never released, and endless volumes of energy are wasted in posturing and scheming. (As opposed to creating value.)

Where co-dominance is present, cooperation rules and massive accomplishments can arise. For people to live together in a peaceful way, co-dominance and cooperation are necessary.

Forgiveness and Repentance

Since its beginning, this set of writings has glorified men who had deep changes of heart. This not only allows bad men to start anew and improve, but it removes guilt for their past actions. There can be problems associated with this from a justice standpoint, but it has assisted human improvement.

Self-Reference and Integrity

> Whatever you would have men do unto you, do ye even so to them.

This type of self-reference and integrity carries benefits in all areas of life and has effects that extend far beyond a casual analysis.

A Permanent Reset

We've previously discussed moments of cultural resets, when people pull themselves together and develop virtuous, cooperative arrangements that allow them to move forward. We further said (and shall say again) that this early formulation is eventually lost, leading to the downfall of that civilization.

The historical importance of Jesus' teachings is that they created a *creed of the foundational moment,* incorporating, explaining and demanding a set of virtues that – if they are followed – produce a cooperative, productive society.

Because this code was written, it does not need to be relearned at the base of each societal cycle. In an enduring form, the foundation is effectively re-laid in one individual at a time, to one extent or another, every time these teachings are sufficiently understood. The teachings of Jesus are a permanent societal reset.

Of course, there are many possible objections to the statements above, based upon individual cases that differed[69]. And, of course, many of these cases were truly horrific. Nonetheless, this statement is generally true, and it provides the answer to Professor Quigley's question: Why does this one civilization continue to resurrect itself? That answer is, *because it contains a creed of the foundational moment, which remains accessible.* Many people will ignore this creed until absolutely necessary, but when they do need it, it is present.

Furthermore, Jesus does not want men to merely hear and mimic his teachings, he wants them to build them into themselves. Jesus' goal is nothing less than for all men to become independent creators of virtues: Virtues grown within each individual, not merely accepted as hand-me-downs. And this, whether initially apparent or not, this is both highly productive and highly subversive to centralized power.

---

[69] Most of these objections do not address Jesus' code, but the actions of evil people who pretended to follow it.

The Philosophy of A New Age

Before leaving this topic, it is worth noting that Jesus laid a foundation not only for Christian Europe, but for an age we have not yet entered.[70]

Jesus tried long and hard to stop men's minds from thinking about the enforcer above, who would punish them for stepping out of line. As you will certainly be aware, this "do as the law demands or be punished" remains the foundation of our modern systems.

Jesus wanted to replace this thought process with something better. He very clearly set a new method of judging conduct. And again, it is a method that we haven't yet adopted. Indeed, it is a method that Christians have barely recognized.

As we all know, the standard model for defining proper conduct is and has been by reference to a law. In other words, men are told to measure themselves by an *external* standard. Jesus changed this, and told people to measure themselves by an *internal* standard.

Notice some of the things Jesus says:

> Whatever you would have men do unto you, do ye even so to them.
>
> With whatever judgment you judge, you shall be judged.
>
> By *your* words you will be justified, and by *your* words you shall be condemned.
>
> Forgive our debts as we forgive our debtors.

These are only some more overt examples. Jesus, clearly and repetitively, instructs men to judge themselves by reference to things internal rather than external. In fact, he demands it of them.

This teaching of Jesus describes an entirely new moral system, based on a completely different mechanism than the Law of Moses or of any hierarchy that has ever existed. According to Jesus, you are to judge by self-reference, not by referral to a set of edicts made or enforced by others.

This new formulation is highly subversive[71]. Indeed, it is fundamentally incompatible with every centralized application of governance.

---

[70] See FMP #44.

[71] Which explains why it hasn't yet been championed: It's still too heretical.

6

Western Civilization Forms

Western Civilization… might be summed-up in the belief that "Truth unfolds through time in a communal process."
– Carroll Quigley

The quote above expresses a great core of Western civilization, if not *the* core. There are many facets to the formula: *Truth is revealed by a communal (cooperative) process.* And while this statement may be new to most of us, its effects are not. Everyone in the West faces them every day; so much so that we never really consider them.

This formulation has been assumed many times in this book already. By this, the sixth chapter, phrases like "We know that…" or "we have no information on…" have been used many times. Every time we use such words, we presume that truth is built, that all of us may contribute to this building of knowledge, and that we will certainly have more in the future than we have now. Truth is revealed by a cooperative process.

Obviously, this belief makes Western civilization[72] optimistic, but there is more than just that; it also makes authoritarian rule incompatible with our beliefs. If the final truth is yet to be revealed, who can say that he or she has full knowledge and should be given full powers? It also makes the West open to new ideas from any source. If something contributes to the accumulation of truth, who cares where it comes from?

---

[72] I do not consider the classical civilizations of Greece and Rome to be "Western civilization." Certainly we in the West have borrowed from them, but they operated on a radically different model from ours. Their system was built upon slavery.

This idea that full knowledge comes in the future is also found in the root documents of Christianity, where Jesus talks about things that are "unknown to the son, but to the father only." Even the most strident evangelicals, if questioned properly, will make the distinction between having *some* perfect truth and having *all* perfect truth.

Another important aspect is revealed by saying, "We know." Who is *we*? It is any individual who shares in the stream of truth. That assumes a civilization based upon merit, individuality and equality[73]. Truth does not descend from a ruler or from any authority; we all can contribute to truth and we all can preserve it. Again, dictatorships and blind faith are fully incompatible with the Western ideal: No one has full truth now, because it lies in the future. Thus, no one should be followed with blind faith.

Closely related to this ideal is the assumption that we are a community of interests. We don't all have the same dreams and desires; we don't all have to fit into the same mold. Even so, we all may contribute to the accumulation of truth, and so long as we do not intrude upon others, we feel we should be free to pursue our narrow personal interests. This builds civilization on a decentralized model, which is exceptionally resilient and open to improvement.

A Strange Incubation

When a massive civilization falls, as did Rome, whatever is to follow it has to form anew, and seldom completes the process until the previous civilization has fully unwound. In the case of Western civilization, this unwinding and reformation took place beneath an odd, virtual empire.

Rome did devolve, but this devolution occurred as the Church's Platonic empire struggled to form on top of it.

Over the 5th and 6th centuries in the West, the enforcement of Roman law ceased, the currency more or less vanished and trade began to migrate from the Mediterranean to the North Sea. A few large manufacturing operations are known to have continued in the extreme southwest of England, but not many others.

Gothic kings attempted to keep the Roman model going, but by the end of the 6th century (600 A.D.) local strongmen (often in partnership with the richest old families) were grabbing whatever territories they could. Everything that had been paid for out of the central treasuries was abandoned: Libraries, public baths, arenas, and educational institutions were forsaken and their buildings either torn down for materials or used for other purposes.

---

[73] Equality in the sense that all stand equally upon their merits and their actions; that there are no inherent classes.

Things that were paid for and controlled on a local level, however, did well. Crop yields rose as central interference failed and farmers were left alone to make their own, more sensible, decisions. As the massive load of Roman taxation vanished, more effort could be put into improvements. For individual farmers, the collapse of the Roman empire was *not* a catastrophe, and where the archaeological record shows us "elite dwellings" broken apart, we are usually seeing comfortable, reasonable dwellings being gained by many more non-elite persons, who stepped *up*, not down.

The Centuries of Reset

Between the 5th and 10th centuries, large ruling organizations were unable to sustain themselves. At first gothic and gallic tribes built kingdoms where the Empire had been[74], but they also proved too large to sustain in the absence of state legitimacy, which had vanished with Rome.

Roman elites in the countryside were occasionally removed violently and sometimes fled to the Eastern empire. Many, however, made alliances with the new rulers and/or became local rulers themselves as power continued to devolve.[75]

A great deal of Europe at this time was simply unruled.[76] Rulership existed in small spots and was either absent or intermittent elsewhere. A king's power base was his court (which generally moved from place to place) along with a few close associates and the fighting men they employed. To a very large extent, where the king wasn't, power wasn't. The average person interacted very little with any king (usually never), no matter how often modern writers call them "subjects."

To make the point that most of European life disconnected from power during this period, here are a few references:

> For the collectors of the tribute had suffered great losses, since in the course of long time and succeeding generations the estates had been divided into small parts and the tribute could be collected only with difficulty. (Gregory of Tours, 6th century)

> Never in our history has the conception of the state known so complete an eclipse. Numerous churches obtained privileges of immunity; many enjoyed that of minting money. (Latouche, *The Birth of the Western Economy*)

---

[74] The Ostrogoths and Lombards in Italy, the Visigoths in Hispania, the Franks and Burgundians in Gaul and western Germany, the Angles and the Saxons in Britain, and the Vandals in North Africa.

[75] See FMP #52.

[76] See FMP #53.

The State itself had no rights... It could, for example, raise no taxes, for according to the medieval view, taxation is a sequestration of property. (Kern, *Kingship and Law in the Middle Ages*)

In Frankish Gaul in the 580s, assessment registers were no longer being systematically updated, and tax rates may only have been around a third of those normal under the empire. Tax was, that is to say, no longer the basis of the state. For kings as well as armies, landowning was the major source of wealth from now on. (Wickham, *The Inheritance of Rome*)

Summing this up, professor Quigley writes this in *Tragedy and Hope: A History of the World in Our Time*:

[A]bout 900... there was no empire, no state, and no public authority... [T]he state disappeared, yet society continued... It was discovered that man can live without a state... It was discovered that economic life, religious life, law, and private property can all exist and function effectively without a state.

This condition was critical for the formation of a new European civilization; one very different from Rome.

Local Christianity

In chapter 4 we explained the theories and actions of the Church[77] to maintain an empire of legitimacy, and they pursued precisely that through all of the Middle Ages. Nonetheless, while these efforts were surprisingly effective among rulers, they started with difficulty and were, for a long time, considerably less effective at the local level.

Let's begin with the Church's early difficulties:

- The pope was appointed by the Eastern emperor and was often made to answer for his actions, overruled, or disregarded.

- The pope seldom appointed bishops; locals did.

- Roman Catholicism was *not* the only Christianity – there were several other forms in the early centuries.

- The primary centers of Christianity were the monasteries. And there were very many monasteries in Europe.

- Monasteries were rarely controlled by Rome or even by the bishops. They were mostly independent.

---

[77] When I use the capitalized word, Church, I am referring to the Roman Catholic Church.

- There were four bishops[78] who were specifically referred to as *papa*, the Latin word for "pope." The pope we think of was simply the bishop of Rome.

The situation is summed-up by historian Chris Wickham: *The pope between 550 and 750 was little looked to by people in Francia, Spain, even northern Italy.*

Monasteries became crucial components of the new European civilization because they filled crucial voids. Many functioned almost as retirement homes. Soon they were also homes for orphaned children and charity distribution centers.

In order to understand this, however, it is necessary to differentiate between European monasticism and the Eastern variety. The two types were wildly different (with Irish monasteries closer to the Eastern model). European monasteries were more of a social development; Eastern monasteries were very strict.

Since monasteries filled the gaps in early medieval living, they were supported by a wide variety of people, even if only to make themselves look good. Monasteries also became hubs for the newly forming capitalism, first as centers of production (farming, crafts) and then as centers of commerce.

It is also important to remember that, because of their Christianity, Europeans of this era expected to see goodness in the world. And, in fact, they did see it. Some people fell far short of that goal, of course, as some always do, but Europeans believed that goodness was attainable by them as individuals. They might not expect to become a venerated saint, but they could see themselves as virtuous men or women, and they often lived up to those expectations.

And as much as there are legitimate complaints to be made about the clergy through the entire Middle Ages period, there were also local priests, monks, nuns and lay members and who spent their lives helping the people of their parish; who, rather than abusing people, worked to feed the hungry, to support the widow and orphan, to guide the errant child and to strengthen the struggling adult. The stories of these men and women haven't made most of our history books, but they were real and they had a powerful impact.

The Infrastructures of The Reset Period

Whether a king is present or not, daily life continues and certain human processes must be handled. So, the emperor and his ways being gone, the Europeans of the early Middle Ages invented ways to handle them as they went.

---

[78] Those of Antioch, Alexandria, Rome and Constantinople.

One of the first areas where this was necessary involved the resolution of disputes, or, in general terms, law. *Law*, however, is not the precise term to use where power has evaporated. Rather, the concern in such situations is always *justice*.[79] And methods of assuring justice formed separately in each village, creating local customs that endured for many centuries. For example, historian R.H.C.Davis reports that,

> [T]he law might change from village to village; a thirteenth-century judge pointed out that in the various counties, cities, boroughs, and townships of England he had always to ask what was the local customary law and how it was employed before he could successfully try a case.

Chris Wickham reports on a case from the 9th century, detailing how local law operated:

> When disputes were dealt with, it was the villagers who reached judgment; they also acted as oath-swearers for the disputing parties, as sureties to ensure that losers accepted defeat. In one notable case of 858 in the plebs of Treal, Anau had tried to kill Anauhoiarn, a priest of the monastery of Redon, and had to give a vineyard to Redon in compensations, as an alternative to losing his right hand; here, six sureties were named, and could kill him if he tried such a thing again… most judgment-finders and sureties were peasants; the villages around Redon policed themselves.

These traditions of justice grew around a basic idea that we call "negative rights." It says that *you are free to do whatever you want, so long as you don't transgress against others.*

The opposing theory of positive rights says, *men are permitted to do only those things which are specifically allowed.* You can see that this contrasts with the basic core of Western civilization: That truth is revealed over time. If more truth is coming in the future, then no lawmaker knows enough to prescribe the correct limits of human activity.

Defense, another necessity of life, was sometimes handled individually, sometimes (cooperatively) on the town level, and sometimes by a large landholder, who agreed to protect his tenants. There were many variations.

There were, for example, as many as 100,000 castles in Medieval Europe; 26,000 in Italy alone. In addition, there were an unknown number of fortified houses. These fortified dwellings – most of which were made of wood rather than stone – were family protection systems. At this time, if you wanted to find an empty plot of land, till it and build a castle of some sort, you probably could. And many did.

---

[79] See FMP #27.

But while discussing defense, it is crucial to point out that the wars of this period were tiny by later European standards and microscopic by modern standards. Fighting was limited mainly to nobles who chose to fight. In fact, most "wars" of this era involved casualties measuring only in the hundreds, sometimes only dozens. Christ Wickham (again from *The Inheritance of Rome*) reports:

> An army of less than a hundred, contained in a single stockade, was determining the fate of a whole kingdom as late as the 780s.

> Armies in this period were generally small, up to 5,000 for the Merovingians and far less than that for the Anglo-Saxons, and could usually have been made up of aristocrats and their entourages.

During this era, if you didn't want to be involved with war, you probably wouldn't be. And while there *were* cases of villages being burned, any comparison with the horrors of the 20th century would be ludicrous.

Another important area of life is literature. And contrary to modern beliefs, there *was* literature in the "Dark Ages." Rates of literacy were certainly lower in this period than in our own, and books fewer, but literature was far from absent. Furthermore, pilgrim's guides were published all through this period (these people *did* travel) and were read in more or less every village.

Most literature of this era is ignored because it was religious in nature. For example, there were a great number of stories written as "Lives of Saints." When Rev. Alban Butler collected these stories for his book, *Lives of the Saints,* compiled between 1756 and 1759, he found 1,486 of them.

Latin and Greek authors, moreover, were not lost, although certain manuscripts were. There were libraries in Europe, including one at Mont Saint-Michael that contained texts of Cato, Plato, Aristotle, Cicero, Virgil and Horace.

In addition, a large number of schools were founded during this period, many of which still exist in England, including The King's School, Rochester (founded in 604), St Peter's School, York, (627), Thetford Grammar School (631), Royal Grammar School, Worcester (685), and Beverley Grammar School (700).

Women & Men

The most central type of human relationship, at any time, is the relationship between women and men. These relationships were regimented under Rome, limiting women a great deal. (Greece was still worse.)

With the passing of Roman law, however, restrictions on women passed as well. As a result, women fared much better in this period than in the later

Middle Ages, when Roman law was revived. Here, to make the point, are two passages from historian Regine Pernoud's *Those Terrible Middle Ages*:

> The woman in classical times was relegated to the background; she exercised power only in a hidden way... in feudal times the queen was crowned just like the king, generally in Reims... as much importance was attributed to the crowning of the queen as to that of the king.

> We find there, taken from everyday life, thousands of small details... here the complaint of a woman hairdresser, there of a woman salt merchant, of a woman miller, of the widow of a farmer, of a chatelaine, of a woman Crusader, and so on.

The Death of Slavery & The Rise of The New Economy

The great accomplishment of the Early Middle Ages was its triumph over slavery. Christian Europe inherited massive slavery from Rome and eliminated it by the year 1000 or so. Were there a "most ethical civilization" award, they would deserve it above all others.[80]

It is essential to understand that slavery was an *economic* system. It was used to gather surplus, which could then be used for investment or luxury. *Slavery was enforced thrift*. Greece and Rome were built firmly upon this foundation, and it is the glory of Western civilization that it replaced slavery with a capitalist system[81] – one that produced surplus without enslaving anyone.

Slavery, however, was not defeated as part of an economic plan; it was defeated because of the Europeans' new morals. Slaves, under this new model, could not longer be passed-off as a lower grade of being, as they had in Roman law. The new Christian ethic said that all men were equal children of God. They attended the same church services, partook of the same rituals, listened to the same sermons, and had the same standing... which included the same standing in any justice or legal process. Slavery couldn't survive that environment[82].

The actual processes of removing slavery were individual and local, not imposed by some great power. When rulers issued anti-slavery edicts, as they

---

[80] See FMP #70.

[81] I am using *capitalism* to refer to free commerce, not the corrupt crony capitalism that is so common in our time.

[82] The orthodox-catholic church centralized themselves under the Roman emperors. Once Rome fell, however (at least in the West), their power was lost and the Christians of Europe were left more or less on their own. Thus it was a decentralized Christianity that defeated slavery between 500 and 1000 AD. See FMP #77.

did on a few occasions, it was only after the people had moved in that direction before them.

Slavery died because millions of people, over four or five centuries, decided that it was wrong. Most of the liberations were personal and small. Among the most common were intermarriages between slaves and free persons, with the children of these unions acknowledged as free. Many more were freed in wills, often allowing the freed slaves to keep their savings and encouraging them to increase them by hard work.

The enforced thrift of slavery, however, had to be replaced if the new economic system was to work. Ultimately that was done two ways: With cleverness and with intentional thrift.

Cleverness was able to thrive in this time because men were mainly free of dominators and learned to think for themselves. Thrift was developed because it was one of the widely-taught Christian virtues – that of temperance, or self-control. This process was slow and complicated, of course, but in the end it formed an economic system that had replaced slavery with profit.[83] Profit, after all, is simply surplus.

By about 1100 AD, as if to complete this transformation, Europe moved from gift and barter transactions to monetary transactions. Historian Marvin Becker was able to closely survey one area of Italy and found that before 1000 AD, 80-85% of recorded transactions (primarily land deals) were in the form of gift exchanges and donations. By 1150, however, monetary sales accounted for 75% of all transactions.

Another crucial aspect of the new economic model was merit. Rome had been built almost entirely upon patronage, but once its power evaporated, merit returned. One famous story from this time involved Saint Martin (who died in 655) looking for a suitable bishop for the diocese of Le Mans. After much searching, he finally noticed a clerk named Victor working his vineyard with vigor, covered in dust from head to foot. Upon finding a hard-working man, Martin immediately made him bishop.

In Rome, connections had been rewarded; in the new Europe, merit was rewarded. The effect of this change upon the poor but motivated would be hard to over-estimate.

The Church, The Rulers & The Serfs

The Church, as we've noted, developed and extended its legitimacy all thought this period. Legitimacy, however is a more or less zero-sum commodity: If the Church has full legitimacy, there's very little left for the king, and vice-versa. So, the Church increased its share by keeping (as best they could) kingdoms in need of the Church's assistance.

---

[83] See FMP #33.

Rulers in the early centuries had little legitimacy on their own and had to join themselves with things their subjects respected. At first they tried to associate themselves with Rome. When that was no longer working, they tried to show themselves as godly, by gathering relics, making grand donations to monasteries, and so on. Still later, they tied their legitimacy to being "upholders of the law," or, in some cases, "givers of the law."

There were, of course, endless fights between nobles and bishops through this era. But if things went too far, the noble was likely to lose. For example, after King Henry II of England had Thomas Becket murdered, he was forced to walk to Canterbury Cathedral in sackcloth and ashes and to be flogged by monks. Had he not done this, the Church would have turned publicly against him. Lords could have withheld what they owed him and could have attacked him with impunity.

Among a religious people, being the entity closest to God has real advantages, and the Church was able to use it to gain access to powerful armies, such as those of the Carolingian family.

Serfdom, contrary to what many of us were taught, was not universal and was *not* slavery. There were many types of serfdom, and people moved between them. Serfs had specified rights and often held to them rather than leaving serfdom. Once serfs became old and unable to work, for example, they remained entitled to live where they were and to be provided with food as they always had been.

Moreover, many people lived in towns. Some were members of craftsmen's guilds, others were long-distance traders. The above-mentioned Thomas Becket makes a good example: His grandfather had been either a small landowner or a petty knight, recently come from Normandy. His father, Gilbert, began his adult life as a merchant (probably selling textiles), and by the 1120s he was living on rental income from his properties in London. All of that, very obviously, was nothing like serfdom.

Beside everything above, people in the Middle Ages could run away from their situation if they wanted to.[84] There were no fenced borders or identity documents in pre-modern times; if you wanted to leave badly enough, you could probably run away and start fresh, never to be forcibly returned.

It's also necessary to understand that serfdom was very often preferred by the serfs. The truth is that most people, then and even now, avoid responsibility. That was precisely the choice that serfs made. Most serfs stayed in their position because they preferred it. They complained about it, but probably no more than modern employees who hate their job but never leave it.

---

[84] It is only in the past century or two that escape has been suppressed.

Serfdom was, of course, a fundamental part of the overall structure of power in the deep Middle Ages; at the bottom end of the scale, living on a local *fief*[85]. Above the serf was a local landholder or tenant, and then someone above him, and so on. The primary ruler – where and when they could be clearly seen, as happened in most places by the 12th century or so – had the right to call up soldiers from the lower levels, but not a great deal more, and this only about forty days per year. Following is an example of how the hierarchy of land rights and ownership went during the reign of king Edward I of England (1239-1307):

> *Roger of St. Germain holds land at Paxton in Huntingdonshire of Robert of Bedford,*
>
> *who holds of Richard of Ilchester,*
>
> *who holds of Alan of Chartres,*
>
> *who holds of William le Boteler,*
>
> *who holds of Gilbert Neville,*
>
> *who holds of Devorguil,*
>
> *who holds of the king of Scotland,*
>
> *who holds of the king of England.*

You can see from this list that land ownership during these centuries was maintained with private agreements: Devorguil (noted above) held his land based upon personal relationships with the king of Scotland and Gilbert Neville, the man below him. Neville most likely had never seen the king of England and Devorguil may have met him only a few times. Everything these men did – including raising armies – was done by private contract.

There was also immense inter-connectivity: The same noble might owe services and allegiance to more than one ruler. One medieval noble named John Toul had allegiances to four different lords, and complained about the situation in this way (edited and condensed):

> *If Grandpre goes to war with Champagne for his personal grievances, I must personally assist Grandpre, but I must also send knights to Champaigne.*
>
> *But if Grandpre goes to war with Champagne on behalf of his friends, I must personally assist Champagne, and send one knight to Grandpre.*

---

[85] A *fief* referred to small piece of land. But more properly, it meant the right to exploit this particular piece of land, and the obligation to provide some level of service to the lord above the fief-holder, in return for this right.

There were many cases like this, and thousands of small, interconnected ruling hierarchies. I think you can see why *decentralized* is an apt term to apply to these centuries.

The Europeans See To It Themselves

> *It is only an ethical movement which can rescue us*
> *from the slough of barbarism, and the ethical comes*
> *into existence only in individuals.*
> – Albert Schweitzer

The fundamental re-organizational element to the growth of Western civilization was *initiative*. People simply took it upon themselves to pursue the things they wanted. They didn't wait for permission or beseech a ruler to do it for them; they simply went out and did it. And this theme was showing itself widely by about 1000 A.D.

One of the first places it showed itself was in learning. Educational facilities, dominated by the Church for many centuries at this point, had grown hard, arrogant and restrictive. Then, apart from the established systems and mostly by the efforts of radicals, the first universities of Europe began to form. Among these were:

1088	The University of Bologna
1160	The University of Paris
1167	The University of Oxford
1209	The University of Cambridge
1212	The University of Palencia
1218	The University of Salamanca
1220	The University of Montpellier
1222	The University of Padua
1229	The University of Toulouse
1235	The University of Orleans

All of these schools began as private enterprises – simple commercial arrangements between the teachers and their pupils. It was only after these schools were established for many years that rulers began to acknowledge them and to certify them. A few minor reasons aside, the rulers finally did this to maintain control. By "certifying" the university, they could effectively control what was taught, or else the certification would be pulled in the most embarrassing fashion possible. Popes and princes hurried to place their stamps of approval upon these schools, who had built their operations entirely without certifications prior.

The University of Bologna operated for seventy years before Frederick I, the Holy Roman Emperor, legally declared it a place for research in 1258.

What became the University of Paris actually began with a few small schools in Paris that functioned quietly on the fringes of legitimacy. The man who turned them into open places of learning was Peter Abelard (1079-1142). Unhappy with the censorship of intellectuals by the Church, Abelard and others helped form what became a *universitas*, modeled on the medieval guild, as a self-regulating, permanent institution of higher education.

Abelard began his intellectual life by running away from home and wandering throughout France, debating and learning as he went. By the time he was twenty he was in Paris, studying at the cathedral of Notre-Dame. Soon enough, he ran into opposition from the principle teacher. So, in 1101, at twenty-two years of age, Abelard set up a school about forty kilometers from Paris, and then moved it to a closer town for some time before he was able to lay the foundation for a *universitas magistrorum et scholarium* (guild of masters and scholars) in Paris, which finally came together in a permanent form in 1160, eighteen years after Abelard's death.

Note that is was not until 1231 that Pope Gregory IX formally recognized Abelard's creation – 130 years after he had opened his first school and 71 years after the universitas was fully in place.

A notable student of Abelard's was John of Salisbury (1120-1180), who somehow traveled, alone, from England to France in 1136, when he was only sixteen years old. He had a long and distinguished career in Paris, mostly after Abelard's death, eventually publishing a very important book called *Policraticus*. This book set the moral foundation of what later came to be called The Rule of Law, as well as exposing the decadence and immorality of the royalty.

The itinerant student Abelard had created a place of unapproved learning in the midst of distributed kings and an overseeing virtual empire. In this situation, and partly by playing prince against Church, he found open room in which he could act and expand. And he found, within himself, the initiative to go out and do it. Soon enough, students with new ideas created a new ethical system that would bring kings into subjection to the law.

The Guilds

Medieval guilds were exclusive organizations, created to preserve the rights and privileges of their members. The guild was self-created power. (Again, the Europeans seeing to things themselves.) The guild was separate and distinct from the civic governments, although wealthy guildsmen soon enough sought positions in city governments and blurred the lines.

Guilds were entirely city organizations. There was no place for a guild where specialization of labor didn't exist; they arose only in cities where specialists were required.

Merchant guilds were the first to appear, at around the year 1000, being mutual protection societies for traveling merchants. In other words, these were traders who banded together and developed ways to protect themselves while traveling through Europe on business. They went so far as to found their own towns, as we will examine later in this chapter.

Craft guilds followed the merchant guilds, and normally included people engaged in the same occupation, such as bakers, cobblers, stone masons and carpenters. Again, these were self-created organizations for mutual aid. Then, as the guildsmen became wealthy (or, more usually, their children), they often sought positions of municipal power. Once in such a position, the guild would use that power to forbid any non-members from practicing their trade. Local rulers were also eager to control the guilds, and laws were soon passed that forced guild members to takes oaths of loyalty.

This process is one that is seen over and over:

1. A fresh start is made, independently, by unauthorized individuals.

2. The new venture gains popularity with other individuals.

3. Rulers seek to bring it under their control. This is done in a subversive way, usually by offering official recognition.

4. The group grows into a formal organization, and second- or third-generation members, focused on authority, seek to join themselves with still greater authority, usually a state.

5. The organization uses state power to magnify itself and to enrich its members by punishing and suppressing competition.

6. Eventually the organization goes too far and the situation changes. The organization fails, abusing all the power it can on the way down.

Soon enough, the purpose of the guilds became to maintain a monopoly of a particular craft, but some more so, some less. Manufacturing guilds, for example, tended to establish reputations for quality rather than restricting competitors. These people wanted to expand their sales and needed to convince people in distant places to buy their products. *Victualling guilds*, on the other hand – the groups who sold foods – were big on restraining trade. People didn't need to be convinced to buy their products, since biology did that for them. And so, with no need to convince people to buy, they went about to forcibly restrain trade and to raise their prices as high as they could.

There was usually a strong religious aspect to guild membership. This functioned as a way of enforcing the good behavior of the guild members, but it also acted as a hedge against local officials and their power: *I'm connected to the Church; don't mess with me.*

As the guilds failed after the Reformation, many turned to governments, asking them to enforce monopolies on manufacturing[86] or trade and to force members to pay back obligations. Where governments provided such force, the guilds hung on. In the absence of force, they did not.

The Sovereignty of Law

> *It is established by authority of the divine law that the prince is subject to the law and to justice.*
> – John of Salisbury

Since the rulers at this time had limited direct legitimacy, the previously-mentioned John of Salisbury faced relatively few difficulties when he published his book *Policraticus*, which was highly critical of them. (And from which the quote above is taken.) Prior to this time princes were often held to be beneath law or justice, but John was among the first to promote the idea logically, carefully and widely. The Church, conveniently, supported this idea, primarily because they always wanted to keep the princes under control.

During the Classical era, the citizen was considered the seat of sovereignty. As Western civilization evolved, however, sovereignty slowly accrued to "the law," instead of to the people or to the rulers. The ruler was legitimated by upholding law. The ruler was considered *il*legitimate if he failed to uphold law. Over time, the Sovereignty of Law became the code of Western civilization.

But this did not spring into place in a moment, even after John's formulation was published in about 1159. It spread slowly and in different forms in the various parts of the West, and notably as the common law of England.

But before we cover two of the more important developments in law, it is very important to understand that what modern people think of as law is actually a very recent development. When the Rule of Law began, law meant something very different.

Here is a passage from Bruno Leoni's *Freedom and The Law* that provides some historical perspective:

> The Roman jurist was a sort of scientist: the objects of his research were the solutions to cases that citizens submitted to him for study, just as industrialists might submit to a physicist or to an engineer a technical problem concerning their plants or their production. Hence, private Roman law

---

[86] Though seldom noted, it is important to remember that monopolies only endure with force backing them.

was something to be described or discovered, not something to be enacted... Nobody enacted that law; nobody could change it by any exercise of his personal will.

The critical distinction to make is that law and legislation are not the same thing, or at least *were* not.

Properly, *law* was a process of determining whether actions were just or unjust. In practical terms, *laws* were the findings of judges. These were not edicts or commands; they were opinions, and were valuable because they explained justice and its reasonable application. A judge discovered, defined and explained justice.

Legislation, in old times, were merely collections of laws (legal findings), put together into one group for convenience. It was only much later that legislation became a type of edict. (We'll cover this in a forthcoming chapter.)

So, in understanding the creation of the Rule of Law, we should not think of legislation; that came much later and confuses the issue. The rule of law was certainly *not* the rule of legislation.

Local Law

As noted previously, the great eruption of civilization in Greece, after their Dark Age, was made possible by the difficult geography of the area, which made assembling an empire and a national priesthood very difficult. As we explained in chapter three, this allowed the development of literature and science with no interference from above. Unapproved ideas were unhindered and the best of them could take root. It a more abstract way, the same thing happened in England in the 5th through 10th centuries A.D.

During this time, kings, nobles and the Church all fought for control and advantage. There were endless fights over who was permitted to appoint bishops and over the legal status of clergy, among many smaller disputes. These two groups fighting meant that large areas of life were left alone as the combatants busied themselves with their battles. Customary, local law took shape in the towns of Europe in the wake of Rome's fall. In England, this developed into what was called the common law.

Common law refers to law and the corresponding legal system developed through decisions of courts and similar tribunals, rather than through legislative statutes or executive action. The common law is created and updated by judges, not by legislators.

Under the common law, a decision in any case refers to decisions in previous cases and affects the law to be applied in future cases. When there is no authoritative statement of "the law," judges define the law by creating *precedent*. This body of precedent is called common law, and it binds future decisions to itself. If a similar dispute has been resolved in the past, the court is bound to follow the reasoning used in the prior decision. (This is known as the principle of *stare decisis*.) If, however, the court finds that the current dispute is fundamentally distinct from all previous cases, the court will write and publish its own decision, forming a new precedent. (This is often called a *matter of first impression*.) This new decision must then be followed by future courts under the principle of *stare decisis*.

On the occasions where a bad decision is made by a judge, other judges will reject the decision, usually publishing an explanation. If still other judges agree, the bad decision is eliminated from the law books. Note that no legislation is required in these processes and no central authority is required. This is because the common law was formed in the same way as the universities of the era – men who needed them simply built them, with no one either forbidding or authorizing. They built the system according to the necessities of active men, not the necessities of rulers. The common law, unlike Clerical Law or the old Roman law, was written primarily in the conversational language of the people, and was, therefore, accessible to them. It was a law written for normal people, not for experts.

By the beginning of the 12th century, common law was so well established among the populace that the kings of England had to acknowledge it. When Henry I proclaimed his *Charter of Liberties* in 1100, he says that things ought to be done "through force of law and custom," or "in a lawful manner." Henry is accepting, not just the common law, which was the law of custom not a law of edict, but he is also accepting the idea that law is binding even upon himself, the king. A Mesopotamian ruler of 3000 B.C. would never have made such a comment: *He* was the law; he was sovereignty personified.

The Clarendon Constitution of England, in 1164, called itself the "record and recognition of a certain portion of the customs and liberties and rights of his ancestors which ought to be observed and held in the kingdom." Thus laws and customs developed by subjects, rather than rulers, became the law of England. This was explicitly acknowledged by Article 39 of the Magna Carta (1215 version), which read, "No free man shall be taken, or imprisoned or dispossessed, or outlawed, or banished, nor will we go upon him, nor send upon him, except by the legal judgment of his peers or by the law of the land." Note that the ultimate arbiter was not the king, but "the law of the land," which was the early common law.

Magna Carta did not, as is sometimes said, give rights to the people. Instead, it bound the king to the common law of the people and granted powers to the nobles. Again, this was not the usual foundation of rulership, and it very soon got the attention of other rulers, who did not like what they heard.

Once news of Magna Carta reached Pope Innocent III (two months later), he immediately issued a *bull* (a papal decree) against it, calling it "a shame for England," and saying: *We utterly reprobate and condemn any agreement of this kind, forbidding, under ban of our anathema, the aforesaid king to presume to observe it.* The Pontiff, schooled in matters of rulership and empire, seems to have understood that a diminution of the king's authority would undercut rulership.

King John and those who followed him tried to repeal Magna Carta, but the barons of England stood their ground. Popes threatened eternal judgment; princes raged with threats, schemes, and shows of authority. Masses of clergy and believers reviled them, but the barons remained firm; they outlasted the treats and liberty gained a modern foundation.

The Secret Courts of Germany

At about this same time, a string of secret courts and secret societies sprang up in the Westphalia region of what is now Germany. They were called the *League of the Holy Court*, or *Vehmgericht*, or the *Vehm*. Once again, something new was initiated by commoners, in response to their needs.

The beginnings of the Vehm are essentially unknown, which is not surprising for a secret group. They probably needed to remain secret for two reasons:

- They were not legally armed, and might have difficulty defending themselves from powerful criminals.

- They were forbidden by law from acting as agents of the law. This was the right of the king, not of commoners.

The Vehm had to protect itself from both kings and from criminals; secrecy was necessary if justice was to be provided.

A story circulated that the Vehm was founded in the year 772 by Charlemagne, but this was almost certainly a fabrication made to provide justification and to give them the shield of authority. The Vehm seems to have originated a couple of centuries *after* Charlemagne.

Court sessions were held in secret, and the uninitiated were forbidden to attend. The court consisted of a chairman and a number of lay judges, and any free man of good character could become a lay judge. The new candidate was given secret identification symbols. All members of the Vehm were required to keep their knowledge secret, even from their closest family.

Lay judges gave formal warnings to known troublemakers, issued warrants, and took part in executions. After the execution of a death sentence, the corpse would be hung on a tree to advertise the fact and to deter others.

This idea of secret courts has been much attacked ever since, but historical research has vindicated the Vehm, who never used torture, even though it was common at the time. Furthermore, their trials were only secret where and when they needed to be and their meeting places were always well known. A depiction of a Westphalian Free Court is shown below:

A Secret Vehm Court

In this case, again, the innovation of the responsible men of Westphalia was taken over by a ruler. In 1180, the archbishop of Cologne, Philipp von Heinsberg (also the duke of Westphalia) placed himself at the head of the Vehm, as the emperor's representative. After this time, the organization spread and was overseen by the state. Princes and nobles were initiated, and in 1429 even emperor Sigismund joined.

As kings and princes grew in power, the functions of the Westphalian Free Courts were brought under the control of state courts, and the Vehm was confined to mere police duties. They were fully abolished by Jerome Bonaparte, the younger brother of Napoleon, in 1811.

The Hanseatic League

Earlier we mentioned the merchant guilds. These were mutual protection societies for traveling merchants, and they began to rebuild trade on a decentralized model. One of the primary problems these traders faced was the plunder of local rulers. Princes and officials always seek revenue, and since traders were not defended by anyone with the authority to use violence, they were easy targets. In response, the merchant guilds boycotted the lands of rulers who did this. Since boycotts impoverished the kingdoms (who depended on commerce), this use of ostracism was effective and the rulers backed off. This was an early instance of commerce winning a battle with the state.

Merchant guilds had long enforced contracts among members and between members and outsiders. Guilds policed their members' behavior, especially since reputation was a critical component of commerce at the time. The debts of bad merchants were generally paid by the guild. By the middle of the 13th century, groups of merchants were becoming prosperous and their mutual-protection league went so far as to include ruling over their own trading cities, which the various princes were forced to permit.

This *Hanseatic League* (also known as the *Hansa* or *Hanse*) was an alliance of trading cities and trading guilds that established and maintained trade along the coast of Northern Europe, from the Baltic to the North Sea and inland, between the 13th and the 17th Centuries. The Hanseatic cities had their own system of law and furnished their own protection and mutual aid. Here, again, we find independent Europeans seeing to things themselves, with no ruler approving their plans in advance. The main trading routes of the Hansa and their cities are shown on the next page.

The early center of the league of Hansa was a German city named Lubeck, and from there, the merchants of Saxony and Westphalia spread to the east and the north. The name, *Hanse* is first known to appear in a document in 1267, but merchants had been cooperating in the Hansa manner well before. An early goal of theirs was to trade with towns in the less-developed area of the eastern Baltic, a source of timber, wax, amber, resins and furs. Even grains such as rye and wheat were brought on barges from inland producers to port markets.

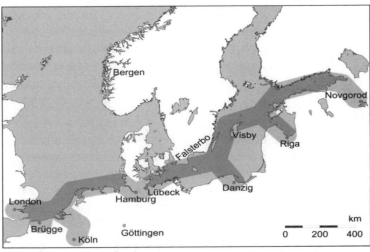

The Primary Hansa Trade Route

Courtesy Wikimedia Commons

Hansa towns furnished their own protection officers, with each guild providing members for this work as required. When necessary, trading ships were used for carrying armed men and Hanseatic cities came to each other's aid.

Hansa societies worked to reduce restrictions upon trade. For example, in 1157, the Hansa convinced Henry II of England to free them from all London tolls and allowed them to trade at fairs throughout England. Over the next decades, additional agreements were made with other princes and kings. Most of these agreements were called "the granting of special privileges," or similar terms, but they were often precisely the opposite. Rather than the Hansa being given government-enforced advantages, they were freed from the government's tolls and restrictions. In other words, actual free trade was called a "special privilege."

The League never became a closely-managed formal organization; that is, it never created central power. Representatives of Hanseatic towns met occasionally in Lübeck (beginning in 1356), but many towns didn't bother to send representatives and in any case there was no central power to enforce their rulings.

Over time, the League grew to include a flexible roster of 70 to 170 cities, who traded in timber, furs, resin (or tar), flax, honey, wheat, metal ores, fabrics and manufactured goods. The League also trained pilots and built lighthouses. Most Hansa cities either started as independent cities or gained semi-independence through the collective bargaining power of the League, which was simply the ability to refuse business with the lands of adversarial rulers – the power of ostracism.

Most foreign cities confined the Hansa traders to certain trading areas and to their own trading posts. Hansa merchants could seldom interact with the local inhabitants, except when actually conducting business. And, of course, many people of all classes envied the League. In London, for example, local merchants continually petitioned to revoke the League's exclusion from tolls. The situation was highly complex, of course, and we are passing over many details.

Over time, political events such as wars and changing alliances doomed the Hansa, as did their own misguided attempts to enforce exclusivity upon their markets. The growth of larger states with greater power made the Hansa less effective, and individual cities began to cooperate less. By the 16th century, the League was a shadow of its former self and withered away over the next century or so.

The great port cities of northern Italy, Genoa and Venice, developed trade at about the same time as the Hansa, but their trade was always a state function. Once the governments of these cities weakened or failed, trade was disrupted along with them. It is of interest that ever since the decline of centrally-controlled trade in Venice and Genoa, commerce in southern Europe has lagged. On the other hand, commerce in northern Europe, founded upon a decentralized, independent model, continued to thrive as rulers came and went, and even after the Hansa had come and gone.

The Law Merchant

The *Law Merchant*, or *Lex Mercatoria*, was a body of rules and principles laid down by the merchants and traders of Europe to regulate their dealings. It evolved among people who were doing business with no state power backing them or overseeing them. In such a situation, they did what other productive Europeans of this period did; they built what they needed.

The primary principle of this merchant law was the same as the common law – that it should grow organically, adapt to the needs of the merchants and be comprehensible to the people who used it.

Lex Mercatoria was administered by merchant courts, which were located along trade routes and at trade centers. At these places, merchants could solve their disputes within hours and at minimal expense. Proceedings were informal and focused upon justice and productivity rather than upon rules and procedures. "Fair price," "good commerce," and "equity" were the primary concerns.

Judges were chosen for their honesty, their commercial background and their practical knowledge. Their reputation rested upon their fair-mindedness. Before long, being a merchant judge became a profession of its own.

Much of international commercial law to this day has taken its fundamental principles from Lex Mercatoria. This includes choice of arbitration institutions and procedures, the necessity of reflecting customs, and good practice among the parties.

The Law Merchant declined as states grew in power and imposed their control over the merchant courts. Kings and princes became strong enough to control the activities of the merchants and soon did so, by force or by threat. In short, they enforced a monopoly on the provision of justice and drove the merchant judges out, after centuries of functioning smoothly. The term "protection of state interests" tended to be the justification for this takeover and others like it. "Amoral force" would be a more honest term.

Given the similarities between the law merchant and the common law, it is little surprise that Law Merchant rulings were included in the common law. This was acknowledged by England's Chief justice Edward Coke, who commented in 1608 that, "the Law Merchant is part of this realm." Principles of the Law Merchant continue in equity and admiralty courts. They are also widely respected in international arbitration.

A Foundation Is Established

By the late Middle Ages, Europeans held the root ideas of Western culture and were passing them down through their generations. Their children were absorbing many of these ideas even when they weren't specifically taught. Among these were Christian ideals and the influence of a farming culture.

The Europeans, even those who were illiterate, were exposed to the sayings of Jesus on a regular basis, and many of those ideas had taken root. Even if the local priest had a less than useful interpretation of those sayings, people would remember which parts Jesus had actually said and which parts were interpretations. Again, these people, even through the worst parts of the Middle Ages, *were the same as us*. They were not defectives. So, when they had access to little information, they held the little they did have all the more dearly. They knew, surprisingly well, what Jesus had said.

Farming also builds certain character traits into its long-term practitioners, and it taught the Europeans (with the usual exceptions) to cooperate and to respect property.

So, the mentality of the Europeans generally coalesced over centuries with a mix of Jesus' foundational ethics, the virtues of farming, the understanding that truth developed over time and the virtue of self-initiative. Thus Western civilization was formed. And being formed, it took on a life of its own. Like all civilizations, this "life" was not permanent – it would either be refreshed or lost over time – but it had inertia.

Holding of these basic Western ideas created many second-level effects over time, and certainly far more than this book will attempt to address, but a few of them were the following:

> **A high-trust culture:** A *high-trust culture* is one is which people can be relied upon to do what is right. Others can trust them to do things like open stores on time and clean their own messes. Europe (especially northern Europe) created a high-trust culture because initiative was self-generated in them. When people are in the habit of seeing to things themselves – of being self-directed – they contain the root of responsibility within themselves; they do not refer to the approval of a third party before acting. This produces reliable conduct. But far more importantly, self-referential conduct leaves men and women feeling good about themselves. Producing good acts from within themselves, not at the impetus of another, produces honest self-esteem and satisfaction[87].

> **A voice in governance:** Democratic government became the norm in Europe because people demanded to have some type of input into the

---

[87] This fact also illustrates its opposite: *Being ruled steals from men many of the best parts of their being.*

process. In other words, they expected to act as self-sovereigns, to some extent. They knew they could see to their own affairs and create what they needed. So, they demanded at least the minimal voice of being able to elect a representative with actual power[88].

Understanding wealth-production: Europeans understood how wealth was produced and respected the process. Most of this, however, was lost as Europe moved to specialized labor. But when Europeans actually understood the wealth-generating process, they generally engaged in a healthy fashion.

Long-range thinking: When people consider the future results of their actions, instead of just the immediate results, they act better and produce better results. Europe produced a great deal of this because they understood farming and valued property. To survive on a farm, one must think ahead and save seed for the next year and be prepared for both planting and reaping. This pattern leads men to think about their actions before taking them rashly.

Distributed enforcement of good conduct: Because this was a highly-cooperative culture, the people in it expected everyone else to cooperate. When members of the society acted uncooperatively, by placing obstacles in the paths of others or by disrupting their activities, any number of nearby persons would express dissatisfaction. This assured good conduct far better than a modern police force can. When a man's family, neighbors, coworkers and even local shop owners become enforcers of good conduct, he either learns to cooperate or he leaves.

The Kings Re-Learn Legitimation

After the devolution of the 5th through 10th centuries, units of rulership slowly grew larger and fewer in number. And, as briefly mentioned in chapter 4, the Church lost much of its power in the Reformation of the 16th century. This put the kings of Europe back into the legitimacy business.

As we noted, one source of legitimacy for this era's rulers was as an upholder of the law. They became a "good king" by talking about the sanctity of the law and by punishing notable crimes.

Another new source of legitimacy was simple geography. By the ruler championing "our land" (or "the motherland," or…), the inhabitants felt a connection with him.

The role of royalty as the bestower of honor is one of the legitimacies that has held into the modern era, and it was certainly in the repertoire of these rulers.

---

[88] We will explain in Chapter 10 how this ended up being problematic, but that was difficult to foresee.

One other aspect of legitimacy explains many of the odd actions of some rulers. Max Weber, in his book *Essays In Sociology*, explains the ruler's personal need of legitimacy:

> The fortunate is seldom satisfied with the fact of being fortunate. Beyond this, he needs to know that he has a *right* to his good fortune. Good fortune thus wants to be *legitimate* fortune.

Rodney Barker, in his *Legitimating Identities*, makes a similar point:

> People issuing commands are legitimated by their being identified as special, marked by particular qualities, set apart from other people. When rulers legitimate themselves, they give an account of who they are, in writing, in images, in more or less ceremonial actions and practices. The action creates the identity.

The rulers of this era, like the Church and like rulers of old, needed to play the role of the higher power. That is, they needed to be seen as a higher type of being, and to see themselves as a higher type of being.

When discussing legitimation, however, it is important to repeat that a very significant number of rulers are sociopaths, feeling a right to rule for internal reasons.[89]

Legitimization has always been necessary for two critical reasons:

> *Giving the subjects an excuse to obey.* No man likes to call himself a coward. So, when the orders of a ruler reach a man, he must find an honorable reason for obedience. He knows that orders from rulers are backed by force – by experts with superior weapons – but he must also find a reason to obey that is better than simple fear. And so, a reason to call the king legitimate is required. These reasons range from the silly to the mostly true, but they are always essential. The ruler must empower the subject to obey, without offending the subject's image of autonomy.

> *Enabling the ruler to issue commands.* The ruler must be confident in what he is doing, if he is to produce the necessary theater. He must believe that he has a right to transcend the morality that law enforces upon the people – that one may not coerce his neighbor. Some rulers will go to great lengths to secure this feeling[90].

---

[89] See FMP #51

[90] The strange case of Rasputin and the Romanov family comes to mind.

The Renaissance

The Renaissance, or *rebirth*, began primarily in northern Italy in the 15th century. This was a very important moment in human history, but not really from an organizational standpoint[91]. The crucial thing about the Renaissance was that it freed the imaginations of men and women to venture into new territories and to imagine new things about themselves.

Art played a major role in the Renaissance. It first gave men a glimpse of art that had been better in the past. This was, by itself, a significant development, since every society tends to see themselves, in whatever way they can, as superior. The people of the Renaissance, however, accepted that parts of their current condition were suboptimal. Then, in healthy fashion, they went about to correct the deficit.

The great artists, Carravagio, Donatello, Titian, Bellini, Raphael, Michelangelo, Leonardo, and many others, became better than any who had come before. They were more aggressive and creative with technique, color, design, light, depth, and even with subject matter. This had a terribly important effect on the men who saw these great works. Yes, the impact of the art itself was good, but the crucial impact was confidence in themselves and in humanity in general.

At first they saw that the Romans had been better than they. Then they applied themselves vigorously and exceeded them – openly and honestly. Now they knew that they could improve, and quickly. Where the end of that growth might be, they couldn't tell, but they knew they could go up from where they were, and quite possibly very, very high.

---

[91]Many people of the era thought their republics or benevolent dictatorships were important, but they didn't actually change much.

7

The Quickening Of The 17ᵗʰ Century

Genius is present in every age, but the men carrying it within them remain benumbed unless extraordinary events occur to heat up and melt the mass so that it flows forth.
– Denis Diderot

The 17ᵗʰ century (1601-1700) was the beginning of the modern age; when men (or at least a noticeable number of them) finally left their status quo behind and stepped forward into something new. The previous order fractured and the Christian world began to re-form in two distinct parts. Gutenberg's new printing technology had burst upon Europe, and people were learning more about the distant world than they ever had before. Curiosity bloomed, hunger for knowledge erupted, and science as we know it was born.

On top of this, virgin continents were available to any who dared to go. These were free territories with no established order to restrict human action. Non-conformists could now flee persecution, and many were willing to brave dangers if it meant they could be different and yet unopposed. Men and women began to imagine lives in far-off lands, where they would be released from constraints and live as they pleased. As a result, innovators began to show their faces in public.

The Internal Enforcer Retreats

> *It is hard to fight an enemy who has outposts in your head.*
> – Sally Kempton

We have previously mentioned the fact that men and women under authority refer their thoughts to the ruler, even if only as a safety measure. The critical factor of the 17th century was that this "internal enforcer" had lost some of his lofty image, which allowed men's thoughts to stray from their usual script.

The Protestants had wounded the Church's monopoly on legitimacy. Even in the areas of Europe that remained Catholic, the awe and majesty of the Church was diminished. At the same time, the legitimacy of kings and princes was rising.

So, it was reasonable at this moment to imagine an escape. Even if people couldn't bring themselves to pursue it, they could entertain a desire to go to the new world.

Rulers can survive being hated but they cannot survive being ignored. The image of a punishing ruler can usually be maintained without much difficulty, causing almost everyone some level of fear if they stray from obedience. But at this moment the image of the ruler withdrew from men's minds, at least to a notable extent.

Europe Splits In Two

The loss of the Roman Church's legitimacy had serious political consequences. As people rejected the Church's demands on how they must live, they began to discover commercial prosperity. So, the areas that remained faithful to the Pope tended to maintain a medieval culture and those that separated from the Pope began to build a more modern, commercial culture.

As Europe split, it formed into northern and southern halves. The two halves had been developing differently for some time, but this was when they clearly separated.

In the south, the Church maintained a high level of control and was able to hold onto their lands throughout all the troubles of the Reformation (between roughly 1517 and 1648). In the north, the Church found less of a stable base and had to work harder to maintain control. Once local rulers found a competing religion to support, many of them were glad to adopt it. In addition to the legitimate religious convictions some of them had, many more found an opportunity for tossing off the troublemaking Church and ruling alone. Protestantism provided them what they wanted, and so they supported it.

The two sections of Europe hardened in their differing characteristics. The north took on strong commercial characteristics, individual initiative, and even allowed some applications of decentralized power. The south remained hierarchical, traditional and centralized.

The compelling new thoughts spreading through Europe – not only wealth through commerce and new religious ideas, but the discovery of wild new continents – made literacy and learning prized things, and being "smart" made the young man a desirable mate. Instead of superior thinking being punished, as it so often is, this explosion of new ideas led to "smart" being rewarded. This created a dynamic intellectual culture, especially in the north, where it was less opposed.

The Church fought long and hard to remain overlord of Europe, including travesties like the St. Bartholomew's Day Massacre.[92] But, as in pervious cases of this type, the armies of the old empire were slow to adapt their tactics and weapons, while the armies of the new idea were quick to do so. In the first war of the Reformation, the *Hussite* armies (named after Jan Hus, an early reformer) fought much larger armies to a stand-still, because they adopted early gunpowder weapons and created new tactics suited to them. The armies taking the Church's side fought the old way and died in large numbers.

The areas that went Protestant tended to adopt things like the common law, free courts, and the less-restrictive trade. Everyone in Europe, both north and south, had known that the Church was corrupt; this was old and universal knowledge. Everyone knew the ideas of the reformers as well, but only a few dared take the fate of their souls upon themselves.

The northern and southern areas of Europe (Protestant and Catholic, respectively) are roughly depicted in the map on the next page. Political control over these two groups of Europeans shifted back and forth over time, and this map depicts something of an average condition for the Reformation period.

Science Arises

> *If a man will begin with certainties, he shall end in*
> *doubts; but if he will be content to begin with doubts*
> *he shall end in certainties.*
> – Francis Bacon

The statement above describes the new, scientific way of analyzing the world. Prior to Bacon and a few like-minded men, the order of knowledge was that men first got the "big picture" from the Church or from tradition, and then interpreted the rest of the world within that framework.

---

[92] The Protestants undertook abominations of their own, such as the horrifying sack of Rome in 1527.

Bacon said that this should be reversed: We should assume nothing (as Bacon says, "begin with doubts") and start from this base, testing everything to make sure we are correct about it. Thus, science as we know it was born.

Science is not a set of institutions, is not a set of knowledge, is not a set of laws. Science is a *process* – a technique for verifying our ideas about the nature of the world.

Science uses a chain of logic that starts with specific small truths, arranges them into larger theories, and comes to its most general truths last of all.

Protestant and Catholic Europe, Mid-Reformation

Courtesy Wikimedia Commons

The scientific method demands that observation and experimentation should be taken as the only ground upon which to build, and if new evidence is found which contradicts the existing structure, the whole structure must be rebuilt. One of our great modern scientists, Richard Feynman, put it this way: "It doesn't matter how beautiful your theory is, it doesn't matter how smart you are. If it doesn't agree with experiment, it's wrong."

Bacon was the leading developer of this new method, and his most important book was called the *Novum Organum,* which means *The New Instrument.* (Published in 1620). The title referred to Aristotle, who had written a book called *Organon.*

By shifting to this new method of dividing truth from falsity, men surged forward into new discoveries.

Bacon himself considered the printing press, gunpowder and the compass to have been the most important inventions of the early 17th century; an opinion that would be hard to argue with. They utterly revolutionized the Western world, allowing for knowledge and long-range travel, as well as for making war dependent upon knowledge more than brute strength. The brain overtook muscle, even in war.

Here are some of the discoveries of the 17th Century. Contrast these with the centuries of slow progress Europe had previously experienced:

- William Gilbert creates a theory of magnetism and electricity.

- Tycho Brahe makes extensive and accurate naked eye observations of the planets. These became the basis for Kepler's discoveries.

- Francis Bacon outlines a new system of logic, laying the foundation of the scientific method.

- Galileo Galilei improves the telescope, with which he makes important astronomical discoveries, including the four largest moons of Jupiter, the phases of Venus, and the rings of Saturn. He developed the laws for falling bodies based on experiments and mathematic analysis.

- Johannes Kepler publishes his three laws of planetary motion.

- William Harvey demonstrates that blood circulates, using dissections and other experimental techniques.

- Christiaan Huygens develops the first functional pendulum clock

- René Descartes publishes his *Discourse on the Method*, which further establishes the scientific method.

- Antony van Leeuwenhoek constructs powerful single lens microscopes, makes extensive observations, and discovers bacteria. Modern biology begins.

- Isaac Newton develops calculus, opening new applications of mathematics to science. He went on to develop the inverse square law of gravity, explained the elliptical orbits of the planets, and advanced the law of universal gravitation. This in addition to defining the basic laws of mechanics.

- Gottfried Leibnitz invents the binary system and invents calculus independently from Newton.

- Pierre Fauchard begins modern dentistry.

- Wilhelm Schickard builds the first calculating machines.

- Pierre Vernier (1580–1637) invents the vernier scale used in measuring devices.

- Evangelista Torricelli invents the barometer.

- John Napier invents logarithms.

- Edmund Gunter creates logarithmic scales.

- William Oughtred invents the slide rule.

- Blaise Pascal designs mechanical calculators and clarifies the concepts of pressure and vacuum.

- Pierre de Fermat develops probability theory.

- Abraham Darby I develops a method of producing high-grade iron in a blast furnace.

- Thomas Newcomen invents a practical steam engine.

- Marin de Bourgeoys invents the first flintlock musket.

- Cornelius Drebbei builds the first submarine, made of wood and greased leather.

- Otto von Guericke becomes the first human to knowingly generate electricity using a machine.

- Stephen Gray demonstrates that electricity can be transmitted through metal filaments.

- Robert Boyle discovers the law of gasses. He also develops an atomic theory of matter.

- Henry Cockeram publishes the first English dictionary.

- Johann Carolus of Strasbourg publishes the first newspaper.

- William Shakespeare writes most of his plays.

- Monk Dom Perignon discovers Champagne.

- Ice cream is invented. Tea and coffee become popular.

- The first public opera house opens in Venice.

- The first measurements are made of the speed of light.

- The Royal Society of London for the Improvement of Natural Knowledge is founded.

Note also that the overwhelming majority of these discoveries came in the north. This has nothing to do with the relative intellect of the two groups, it had to do with their minds being less encumbered in the north, and being less opposed when treading new paths.

This flowering of science radically altered the development speed of mankind – not only that men found new information, but that they learned *how* to find new information. The phrase, "check it," became something that we keep in mind and use all the time. People used it previously, but not nearly as often or as well. We now know, with certainty, how to find and verify new facts. Before Bacon and a few others, this was much confused and partially understood.

As an example, Aristotle was certainly a bright, thoughtful man, but he did not understand the scientific method and made quite a few dramatic errors, such as believing that heavier objects fell faster than lighter objects. This error persisted for almost 2000 years, even though it could easily have been verified by experiment. No one is recorded to have performed a verification in all of that time.

The accumulation and storage of knowledge has greatly increased since the 17th Century. We know far more and we are making far more rapid progress than ever before in human history. Science sped up the process of development, printing saved and distributed the knowledge, libraries made it accessible.

The Great Civilizer

> *As always, the honesty instituted by trade is far superior to any other conception of honest conduct.*
> – John Maxcy Zane

The commercial culture that developed in the north of Europe tended to be an ethical culture. Certainly there have always been glaring exceptions to this statement, but commerce instills ethics. The vast bulk of commerce relies on fair dealing, trust, reputation, and cooperation. These things root good conduct in the participants, which they tend to spread throughout their families and communities. Shopkeepers make good neighbors.

To understand commerce properly, it is helpful to differentiate between "one-shot deals" and long-term commerce. The incentives are very different and thus they breed different types of conduct.

A common *one-shot deal* is the car sale: The automobile salesman knows that he has one shot at any customer that walks through his door, and that he is likely never to see him or her again. In such a case, it is in his immediate interest to get as much profit out of the sale as possible. If the customer is unhappy a month or two down the road, there will be no effective loss from it. It was a one time deal, and it's over. You can see why deception in this kind of transaction has become proverbial.

Long-term commerce is the kind engaged in by a local grocer. This businessman needs to do business with the same people many times per month. If he gives customers a bad deal, even once, he risks losing them. After all, there are other grocers. This type of business incentivizes honesty, kindness, and fair dealing. Over the long term, goodness pays.

Another critical advantage of commerce involved the movement of surplus. Under commerce, more surplus remained in the hands of people who were best-suited to use it productively. In fact, the great projects of this era were financed by collections of successful businessmen.

The Crazies Escape

> *Human salvation lies in the hands of the creatively maladjusted.*
> – Martin Luther King

The role of non-conformists, eccentrics and "Crazies" in human history has been greatly under appreciated. If you look carefully for the roots of important new developments, you will very often find a Crazy as the forgotten, original innovator.

For example, the Flagellants of the Middle Ages (for whom the title Crazies is fitting) made a critical breakthrough that led toward the Reformation: Divine forgiveness, separate from the intercession of the clergy. Huge numbers of Flagellants believed this, including monks and priests. The Pope eventually fought back against it, but the idea of forgiveness via penance stuck and the clergy were not included in that process; their absolution monopoly was cracked[93].

It is the tightness of a culture that causes Crazies to be bent in their particular ways. These people, different by nature or by unique formation, don't want to be part of a homogenized mass. But because of the culture's demands upon them, they are punished for behaving differently or expressing different thoughts. This either crushes them or drives them to react further.

So, the more restrictive the culture, the more radical are those who eject themselves from it. There are, of course many variances – humans being adaptive, self-correcting beings – but the young man or woman who is able to break out of a restrictive culture almost always bears scars and almost always acts erratically in one or more ways. Breaking out is simply too difficult for it to be otherwise.

This assures the main mass of a culture that anyone who wouldn't accept their model must be a dangerous, deranged person... which, of course, drives the unique man or woman still further away. There have been occasional radicals who attained peace with themselves, but most were driven away and damaged in the process. The tighter the culture, the more tyrannical it is to a non-conformist.

In the 17th century, however, such people could leave. Bear in mind that this was a much more complete exit than is possible in our time. A fitting example of this is the modern tax protester. People say to them, "If you don't like it here, go somewhere else," but that is actually no choice at all: The deal

---

[93] This was very much in the mind of Martin Luther, who was given to fasting and flagellation.

is the same everywhere. If an American tax protester goes to Canada, he finds a nearly identical situation. If he goes to Germany, it is the roughly same, and the same can be said, more or less, for all of the earth's two hundred states. If, however, there was an empty continent available, the same tax protester could truly escape, and then do his best to build a new life as he wished.

So, many such people came to the New World, bringing their new ideas and transformative energies with them. The New World of North America owes a much bigger debt to the Crazies of Europe than respectable types would like to acknowledge.

The Two New Worlds

The New World of North and South America were, fittingly enough, settled by northern and southern Europeans respectively. Effectively, there were two new worlds, not one. And this is not related to the separation of the North and South American land masses – it is a result of the way they were settled and/or conquered.

The monarchs of southern Europe who were aligned with the Church had a very specific pattern of dealing with the new continents of the Americas. Settlers from the north of Europe had a different pattern, and these patterns spawned effects that remain to this day.

The South

The kings of Spain and Portugal were the leaders in sending explorers around the world, and to claim all lands for their kings; for "the Crown," as they used to say. They went so far as to claim all land that touched bodies of water they discovered. When Balboa found the Pacific Ocean, for example, he raised his hands, his sword in one and a standard with the image of the Virgin Mary in the other, walked knee-deep into the ocean, and claimed possession of the new sea and all adjoining lands, in the name of the Spanish sovereigns.

As has been well-noted by many others, the Spanish and Portuguese Conquistadores treated the inhabitants of the new continents abominably, but it was the purpose of their missions and the structure of their arrangements that led directly to this. Spanish and Portuguese actions in the New World were systematic exploitations, with a bit of missionary interest (the Church's version of conquest) thrown in[94].

---

[94] The Church was actually quite involved the whole time. In 1493, immediately following Columbus' return, Pope Alexander VI officially awarded the New World to Spain. (Notice the level of legitimacy attributed to the Pope, that he had the right to give away continents.) Portugal, however, was a powerful exploring nation and immediately entered negotiations with the Spaniards to divide the New World between them. Eventually the Spaniards agreed and Pope Julius II sanctioned the deal in 1506.

The pattern of plundering the New World began with the very first set of arrangements: The deal between Columbus and King Ferdinand of Spain. According to the contract, if Columbus discovered any new islands or mainland, he would be given the rank of Admiral of the Ocean Sea and appointed Viceroy and Governor of all the new lands. He had the right to nominate three persons, from whom the sovereigns would choose one, for any office in the new lands. He would also have the option of buying one-eighth interest in any commercial venture with the new lands and receive one-eighth of the profits.

In other words, Columbus was to get very, very rich by the regimentation and plunder of the new world, and, after fights with the king, he did get rich. Cortez, Pizarro, Balboa and all the others had deals of the same type: They became regimenters and plunderers and were given high office, from which they could dole out favors to friends.

It is no exaggeration to say that this pattern took strong root in Latin America, that it remained, and that it has punished Latin America's inhabitants unto this day.

The North

The settlement of North America was undertaken by commercial ventures, after the models of commercial capitalism. The structure of these arrangements was entirely different than that of the southern Europeans and their hierarchical conquest model. These were private companies, owned by individuals, venturing to the new world for purposes of commerce. The high points of this process were the following:

- The London Company, an English joint stock company, is established by royal charter in 1606 with the purpose of establishing colonial settlements in North America. It financed and created the Jamestown colony, the first permanent English settlement in the new world, in 1607. (Along the way they accidentally found and colonized Bermuda.) Later in 1607, the Plymouth Company – identical in form to the London Company - established its Popham Colony in present day Maine. Popham was abandoned after a year, but Jamestown, after struggling for several years, found commercial success in growing tobacco.

- In 1609, under a contract with the Dutch East India Company of Amsterdam, Henry Hudson explored the waters off the east coast of North America. His report stimulated interest in the area as a trade resource, and Dutch merchant-traders began to fund expeditions. The Dutch began trading furs with the Native Americans who lived in the area. In 1614, they established a fur-trading fort at Nassau, in what is now Albany, New York. The Dutch traded peacefully with a large number of migratory Indian tribes and the area became known as New Netherlands. At the same time, they built a trading fort at a place called New Amsterdam, now known as New York City. Company policy required that all land be properly purchased from the existing peoples.

- In 1619, a group of religious outcasts called Pilgrims, who had been chased from England to Amsterdam some years prior, made commercial arrangements with the investors of the Company of Merchant Adventurers of London to establish a new colony in North America. In their own words, they had: *great hope, for the propagating and advancing the gospel of the kingdom of Christ in those remote parts of the world.* They arrived in 1620 and formed the Plymouth colony in what is now Plymouth Massachusetts.

- In 1629, another group of religious non-conformists and separatists established the Massachusetts Bay Colony with 400 settlers. They hoped to reform the Church of England by creating a new, pure church in the New World. Within two years, an additional 2,000 settlers arrived. Thsee Puritans created a deeply religious, tight-knit and innovative culture that is still present in the United States. They hoped this new land would serve as a "redeemer nation," a "nation of saints" and a "City upon a Hill."

- In 1636, a preacher named Roger Williams, who advocated a complete break with the Church of England, was banished from Massachusetts Bay and founded the Rhode Island Colony, which became a haven for other religious refugees from the Puritans. One year later, in 1637, a more-or-less Baptist[95] leader named Anne Hutchinson purchased land on Aquidneck Island from the local Native Americans, establishing a settlement in what is now Portsmouth, Rhode Island. Still others followed and formed a loose alliance.

- In 1658 Franciscus van den Enden and Pieter Corneliszoon Plockhoy began work on a Utopian settlement in New Netherlands, in the area of the present state of Delaware. In 1663 Plockhoy and 41 settlers made their way to Delaware Bay and established a colony.

- William Penn was a wealthy convert to the despised Religious Society of Friends, also known as the Quakers. Quakers were frequently imprisoned and beaten at this time and the outspoken Penn was no exception. In the late 1670s and early 1680s, Penn settled a debt owed to his family by the Crown, receiving a huge area of land in the New World in return. This area, immediately settled by

---

[95] She was, or quickly became, what we would call a Christian Anarchist.

Quakers escaping persecution in Europe, included a good deal of several present US states, including Pennsylvania, named after Penn.

- In 1632, George Calvert, 1st Lord Baltimore, received a royal charter for what was to become the Province of Maryland, which became a Catholic colony. Calvert had apparently been stripped of his Secretary of State office in 1625, when he converted from the Church of England to Catholicism. This group of colonists purchased land from the local Indians and attempted to govern the area under feudalistic precepts. However, these efforts failed in the New World, and after intermediate reforms he was forced to abandon the medieval model and to govern according to the laws of England[96].

There is much more of interest to be said about each of these ventures and others, but again we risk straying from the primary subject of this book.

One point of interest is that the commercial ventures of northern Europe soon found ways to bring people to the New World at no initial cost. In other words, any reasonable poor person who wished could get to colonies in the New World. This was done by the process of *indentured servitude*. These were labor contracts, whereby the new colonist would agree to work for three years in return for his or her passage. A great many young men and women took the deal[97], possibly up to one half of all who came. The main section of one such agreement read as follows:

> INDENTURE Witnesseth that James Best a Laborer doth Voluntarily put himself Servant to Captain Stephen Jones Master of the Snow Sally to serve the said Stephen Jones and his Assigns, for and during the full Space, Time and Term of three Years from the first Day of the said James's arrival in Philadelphia in AMERICA, during which Time or Term the said Master or his Assigns shall and will find and supply the said James with sufficient Meat, Drink, Apparel, Lodging and all other necessaries befitting such a Servant, and at the end and expiration of said Term, the said James to be made Free.

---

[96] Note that this group – strongly influenced by the Catholic Church – at first tried to do things the Church's way. But there was no inertia for such actions in a barren land, and these efforts, forced to stand or fall on their own merits - failed quickly. The northern, decentralized, individualistic model of England was adopted instead.

[97] It is also of interest that a great number of women escaped the Old World. We have already noted a Baptist leader and colony founder who was female. There were a great many women who came to the New World. They took indentured servant contracts, left their families behind, and jumped on boats for a new continent.

Upon arrival in the colonies, advertisements were placed, to find employment for the indentured colonists. This was a complex set of business arrangements, and (minus the occasional problems that are associated with all human actions) the arrangements worked well: Poor men and women got a fresh and free start in life, and the businesses made money.

In general, the northern colonists sought peaceful relationships with the local Indians they encountered. Sometimes this was possible and sometimes it was not. Problems did certainly arise and there were travesties that can be blamed on both sides. But the actions of the northern settlers were of a wholly different character than those of the southern conquerors. In the north, cooperation was much preferred; in the south, only domination and submission were acceptable.

Trials, Errors, Results

In the south, a Conquistador culture was founded. In the north, no single culture was possible. There were Englishmen, Dutchmen and a smattering of other Europeans; there were Utopians and the adherents of many religions, who sometimes fought. Beyond that, there were dozens of business models, some competing and some complimenting each other. New ideas required no charters or permissions, and they flourished. Many were silly and some were brilliant, but it was difficult to tell which was which as they all sprang up together.

The key attribute of the northern colonies was that the people were not enamored with authority. They developed their colonies from the ground, up, organically rather than hierarchically and by permission. If someone had what they thought was a better idea, they could simply go out and try it. The ideas which were unsustainable failed; the ideas that made life more productive survived. This was an ugly, erratic process, and one that was always easy to criticize, but it spawned a fast and effective evolution of strategies.[98]

The old world had lost control of these people. They were facing nature and God on their own; they didn't need distant rulers and religious authorities any more. They were creating a new synthesis without them. No central pattern had to be held in pre-eminence. The best and brightest of them were allowed to use their talents, without the usual limitations. They could be whatever they wished to be, and along the way they founded a new way of life.

---

[98] See FMP #16.

8

The American Revolution

Our contest is not only whether we ourselves shall be
free, but whether there shall be left to mankind an
asylum on earth for civil and religious liberty.
– Samuel Adams

The American Revolution is a historical event that inspires odd reactions from people. On one hand, it is grossly under appreciated, even passed-off as meaningless; but on the other hand it is over-promoted for the sake of cheap self-esteem. Both these errors are the result of people interpreting the American Revolution in the light of their own needs.

Any simple interpretation of the American Revolution is wrong. This was a complex set of events that changed the world. It featured an exceptional group of men, produced by exceptional circumstances and exceptional ideas. And, ultimately, it was a remote and virgin territory that allowed it to come to fruition... just barely and with a lot of luck.

The Quickening of the 17th century certainly provided the foundation for the American Revolution, but the Scottish Enlightenment was also critical to the American enterprise. This was an exceptional intellectual event and we will now turn our attention to it.

The Enlightenment

There are several episodes in history called "Enlightenment," but it was the Scottish Enlightenment of the 18th Century that served as both inspiration and root for most of them.

There are several theories as to which events led to the Scottish Enlightenment, but it is likely that many events deserve parts of the credit.

Among these are the free trade that came along with the Union of 1707 and removal of church power at the adoption of the English Bill of Rights following the Glorious Revolution of 1688. But perhaps even more important than these was a general battle between the ideas of Humanism and Calvinism during these years. When there are competing ideas, humans experience more free mental space. When one ideology rules among a group of people, adaptations and differences are punished in many ways, ranging from the subtle to the violent. When ideologies compete, on the other hand, no one of them has overwhelming authority and new ideas find space to grow.

But for whatever reasons, the Scottish Enlightenment, which occurred primarily in the city of Edinburgh, was a period of extraordinary progress. Within it, the following were seen:

- Robert Adam changes the course of architecture.

- James Anderson invents the modern plow.

- Joseph Black discovers latent heat, specific heat and carbon dioxide, as well as initiating the study of thermo-chemistry.

- Hugh Blair becomes a highly influential churchman and professor of rhetoric.

- James Burnett creates comparative linguistics and first describes the process of natural selection.

- Robert Burns writes poetry that is revered to this day.

- Alexander Campbell leaves to lead the Second Great Awakening in the United States.

- George Campbell modernizes the study and practice of rhetoric.

- John Clerk creates modern naval tactics. (His great-great nephew, James Clerk Maxwell, will define the laws of electromagnetism.)

- William Cullen co-founds the Royal Medical Society and influences a full generation of physicians.

- Adam Ferguson creates the study of sociology.

- James Hutton founds the study of geology and James Hall contributes the first scientific studies.

- David Hume and his friends create Empiricism.

- Francis Hutcheson organizes the study of metaphysics, logic, and ethics.

- John Leslie discovers capillary action and learns to artificially produce ice.

- Thomas Reid creates the study of Common Sense.

- John Sinclair becomes the first person to write on statistics.

- William Smellie edits the first edition of Encyclopedia Britannica.

- Adam Smith creates the economic theories that made commerce defensible.

- James Watt invents a functional steam engine.

This list shows only the more specific accomplishments of this group. These men crossed disciplinary lines continually. Lawyers studied and worked with artists, biographers with scientists, doctors with poets. These men allowed their interests to run wild, and they found fellows who were eager to do the same. Most of them made substantial contributions in fields other than the one they are remembered for most. Foreigners like Benjamin Franklin of the American colonies corresponded with these men at length.

In general, this group championed human reason and rejected any type of authority which couldn't be justified by it. They were optimistic and thought that human ability was sufficient to improve the world and their place in it. But, perhaps more importantly than all else, this was a group of intellectuals who did not fight amongst themselves.

The truth is that most idea sellers, at most times of history, fight each other for dominance. These men took the opposite course and helped one another. This may have been a primary reason why their ideas developed and survived intact. They did not waste their time and energies on temporary and destructive group dynamics. And it followed that these men tended to attract readers who wanted more than becoming important within a group. Rather, they sought knowledge itself.

Here again it was inner mechanics that created the important moments of human history, not externals.

Non-Authority and Its Fruit

The men of the Scottish Enlightenment – partly due to the virtues they developed among themselves, partly due to the times, and definitely because of beneficial ideas that were passed down to them – became free from both sides of the authority trap. That is, they were generally free from the oppression of authority and from the desire to become authority.

As mentioned previously, the ideological structure of the time was divided and oppositional: Calvinism versus humanism. There was no universal ideology that was in a position to harm them for thinking along new lines. In addition, the center of governmental authority had just been removed more than three hundred miles to London. (And governments of this era had next-to-zero information on the daily activities of its subjects.) This greatly reduced the pains that authority was able to impose upon them. And, as mentioned above, the culture of cooperation that developed at Edinburgh was quite contrary to any of them becoming an authority above another.

All of these things: Intimidation, becoming the leader, cult-followings, division into groups – these all divert effort from discovering the truth about the world and redirect it into struggles for the approval and control of other men. The men of the Scottish Enlightenment and those who followed their example showed, dramatically, that the energies wasted in dominance struggles could be put to much better uses.

Being ruled steals from men many of the best parts of their beings, and seeking to rule corrupts men. The intellectual Scots of Edinburgh were able to provide their own escape from these wastes. Others escaped authority by simple separation. And, finding themselves in open territory, they tended to disregard the goal of ruling (or even leading) others. Frontiersmen, as a rule, are notably anti-authoritarian.

Living in the wild puts men in direct contact with nature and their natural place in it. They begin to face the man next to them directly, not through cultural expectations. Class boundaries diminish in importance. Processes that were once done in regimented, prescribed, restricted ways are thrown open to anyone who steps up to do them. When things cannot be done the old way, nature is exposed and men confront reality directly, not through the filters and limitations of tradition. This is precisely what happened in the New World of the Americas, and it approximated the interrelation of the learned men of Edinburgh. The intimidations, privileges and protected positions of Europe fell by the wayside, and man dealt with man far more directly.

This unrestrained activity between men created different relationships and differences in human character. For example, at the end of the frontier era, in the American west, there existed a specific type of independent man: Self-contained but gregarious, generous and fair-minded. Frederick Turner, an American historian, wrote the following:

> From the conditions of frontier life came intellectual traits of profound importance... coarseness and strength combined with acuteness and inquisitiveness; that practical, inventive turn of mind, quick to find expedients; that masterful grasp of material things, lacking in the artistic but powerful to great ends; that restless, nervous energy, that dominant individualism, working for good and for evil.

Most Unlikely Leaders

The American Revolution featured men and women who dared to be free and independent: Mature, self-responsible, informed, and bent on developing the higher and better aspects of human nature. They often fell short of this goal, but it remained an ideal that they held. When conflicts with the British came, they did not meet them as men pushed to the limit and striking out wildly. On the contrary, these people did the right thing, *because* it was the right thing. And, they did this after long study to determine what that right thing was.

The fact that a group of such men became leaders is most unusual in world history. In most cases, the leader is one who can impose power on others or one who convinces others that he can cause power to be used in ways that they prefer. Or, sometimes, the one who offers some sort of easy path to good feelings. These men were not of any such type. Primarily they were listened to because of their personal abilities and because their words made sense. Granted, it was never simple and there were many who listened because they thought they'd get easy benefits by doing so, but this was no normal group of leaders.

Sam Adams was a failed and bankrupt businessman, John Hancock was a smuggler, Tom Paine failed at almost everything he had ever done and came to America almost as a vagrant, Jefferson and Madison were overly studious farmers, John Adams a not-very-successful lawyer and Patrick Henry a twice-failed businessman. Franklin was a success in business but was considered ungodly by a large number of people. Even Washington, an experienced military veteran, preferred farming and was a surveyor by profession.

World history is full of brave men standing up to tyranny, but these men were different. This was a group of men who had studied, learned, and formed a vision of a better way to live. Then, they went about to create it. They fought the king because he refused to leave them alone. They were not trying to take over the system and run it their way as much as they were trying to create a new and different system. The revolutionary wars were, at least from the viewpoint of the colonials, about the old order trying to oppress a new development.

Of course, this group of men was not enormous (most colonials were too busy working to devote extensive periods to study). Nonetheless, even the working people were literate and well-read in many fields, including that of law[99]. The vast majority of them spent a good deal of time and intellectual energy in church and in discussing sermons.

---

[99] Blackstone's *Commentaries on The Laws of England* was a best-seller in the colonies; for a long time out-selling everything but the Bible.

The result of all this was *not* a massive movement for independence from England. Almost all those who wanted independence wanted it grudgingly. Approximately one third of the American colonials wanted to remain loyal to England. Another third or so didn't want to take sides. But the final third styled themselves as self-sovereigns. This was a crucial and important step to take – not because of its impact upon the outer world, but because of the clarity of mind it gave them.

We will not be examining the details of the struggle for American self-sovereignty, but there are some central facts that are of importance:

- The events took place in a virgin territory. They did not have to compete with an existing order.

- The events took place in a remote territory, where orders from the king were slow in coming. For many years the settlers were ignored.

- The colonials grew from one of the most productive cultures the world had yet seen. The people of British America started from the leading edge, and went forward from there.

- There was a powerful moral culture. These people were in church regularly, they distributed sermons, and those who rejected traditional religion (like the deist Ethan Allen), argued their cases for moral reasons.

- In the tradition of the Scottish Enlightenment, these people did not hold ideas as idols, but used them as tools. They examined them, adapted them and applied them. They mixed them with other good ideas and expanded them.

- Americans had learned that the old organizational myths were fairy tales; they confronted reality face-to-face, with no illusions of a king riding in to save them. Discovering that they could face the world themselves, they began to question why, exactly, a king was necessary.

What Happened In America

The development of the American colonies moved in an arc. The colonies began with a lot of oppression, shook it off as the arc rose toward 1776 and the revolution, then headed slowly back down.

We see this beginning at the Virginia colony. The Virginia Company of London had given their first settlers a wildly harsh set of rules to live by, including these:

> That no man shall use any traitorous words against His Majesty's person, or royal authority, upon pain of death…

> No man… shall dare to detract, slander, calumniate, or utter
> unseemly speeches, either against Council or against
> Committees… First offense to be whipped three times;
> second offense to be sent to galleys; third offense – death.

Offenses such as obtaining food from the Indians, stealing food, or attempting to return to England were punishable by death and torture.

Those laws, however, were mostly bypassed, the minds of the people being incompatible with them. Then came a new governor who attempted to restore them, at which point the Puritans tried to arrest him and forced him to be removed. By 1619, the people of Virginia set up their own legislature and started passing their own laws.[100]

Among the more important accidents of the early America period was a British policy that later became known as salutary (that is, healthful) neglect. This salutary neglect began in 1722, when a Whig named Robert Walpole became the king's chief minister. The Whigs held what we might call libertarian opinions, and Walpole wanted to govern loosely, to avoid government meddling, and to let natural forces bring prosperity to England. Under Walpole, many of the existing regulations upon American trade were simply forgotten or ignored.

This policy lasted, more or less, until 1760, after which the impositions we normally associate with the American Revolution began.

The Speculators

When reading letters from the era of 1750 through 1820 or so, it is surprisingly common to find complaints about "speculators." These are generally references to men of the political means, who used governmental privilege to enrich themselves. As historian Merrill Jensen describes it, they tried to establish claims within the colonies by "appeals for grants from the British government… They grabbed land everywhere, calmly indifferent to fraud and corruption as a method of acquisition, and then demanded strict legality in payments from the settlers to whom they sold it."

The Backcountrymen – that is, individual settlers – fought off land speculators, refused payment of rents, and from time to time were attacked by troops sent out by colonial governments to maintain "law and order."

The result was that colonial history was punctuated by rebellions against dirty political dealing. There was Bacon's Rebellion in 1676 and the Regulator movement in the Carolinas a hundred years later. There were tenant farmer rebellions in New York and New Jersey.

---

[100] And in the old world way, they excluded their Polish artisans. The artisans went on strike and received the right to vote a month later.

What this means is that the men who composed the Continental Congress, who declared independence from Great Britain, were a mixed group: some of them honest people of the economic means, while others were abusers of the political means, taking seats in Congress in order to twist the laws in their favor. Samuel Adams mentions such men in a letter to his friend Richard Henry Lee, in January of 1781:

> ... men, vain, avaricious, or concealed under the hypocritical guise of Patriotism, without a spark of public or private virtue. ... I need not remind you that men of this character have had seats in Congress from the beginning.

So, the Founding Fathers of the United States were a mixed group. Some of them were people who, while perhaps flawed, cared deeply about freedom and risked their lives for it. Others were fighting to preserve the advantages they had established under the British political system, then, after that structure was gone, to build a new legal and constitutional structure they could continue reaping from. Chief among these were Alexander Hamilton, Robert Morris and their associates. These oligarchs were generally shrewd enough not to condemn independence, but they didn't pursue it either.[101]

The Top of The Arc

By 1760 or so, the fruits of salutary neglect had appeared. In 1776 – the high water mark for these sentiments – subversive opinions were widespread and approaching a majority opinion, certainly so away from the cities.

The most enduring expressions of this line of development came from George Mason, Thomas Jefferson, and Thomas Paine. But more important than the words of the most eloquent Americans were the words and deeds of working people. For example, in 1773, the people of Hubbardston, Massachusetts, a town of about 300, published a declaration:

> We are of the opinion that rulers first derive their power from the ruled by certain laws and ruls [sic] agreed upon by rulers and ruled, and when a ruler breaks over such laws ... and makes new ones ... then the ruled have a right to refuse such new laws and ... to judge for themselves when rulers transgress.

In Worcester, a town of a few thousand, a similar letter was published at about the same time:

> It is our opinion that mankind are by nature free, and the end design of forming social compacts ... was that each member of that society might enjoy his life and property, and live in the free exercise of his rights ... which God and Nature gave.

---

[101] See FMP #56.

At the same time, a group of creditors, lawyers, and judges (again, people of the political means) posed a threat to the small farmers and artisans of Worcester county. In response, they formed their own legal system, abandoned government courts and used arbitration to resolve their disputes.

Events like these were common all through the colonies. These people believed in their individual right to judge the world and to act upon it without permission.

The Down-Side of The Arc

From 1776 through 1780 or so, sentiment held fairly steady overall, but some people continued to game the system. By a variety of political moves, the ownership of virgin land was handed from the states to the central government.[102]

By 1787, Alexander Hamilton turned an unremarkable session for upgrading the Articles of Confederation into a constitutional convention, and produced a far more expansive constitution, something he and his associates had long wanted.

Historian Merrill Jensen, writing in *The New Nation*, describes the difference between what the desires of the political class and the working class:

> If we look at the new nation only through the eyes of angry politicians and soldiers at the end of the war, we get a distorted concept of the spirit of the times. ... But if we turn away from such sources, we see a spirit of exuberant optimism everywhere, a belief in the great destiny of the new nation, a conviction that Americans could do anything they wanted to, untrammeled by the traditions of the old world.

Furthermore, many of the arguments for the new Constitution in the *Federalist Papers* are fallacious; a point that Patrick Henry made at the Virginia Ratifying Convention:

> The Confederation; this same despised government ... carried us through a long and dangerous war; it rendered us victorious in that bloody conflict with a powerful nation; it has secured us a territory greater than any European monarch possesses: and shall any government that has been thus so strong and vigorous, be accused of imbecility and abandoned for want of energy?...
>
> Go to the poor man, ask him what he does; he will inform you, that he enjoys the fruit of his labor, under his own fig tree, with his wife and children around him, in peace and security. Go to every other member of the society, you will

---

[102] Again, see FMP #56.

find the same tranquil ease and content; you will find no alarms or disturbances: Why then tell us of dangers to terrify us into an adoption of this new government?

Still, the new Federalists and their constitution carried the day, taking power under the administration of George Washington. A central bank soon followed, as did Hamilton's doctrine of "implied intent," which allowed the central government to do far more than agreed. And, of course, there was the great scandal of revolutionary war soldiers being swindled by their own politicians.

At the same time many Americans were not ready to stop rebelling against tyranny, home-grown or otherwise. And so, there were continuing rebellions.

There was Shays's Rebellion, wherein protesters shut down county courts to stop tax and debt collections, which, in the words of John Adams, were "heavier than the people could bear."

Ultimately the rebellion was put down by the central government, and Vermont, where many of the rebels had hid, was hurried into statehood to prevent a recurrence.[103]

Rhode Island refused to ratify the constitution, was forced to do so with a naval blockade.

The Whiskey Rebellion was a protest against a tax that targeted rebellious areas under Alexander Hamilton's economic program. Many of the tax resisters were veterans, continuing their fight for freedom against a central state. And as they had done earlier, they raised liberty poles, formed committees of correspondence, and took control of the local militia. They created their own courts as well. The rebellion was put down with force, but the tax was repealed after Thomas Jefferson became president in 1801.

By the time of Jefferson's presidency (1801-1809), the United States were not as free as they had been thirty years earlier, but were considerably freer than England or anywhere else in the Western world.

And, for those who wished to continue west into frontier territories, full freedom, or something close to it, was still available.

The Idea of America

The United States has never been able to define itself by ethnic heritage, that is, by DNA. Americans come from every nation. The core of America is an idea: *self-sovereignty*. That the strength of this idea has ebbed and flowed over time is a secondary issue, the United States was never pure and was always at war within itself over a variety of ideas. But the better founders set this idea in the highest places, and endeavored to write their core documents around it.

---

[103] See FMP #57 regarding these rebellions and this era.

The real foundational document of the American Revolution was the Declaration of Independence. The US Constitution contains operating rules; the Declaration defines the soul of the American experiment. And this declaration begins by placing the individual as judge and decider. The phrase "We hold these truths to be self-evident" almost demands that the readers decide for themselves. There is no appeal to authority, no pedigree, no appeal to precedent, no appeal to anything except the mind of the reader.

And the document goes further, defining the genesis of rights: From nature's God, to the people, and from thence delegated to a government: a government that the people have a *duty* to overthrow if it becomes abusive.

The original ten amendments to the US Constitution repeat this idea. They are explicit in stating what Congress may *not* do. People have always called these amendments "The Bill of Rights," but that's a misleading name: This is a list of actions that the people forbid Congress from taking. The language is repetitive and blunt: *Congress shall make no law.*

The overriding idea of America is that the people possess all rights, and choose to delegate a few of them to their government for specified actions. As corrupted and overblown as the US government may now be, this idea of self-sovereignty lives on in the central documents. (Whether people pay attention to such things is another matter.)

When America Was Young, It Had No Myth

National leaders nearly always promote some sort of myth – one or more "uniquenesses" that give the nation a noble identity. (People seeking fast approval are eager to join in.) But in its earlier years, America had no such myth, and this was very healthy. With no myth, politicians have fewer emotional strings to pull, and people who decide based upon reason are much harder to manipulate than those who operate upon emotion.

That the idea of America was good could only be proven by American success, but they did succeed, to the shock of the Old World. Americans success cannot be credited to any sort of genetic superiority (the converse could be argued), nor can it be credited to natural resources. (Brazil, another New World nation, has always had more resources.) Americans succeeded because the structure of their society allowed them to operate by a better set of rules.

America proper is not a nation of dirt or of DNA, it is a nation of mind. Fidelity to better ideas was America's advantage, and this lesson has now been taught to any who wish to acknowledge it.

The Downhill Run

Once the American Revolution turned into the United States of America, power was consolidated, and this was visible because the American experiment was conducted on the blank canvas of an empty continent.

All governments maintain a monopoly of force in a geographic territory. This is the definition of a state, and it makes political processes combative. Once a political process is finalized, only two choices remain: To obey or to break the law. Individuals, acting outside of government, secure the cooperation of others via persuasion. Governments demand and punish.

The above is not an indictment; it is merely a clarification. If we are to understand human societies, we cannot avoid honest definitions. Governments operate on a different model than do non-criminal individuals.

So, once the American experiment moved from convincing people to forcing people, its nature was radically changed. One of the first changes was the creation of political parties. Parties are, after all, the pooling of political power.

The first few sessions of the US Congress were nonpartisan. Legislators came to their meetings and decided their vote upon the merits of the bills presented to them. Certainly they might face the disapproval of their constituents if they voted for a hated project, but they dealt with the issues directly. Once parties became involved, however, a new layer came into play. The legislator now had to consider whether the party would approve or disapprove of his vote. His attention was drawn away from the actual merits of the bill and away from his constituents.

The appeal of parties to voters was that they could pool their power to vote allied candidates into office and thus gain a much greater grip on the government. This, if we are to be honest, meant that they could force others to do the things that they wanted.

In short, the adoption of political parties diminished the cooperative principle and made force a larger component of American life. Ironically, Washington specifically warned his countrymen about this in his Farewell Address. A portion of that address reads as follows:

> They serve to organize faction, to give it an artificial and extraordinary force; to put, in the place of the delegated will of the nation, the will of a party... they are likely, in the course of time and things, to become potent engines, by which cunning, ambitious, and unprincipled men will be enabled to subvert the power of the people, and to usurp for themselves the reins of government.

When parties control legislators, each of them vote as their party demands of them. Even reading the legislation is unnecessary: The party has decided and the individual legislator can choose either to obey or to break faith with the party. This adds a layer of complexity to the operation of the government, a layer of separation between the people and their representatives, and a layer of confusion blocking the view from one side of the process to the other.

To illustrate the change that occurred by the time political parties became part of American life, here are the thoughts of Samuel Adams during the revolution:

> The natural liberty of man is to be free from any superior power on Earth, and not to be under the will or legislative authority of man, but only to have the law of nature for his rule.

To reconcile the intentions of Adams with political rule following George Washington is impossible. But regardless of the general down-hill slide that began with the consolidation of state power, America served as an agent of change world-wide. As Thomas Jefferson said:

> All eyes are opened, or opening, to the rights of man. The general spread of the light of science has already laid open to every view the palpable truth: that the mass of mankind has not been born with saddles on their backs.

Passing-Along The Idea, Poorly

The American ideal of self-sovereignty never fully took root, but at the beginning it had enough force to influence a new branch of Western culture. With great difficulty (along with the religious ideals that informed it) it brought about the end of slavery in the United States in the following century. But in the process of eliminating slavery, the republic changed dramatically.[104]

The South, while certainly morally conflicted due to the enslavement of human beings, was more uniquely "American" than the north in other ways. When the Industrial Revolution began to roll over the north, commercial and urban forces began to change the republic, and often abusively. The agricultural South reacted against this. Combined with the revolution's unfinished business of slavery, this spawned the American Civil War[105].

The end of slavery was, obviously, an important and necessary step, but something of the original idea of America died along with it. Bear in mind that there is absolutely nothing in the Constitution that would forbid the

---

[104] See FMP #70 on the formation of slavery in the New World.

[105] Which was unnecessary. More than dozen other nations, including the UK, ended slavery without war.

South to leave the union. All of the states joined the union voluntarily, and none forsook their right to leave. Even if they had, this would hardly be binding upon their grandchildren. And if the *Declaration* gave the people the right to overthrow an abusive government, how much more, then, the right simply to leave it?

Lincoln's justification for forcing the South to remain in the Union was not logical, but mystical. The famous phrase, "that government of the people, by the people, for the people, shall not perish from the earth," presumes a falsity. Was it really only a Union of thirty-four states that could keep government "of the people" alive? The Union started with only thirteen, after all.

We won't go through an examination of the war and the "saving" of the Union; they are not important to this discussion. What is important is that the Civil War defined a new America: One that was industrial and one where sovereignty was transferred from the people and from the states to the central government. The states were now clearly subservient to the central government, and if *they* couldn't assert their independence, how much less an individual citizen?

So, along with the old and flawed South, something of the original America died during the Civil War.

To make matters more difficult, many of those who still held to the old ideas spent their remaining strength in less than ideal ways. On the heals of the Civil War, millions of immigrants began to arrive in the United States. Political energies during this era of immigration were generally wasted in battles over side issues and details, rather than on passing along core ideals... the things that really mattered. People busied themselves with fights over the control of centralized force rather than the morality of daily life and the ideals of the revolution. They fought immigration and drunkenness, leaving self-sovereignty behind. They had learned to use force rather than persuasion to secure good conduct. They acted politically, not economically; by coercion rather than by cooperation.

The great tide of immigrants during the late 19th and early 20th Centuries were primarily oppressed peoples from Eastern and Southern Europe. (Immigrants from Northern Europe tended to arrive earlier.) They came, not really for the *idea* of America, but for the *results* of America. Then, as now, their arrival in large numbers caused discomfort and anger.

Assimilation was generally expected of the immigrant. But this expectation, while somewhat helpful for passing on the idea of America, was often turned into a bludgeon and used as a tool of insult. Yes, there were good Americans who wished to pass along the great idea of self-sovereignty, but the unkind Americans were at least as loud and the fine points of these arguments were usually lost on the immigrants, who, after all, spoke little English.

So, the core ideas of America were poorly passed on. The immigrants generally worked hard and loved America, but many ideas from the Old World and difficult experiences weighed upon them. On top of this, they were often exposed to discrimination and hatred, making the idea of America considerably less attractive.

Because of the above, late 19th and early 20th century immigrants (and their children) became excellent fodder for new-style politicians who were offering the public precisely what they wanted – promises of nurture, acknowledgement as victims, and someone to blame. This, added to the fact that the idea was in a weakened condition by the time they arrived, assured that the immigrants didn't understand what America originally meant. They were generally decent people and good neighbors, but aside from the most well-read, they didn't understand America's foundations.

9

The Industrial Surprise

*Three hundred years ago, give or take a half-century,
an explosion was heard that sent concussive shock
waves racing across the earth, demolishing ancient
societies and creating a wholly new civilization. This
explosion was, of course, the industrial revolution.*
-- Alvin Toffler (1979)

The Industrial Revolution was, beyond anything else, a great surprise. Its mixture of scientific discovery and unrestrained human action produced a new method of organization that was overwhelming in its ability to produce valuable goods on a never-imagined scale. The new factories made more people more enduringly rich that anything that had come before it, and by a very large margin.

The other ingredient that brought the Industrial Revolution to life was cooperative, inter-disciplinary discussions and projects by groups such as the *Lunar Society of Birmingham*, which was responsible for the development of Watt's steam engine and many other important innovations. This group, like the previously-mentioned group in Edinburgh, met regularly, argued, invented, invested, tested, corresponded with others and worked on an endless series of ideas. These were individuals operating with very few restraints, having the Rights of Englishmen, living with minimal government intrusion into their lives, and with very low levels of taxation. This allowed them to accumulate capital; the ability to finance their own innovations.

The Beginnings

As all new developments do, the Industrial Revolution relied upon earlier developments, such as clocks and the organization of the printing business[106]. But these were limited contributions.

By the 17th century, scientific developments were being made rapidly and clever men throughout Britain and northern Europe were tinkering on ways to use them productively. All sorts of new ideas were coming out of workshops and hovels. Most of them are lost to history, but they led to ever-better innovations and to better and cheaper production.

These new machines and new processes, however, were opposed by entrenched interests: people who had learned to rely upon central force to maintain their advantages. So, once again, progress was not welcomed, but hated. The first effective manufacturing machines, weaving looms, were often hidden in homes and production was carried out in secret. (This was common in mid-17th century London.)

Force was applied to stop these new developments. Here are some events of this type from the early Industrial era:

1586 – A new type of machine loom is forbidden by the city fathers of Danzig and its inventor is secretly murdered[107].

1616 – Official English documents refer to "alien weavers," (weaving machines were accepted in Leyden, from where these men may have come) who were: *bold of late, to devise engines for working of tape, laces, ribbon and such, wherein one man does more among them than seven English men can do, so as their cheap sale of these commodities beggareth all our English artificers of that trade.*

1623 – The Privy Council of England orders the destruction of a machine for making needles.

1625 – The Weavers Company of London beseeches the city fathers: *Order that none may use the said engine, except those who are Weavers by trade, for they which now use them are… Merchants and other tradesmen, but not Weavers by trade.*

1638 – King Charles I prohibits the use of "engine, or great looms," and adds, "whereby much deceit is practiced."

---

[106] Clocks had been developed in the 13th and 14th Centuries by monks who wanted to organize work and prayer. Printing press operations were a precursor to factory organization.

[107] See FMP #2. This story is related in *The London Weavers' Company, 1600-1970*, by Alfred Plummer. (Other items on this list are also drawn from this text.) Plummer obtained the information from J. Beckman's *A History of Inventions, Discoveries and Origins* (4th Edition, 1846) II, which quotes a work by Lancellotti, published in Venice in 1636.

1649 – British Navigation Acts are passed to prevent economic innovation in British colonies and to force all their produce to pass through English hands. This made the colonials subject to English regulations and criminalized any innovations that were not accepted in England.

1666-1730 – France publishes their Crafts Codes: 2,200 pages of regulations, prescribing every detail of the established craft techniques, and forbidding any innovations to them.

1667 – The Weavers Court of Assistants in London sends a group of Yeomen to conduct a search, and to find out how many looms were in use in their jurisdiction, so that, "a course of action may be decided upon."

1675 – A guild of London area weavers petitions the Lord Mayor to outlaw new "engine looms." In addition, they riot for three days and destroy many such machines.

1686 – England outlaws Indian Calico fabric.

1698 – England outlaws cloth buttons.

Here, again, the names of the early innovators are forgotten. They created methods that would enrich mankind beyond all that had been previously imagined; in reward, they were declared criminals, spied upon, persecuted and sometimes killed. Production was in danger of being overcome by plunder once again.

Steam Power

Steam powered devices had existed as parlor tricks as far back as the classical Greeks. But the practical steam engines of Newcomen (in 1712) and especially of Watt (in the 1770s) made steam the greatest power source in the history of the world. It allowed fantastic power to be produced and distributed, easily and efficiently. Systems of belts, drive shafts, gears and pulleys could distribute this power quite effectively through a medium-sized building, and from a single engine. With multiple engines, large factories became practical.

The steam engine made the Industrial Revolution unstoppable. Power was available upon demand for virtually unlimited periods of time. All sorts of beneficial activities could be arranged around such a power source, and, quite quickly, they were. Once this was seen, the sheer numbers of people who wanted it overcame the users of central power, who wished to maintain a developmental stasis.

Very shortly, it was seen that whoever embraced the steam engine and the possibilities it created might become very rich.

Specialization & Economies of Scale

The unique structure of the Industrial Revolution was the factory. Here, for the first time, large numbers of men and women worked in a coordinated fashion. (At its height, factory production was responsible for most employment in the Western world.)

Factories became dominant for the simple reason that they were effective. By hand a single piece of furniture, to pick an example, could be built by a single mechanic in perhaps forty hours of time. But if a factory was set up to produce that same item, it could be produced with perhaps ten hours of labor, a four-fold increase in efficiency. (Other examples are more impressive.)

The first cause of this great gain was merely specialization. A man who works on every aspect of making furniture will become relatively proficient in most of them over time. But if the man works only on cutting wood from the forest, he will become excellent at that specialty, and much more quickly. By specializing in specific tasks, not only does efficiency improve, but special tools and processes for that specialty can be developed. In a short period of time, productivity rises dramatically.

But setting up a factory full of specialty work-stations was neither cheap nor easy. It required a few highly skilled engineers and a number of highly-skilled machine builders and installers, not to mention the necessary materials and tools. This could be expensive.

To continue our furniture example, let's say that the factory setup cost 100,000 silver coins. At a labor rate of 10 coins per hour, costs of one-half labor and a mark-up of 67%, the factory would have to manufacture and sell at least one thousand pieces before it recouped the 100,000 coin setup costs. You can see from this that factories had to produce huge volumes of identical items if they hoped to gain an economic advantage. But, since the cost to the buyer of such furniture was far below the cost of hand-made furniture and the quality equal or better, they sold in volume.

Massification

As a result of this *economy of scale*, factories became places of mass production. And as the central engine of commerce went, so went the culture. What Alvin Toffler calls "massification" became the central paradigm of organization: Bigger was better, smallness an embarrassment. The cult of size affected almost every commercial entity. The assumption was that size had inherent advantages. So, almost everything tended to become big, including news organizations, government, entertainment companies, and so on.

In the early chapters of his book, *The Third Wave*, Alvin Toffler dissects Industrial civilization (he terms it "Second Wave civilization,"), explaining why the mass production model, with its unbeatable productivity, was adopted in nearly identical fashion worldwide. Toffler explains that at the core of industrialism was a set of six interrelated principles that, in the end, affected every aspect of human life in the industrial era. They were:

1. Standardization
2. Specialization
3. Synchronization
4. Concentration
5. Maximization
6. Centralization

One of the primary ways in which the new model of centralized economic action trained humans to operate within it was government schooling. Toffler explains:

> Built on the factory model, mass education taught basic reading, writing, and arithmetic, a bit of history and other subjects. This was the "overt curriculum." But beneath it lay an invisible or "covert curriculum" that was far more basic. It consisted—and still does in most industrial nations—of three courses: one in punctuality, one in obedience, and one in rote, repetitive work. Factory labor demanded workers who showed up on time, especially assembly-line hands. It demanded workers who would take orders from a management hierarchy without questioning.

With a population trained in conformity, large-scale manufacturing became a practical possibility. People were willing to yield themselves to it because manufacturing brought an increase in material prosperity. Working the old way a seamstress may have turned out a single dress on a good day. Now, with the aid of a few steam-powered machines, a handful of partly-skilled workers could produce hundreds of dresses in a day. An equal amount of labor delivered ten times the result or more.

The New Urban Culture

First in England, then in the United States and in Europe, a new, urban culture began to rise. Farm boys and girls, in immense numbers, began leaving the countryside for well-paying jobs in the city. The old order, founded upon farm life, cracked open and split apart. The leading edge of progress moved to the cities, causing governance to change accordingly. The existing urban middle class of merchants, traders, small manufacturers and shopkeepers added supervisors and engineers and expanded to dominance.

Over the next century, industrialization spread throughout the Western world. (And few other places.) Wave after wave of farm children came to the cities for jobs, and most stayed. All of our modern institutions began to form, in service of the new order: local banks, courts, meeting halls, merchants' associations, central markets, warehouses, barge terminals and, soon, railway terminals. Mutual assistance organizations formed, churches sprang up to service the new arrivals, restaurants, barbershops, newspapers, grocery stores, dry good stores, and many others. The world took its modern form.

Government also was forced to renovate. Industrialism displaced the royal families of Europe[108]. Their power at the time was gigantic and their methods of influence were many, but they were nonetheless pushed away from power. The new system was built over and around them, and, once in place, it removed the ground from beneath their feet[109].

Rulership (especially in England and America) evolved into representative government, with the people of each area choosing and sending a few people to regional capitals. Now the masses were a force for the ruler to reckon with. And with newspapers and mail common, the ruler's actions were at least partly open to scrutiny.

In response to this, the various classes of rulers had to pay close attention to the wishes of the people that elected them. To further complicate matters, these citizen/subjects were no longer peasant farmers, but factory workers, managers, shopkeepers, and mechanics. As a result, the rulers paid a lot less attention to the farmers. Power shifted to the cities and to their masses.

Members of governments were forced into the popularity business. Getting huge numbers of people to vote for them determined their employment And, since there is an addiction to power, they wanted very badly to retain their offices. As a result, politicians began to work very hard at gaining popularity. They struggled to determine what the masses wanted, what they were afraid of, what made them like someone and what made them dislike someone.

In some ways, turning governance into popularity contests was beneficial, since it made the politician dependent upon the populace. In measure, at least, the politician listened to the voters, and did what they wanted him or her to do. But on the other hand, politics became a manipulation contest. There were few rules on what could be done to get a citizen to vote for you. Outright bribes were soon enough outlawed, but promises of money from the public treasury always played well.

No longer was the local community of farmers the central unit of power. Now it became groups of people: The factory workers, the bosses, the investors, specific immigrant groups, and so on. Politicians played one group against the other with virtuosity. As time went on, the groups played to by industrial era politicians continually shifted, but income discrepancies and envy have always played major roles.

---

[108] See FMP #76.

[109] The families didn't vanish, of course. They still have massive influence, financial and otherwise, but they no longer dominate the public stage.

Resulting Problems

> *Woe to him who teaches men faster than they can learn.*
> – Will Durant

The Industrial Revolution had negative consequences as well as positives. The technology and economics were fine by themselves, but a lot of people weren't ready to leave the archaic world and join the modern world. They felt dragged into it and were simply unprepared to deal with the emotional dislocation that it caused. They were not ready to adapt; they were not ready to change; but, the open offer of making a lot more money and living in a much grander style drew them into it anyway. Modernity was thrust upon them.

One way to define modernity is by the process of science – that of testing ideas one at a time and building them into larger ideas. The pre-modern mind focused more around beginning with large ideas and fitting smaller ideas into that model. It was a model built for mental stasis and comfort within rigid boundaries.

Specific things that gave shape to the modern world were these:

- Reduced security in the clan, tribe or local group.
- Rapid change.
- Multiplied choices.
- Multiplied information.
- Secure title, lot lines, surveying.
- Business competition, with the attendant possibility of failure.
- Greater accumulation of wealth.

All of the above caused great turmoil and wild, reactionary responses.

Wealth, for example: its very existence threatens those who do not have it. The modern thirst for equality is, to a very considerable extent, an attempt to escape the shame of comparison with people more wealthy than themselves. In the Middle Ages people were often held within their class and couldn't be blamed for a lack of achievement. Industrial society ripped that comfort away. Serfdom had been a restrictive structure, but with in it people found sanctuary from responsibility. Unrestricted wealth accumulation removed that and spawned reactionary movements such as Marxism, which held wealth accumulation to be inherently criminal.

The demotion of place had similar effects: Once your 'special' place is no longer special and people are leaving it for other places (such as the cities), centuries-old self-esteem supports are removed. People who found geocentric belonging or superiority are left grasping for some reason to feel good about themselves.

There have been many variations on this theme, but they all orbit around the issues of externally-based self-esteem, permanent uncertainty, methods of escaping shame, identification with great personalities, living vicariously through others, wishing for successful people to fall, wishing for primitives or their attributes to ascend, and so on. These things certainly existed before the Industrial Revolution, but they gained far greater prominence when a new way of living was thrust upon the world.

The first dislocation occurred when the farm boy left his farm and would no longer undertake his traditional family obligations. This left the older generation unprepared and vulnerable. The young generation focused on themselves and told their parents, "I never signed up for lifelong duty to the farm. I have my own life and I will live it as I see fit.[110]"

The children who went to the cities also suffered shock. They usually found their hoped-for job quickly enough, but found themselves in a completely new situation. In the city, life was ruled by clocks. They rose and lay down according to the sun on the farm. The factory required workers to arrive and be ready to work at very precise times. There was no going to work when you were ready; you had to be in your place and ready to perform at eight o'clock. If not, you were fired and replaced with another newly-arrived farm boy.

There was also the matter of acculturating to city life. A large percentage of these people felt lost, as if they no longer knew where they belonged in the world. They had no certain place, and that void gnawed at them. Before the Industrial Revolution, they at least knew that they belonged somewhere: they had a town, a local church, and a significant number of neighbors. Love them or hate them, they felt at home there. Now that was behind them; they felt isolated in the midst of chaos, and vulnerable. Their identity was in question for the first time. They left the farm where they knew who they were and had a place in a hundred-generation chain. Now they were in a city where almost no one would care if they did or didn't show up the next day.

---

[110] Better jobs in the city was not the only factor affecting these people, although it was the strongest. At about the same time mechanized farming became possible. As the McCormick Reaper and other farm machines proliferated, the demand for farm labor receded. There were, of course, farmers that used the Reaper as a tool to allow them to farm many more acres, but expansion was not always possible, and the number of farm workers declined steadily.

The Road to Auschwitz

The road to World War Two, the central man-made disaster in world history [111], began with the dislocation culture of the Industrial Revolution. This story is important in its own right, but more so because it illustrates the kind of problems that can arise from mass changes. That the creation of better production would lead to something like a Holocaust is not initially obvious.

As the Industrial Revolution proceeded into Southern Europe and to points east, it created groups of people that were less able to be dragged into a new world than Englishmen, Dutchmen and Americans had been.

In most of the south, there was no representative government. That left these people even more isolated than their northern counterparts. In the northern places, one could, and often did, attend a political meeting simply because there was nothing else to do, and because they were assured the local politician would welcome them with open arms. Not so in Southern and Eastern Europe, where there were usually no representative politicians.

So, if there was no group to find representation in, and if the state was not particularly welcoming, an alternative would have to be found. Soon enough, the concept of the *People* came along. So, 19th century Europe became a breeding ground for what came to be called the "Pan" movements. (*Pan* meaning universal.) There were pan-Slavic movements, pan-German movements, pan-Polish movements, and many others. Dislocated factory workers found their identity as part of a "people," not directly or permanently associated with a single nation. Men organized themselves by ethnic self-image, which was better addressed by the Pan groups than it was by the state, which may or may not accept him as a member, and which barely listened to him in the first place.

At about this time, the root of human rights was changing as well. In the Middle Ages, one would speak of his or her "rights as a Christian." But with the rise of national sovereignty, formalized with the Peace of Westphalia in 1648, the root of human rights was passing to the nation-state. Particularly hard hit by this change were minorities in the various states. Who, for example, would protect a Frenchman living in Germany? He was not a German, and therefore not a citizen of the German state and not entitled to its protection. Modern processes for such situations were not in place at this time. Minority populations were not accepted for membership in the state, resulting in large numbers of "stateless people." These were people with no authority to protect them. The most notable of these were the Jews.

---

[111] This statement, obviously, is subject to debate. The 20th century's socialists killed almost unbelievable numbers: Stalin over 20 million and Mao over 50 million, not to mention what happened in Cambodia and in many other places. But these were not single events per se, and were not as flamboyant and concentrated as the killings of WW2. Certainly they were less memorable (for better or worse).

Regarding the Pan movements, it is important to remember that, up to World War One, even the strongest rulers accepted their legitimacy. One of Czar Nicholas II's primary reasons for entering World War One was to "protect our fellow Slavs." These Slavs were *not* citizens of the Czar's Russia. The First World War can be understood as a clash between Pan movements at least as well as it can be understood as a clash between states.

After World War One, the winners attempted to redraw Europe's borders according to the "peoples" of Eastern Europe, and to give them all a nation or to make them legally protected minorities. Hitler called this artificial and became the great implementer of the Pan ideals. He demanded control of the Sudetenland because the German minority there was not protected and should naturally belong to his Germany, not to the Czechs. After that, it was Austria, which he considered a natural part of "The German Nation." Thus the system of States broke down, creating World War Two.

The fate of the Jews was wrapped up in this tumult. The people of the Pan movements saw themselves as superior to the state. When they saw the Jews associated with state power, they became ever so much more the enemy[112].

Schoenerer, the leader of the German Pan movement, seems to have discovered the effectiveness of anti-Semitism by accident. But, whether by accident or not, the Jews became a perfect tool. Hitler condemned the Treaty of Versailles, its humiliation of the German nation, and the current order of states. Then he placed the bulk of the blame upon the Jews: a stateless people who no one was willing to protect. He had nothing to lose and everything to gain. (Anti-Semitism already had deep roots in Eastern Europe.)

Following World War Two, Bolshevism and revulsion at Nazi atrocities killed the Pan movements in a moment. The world would be organized in states for the foreseeable future.

Dunbar's Number

Dunbar's Number[113] is the number of identities that humans can manage and work with. These are relationships in which an individual knows who each person is and how each person relates to every other person. At numbers larger than this, rules and enforcement are required to maintain a cohesive group.

Beyond about 150 people, most humans have a hard time dealing with individual identities: considering how a new policy will affect Jimmy and

---

[112] The truth is that only a fraction of the Jews were associated with power, usually as money-lenders or physicians. The popular images of the time left out the majority Shtetle Jews (poor Jews in small towns), and focused on the few "abusers of the People."

[113] Developed by anthropologist Robin Dunbar. He based it upon brain size and function. He and others have found evidence for it in human history. Some place the number higher than Dunbar's 150, but none more than twice as high.

Suzy and Herman and Sarah and George and Bob, etc. At that point, they move into abstractions[114], and individual identities are grouped behind symbols. (At this point, trouble begins.) Human minds have limits, and keeping complex images of more than 150 or 200 people in their head is too much for most people. They generally resort to symbols and binary decision mechanisms: Yes/No, Allowed/Forbidden, and so on.

This abstraction is the great corrupter of large systems and the root of their de-humanizing aspects. Rules and laws always devalue the individual and *cannot do otherwise*. This is because of information processing requirements, not character flaws. When you stop seeing humans *as humans*, they are inherently devalued and their individual personalities are excluded.

Because Dunbar's Number describes real human limitations, this de-humanizing effect will remain part of large organizations until human brainpower increases dramatically, which may be a long time.

Because of this, systems based upon rules are oppositional to human-to-human cooperation and to human liberty. The great advantage to the common law of England was that it wasn't based upon rules[115]. Rather, it was based upon principles, which would be interpreted and applied to individuals by legal professionals. The core of the issue here is information processing. Principles are designed to be applied intelligently to real human actions. Rules are rigid and binary, not at all suited to a complex humanity.

Rules eliminate reason and interpretation. They forbid complex thought and demand blind obedience instead. Thus, what we might call a terabit processor (the human brain) is forbidden to decide, and merely becomes a tool of obedience. The rule – a single-bit, binary decision – is enthroned. Thus the best information processors are ignored, in favor of single-bit processing[116].

Because industrial production required large numbers of people working in one place and at one time, the effects of Dunbar's Number were a primary and negative feature of Industrial society. The problem could have been worked around (and has been to some extent in recent years) but it simply

---

[114] An *abstraction*, as I use the term, is the substitution of a symbol for one or more real things. Rather than considering the thing itself, someone using abstraction would consider the category to which the thing belongs. If, for example, I was planning a new schedule for my factory: Rather than thinking about its impact upon each of my company's 500 employees, I would simply consider the impact upon an imaginary "worker." This "worker" would be an abstract image, not a real thing by itself.

[115] As a result, people living where the common law was held tended to be more adaptive and creative than placed where Civil Law was in force. This was not because they were inherently better, but because they were allowed to think and operate more freely.

[116] The great fear of abandoning rules is that "something could go wrong." This is held as a deep bias by most people, as is evidenced by the fact that things go wrong every day under the primacy of rules, and that they do not fear this, nor do they question it. And, of course, something always *will* go wrong; human complexity assures that under any system.

wasn't understood at the time, and the people creating industrial production were too distracted to do much about it.

And, of course, the people who felt the sting of this de-humanization tended to blame it on the malice of their employers, or on the "moneyed class," or on capitalism in general. All were distractions from the core of the issue and all created hatreds.

New Opportunities

Although we've spent a number of pages explaining the problems that arose with the Industrial Revolution, it is important to return to its benefits, which outweighed the costs[117].

All humans have talents, inclinations and abilities that are far, far more complex and varied than the assumptions of the societies that contain them. For the vast majority of human history, such abilities found little outlet. The early Armenian gardeners of 7000 B.C. experienced a moment in which their abilities were free to flourish, but they were restrained by force soon enough. Since then opportunities have found an occasional open space, but generally within the limits of agricultural communities. Trade did exist, but it was often limited[118]. Beside, trading is but one occupation.

In complex industrial societies, for the first time, humans had both freedom and access to multiple avenues for the expression of their abilities. Choices opened up, seemingly without limit: engineers of many varieties, specialty manufacturers, repairmen, parts suppliers, transportation specialists, instructors, inspectors, insurance providers, nurses, custom builders, after-hours entertainers, and the list goes on.

Of course there were continual attempts to limit this explosion of growth with professional regulation laws, but these were generally circumvented. For the first time ever, humans encountered more choices than they could seriously consider. This did cause some discomfort (and still does), but it's so much better than the old alternative that comparisons are silly.

This was also highly productive, since it allowed people to find their unique strengths and to use them, rather than being stuck in work for which they were not suited. Granted, finding out what one is best at is usually a lengthy and difficult process, but at least it became a possibility.

It should be added that this ability to choose among unlimited vocations remained more difficult in class-bound societies, such as was frequently the case in England. Every time someone was not permitted in some economic

---

[117] The more horrifying aspects of which cannot be blamed on the Industrial Revolution any further than we blame the peaceful poet who unintentionally inspires a killer.

[118] Rulers of most types throughout the agricultural era resented and insulted both traders and trade. It functioned as a wild card for them: Necessary to some extent, but bringing in strange new ideas and upsetting their systems of control.

activity, productivity was reduced. This form of exclusion was legislated in America (as professional regulation laws), but classes per se were never enforced. This was one of the great advantages of the new world.

The Market Intrudes Upon The State

Under the new model of Industrial civilization, power was steadily removed from ruling families and taxing groups and given to commercial groups and individuals. That is, to the markets in general[119]. By almost any objective standard, a market is a more ethical organization than a state. Markets force no one to do anything against their will, do not possess arbitrary power and are very seldom seen ordering violence[120].

States, always cultivating their legitimacy and having the raw power to impose upon any individual, maintained an advantage in public image. Nonetheless, everyone knew that generating wealth was something that the market did, not the state. So, for the first time, the market began to remove power from rulers and keep it for itself.

Under the rule of a market that bore the impress of Christianity, commercial competition became a game of cooperation. That is, competition was not between individuals as much as it was between strategies. The best strategies displaced others, but could also be adopted by any other player. Thus competition became a discovery mechanism, and the best methods of improving human life were the best rewarded. Certainly this game-play was sloppy, uneven and punctuated by cheating, but overall it provided more and better strides forward than had been seen before, and by a large margin.

Furthermore, the market provided unlimited opportunities for its participants. Where the market was freest, any player had the opportunity to make a fortune for himself or herself, and the method of doing this required that they gave people what they wanted better than others. This was a virtuous cycle[121] such as had never been before. Indeed, the best thinkers of the Industrial era championed free markets, not because they were effective, but because they were the most ethical structures for human cooperation ever built.

---

[119] By "market" or "markets," I refer to systems of voluntary trade. I am *not* including the corporate-legislative complex that has recently become dominant.

[120] I am excluding any consideration of criminal activity, which arises in roughly equal amounts under all systems: state, market, religious or any other. Condemning a system because it fails to provide perfection is silly; no system has ever provided perfection.

[121] The great unethical actions of the free-market era – Colonialism and Mercantilism - were the doings of governments and their allies. Therefore, they cannot be honestly attributed to markets.

10

The Decline Of Western Civilization

There was a golden world which developed between 1815 and 1914. Over that century and with the interruptions of a few short wars... a general peace had been the main feature...

An immense optimism covered the world, economically underpinned by the Classical Gold Standard. Gold coinage, though often of different weights in different countries, WAS money. The entire western world was a form of payments union in the sense that Gold was money.

Governments were small; tiny compared to today. What taxes existed were almost imperceptible. The US had no income tax. Privacy, property and contracts were sacrosanct.
– Bill Buckler

The 19th century was a time of immense progress. In the first half of the century, a huge number of canals and roads were built, opening up trade and travel. In the United States, this allowed for the settling of an open frontier.

In mid-century railroads spread across continents, making travel much faster, easier and cheaper. Never in the history of mankind had the transport of goods at these speeds and distances been possible, much less affordable. Steel went into mass production, making super-strong building materials available at little cost. Electricity was put to practical use in the telegraph.

By late in the century, electricity was used for the telephone and then for electrical light and power. In addition, radio began to develop, along with sound recording.

Scientific advances were far too many to mention: Chemistry, physics, biology, medicine, botany, zoology, mechanics, material sciences and dozens more leapt forward. Engineering positively went wild with new possibilities. For the first time in history, intercontinental travel for leisure and education was possible for people of average means. Humanity surpassed, clearly and even flamboyantly, all heights that had been previously achieved. The race was in new territory. The great forward movements of the 17th and 18th centuries came to full flower.

And then…

As we have seen from so many examples in the past, civilizations do not last forever and once they forsake the virtues that created them, they enter a long, slow period of decline. This is precisely what has happened to Western civilization, and all of our lives have taken place in the midst of this process. Yes, it is still possible for Western civilization to turn itself around, but absent heroic measures it will reach its end; if not soon, certainly in the times of our grandchildren. The factors that enabled Western civilization to renew itself in previous instances are not very strong at the moment and replacements are not apparent. The situation may not be hopeless, but it is dire.

For the rest of this chapter, we will track the descent of Western civilization, focusing on the primary issues and passing over a great deal of minutia.

Reversing Course

> *Ages of experience testify that the only way society can be improved is by the individualist method … that is, the method of each 'one' doing his very best to improve 'one'.*
> – Albert Jay Nock

The first great step backward was the attempt to turn the coercive force of the state into a tool of righteousness. The instigators of this development grew weary of convincing people to be righteous and began to force them, substituting exterior change for internal change.

If you work to convince a man to change his behavior – voluntarily – he may not follow your ideas, but if he does, it's because of authentic, internal changes in that man.

If you get a man to change his behavior by force, he follows your ideas for the wrong reasons. He is *not* changed internally. He learns nothing except that raw power can be used. He's also likely to start forcing others.

This reversed the flow of Western civilization, which had been built upon internal virtues, by which Europeans "saw to it themselves." Under this new model, internals were bypassed and externals were enthroned. Persuasion was abandoned for the use of power.

The process unfolded in three primary steps:

Righteousness Joins With Force, Part One

Slavery in the Western Hemisphere was instituted by Spain immediately upon Columbus' arrival in what is now Latin America, and the first African slaves arrived less than ten years later, coming to Hispaniola in 1501[122]. Throughout the 16th century, slaves, slave traders and plantation owners arrived in North America, which was nearly empty at the time. Europeans, who had rejected slavery a thousand years prior, numbered in the low thousands at best, giving the slavers free run of the North American continent.

It was not until the 17th century was well underway that enough Europeans to make a difference were present. As soon as that happened, however, slavery began encountering strong opposition, and by 1807 the importation of African slaves was banned in both the US and in British colonies.

But regardless of the cessation of new slave arrivals, the existing slaves remained, and this was an open wound for both Britain and the United States. Both countries were populated with religious Christians, many of whom had moral difficulties with the concept of slavery. A large number of non-religious people who had absorbed the teachings of the Enlightenment were also ardent opponents of slavery.

Soon, abolition movements gained numbers and force. In England, one of the lead abolitionists was William Wilberforce, a wealthy Englishman who left the Church of England and became a fervent, non-conformist, evangelical Christian. He waged a decades-long campaign to abolish the slave trade. In the United States, William Lloyd Garrison was the most notable abolitionist. To illustrate the religious aspect of abolitionism, here is an image of one of the most popular medallions of the time:

---

[122] See FMP #70.

A Popular Anti-Slavery Medallion

Courtesy Wikimedia Commons

Abolitionism is crucial to our subject here because it was the beginning of what we might deem *righteous activism*. Religious people or people who considered themselves to be fighting "the good fight" began to use government as a tool for reaching their goals. And reach them, they did. Slavery was outlawed in the British Empire in 1833 and in the United States in 1865.

In Britain the effects of this union of righteousness and force carried on, but not as powerfully as in the United States, which was due in part to the drama of the Civil War.

The success of abolitionism set a pattern for future righteous activism. In fact, William Lloyd Garrison moved into the temperance[123] movement once slavery had been eliminated in the United States. In England, the temperance movement began at almost the precise moment that slavery was outlawed. The strategy was shown to be successful: righteous people could push the government to enforce righteousness. This became a dominant civic ideology in the United States within a surprisingly short period of time.

---

[123] *Temperance* is an old word for self-control. It signifies the opposite of excess. The temperance movement sought to restrain or eliminate the drinking of alcoholic beverages.

Righteousness Joins With Force, Part Two

By the mid-19th century, the ills of America were widely blamed on the consumption of alcohol. Drinking, however, had been a sometimes troublesome activity from time immemorial; so, why a gigantic temperance movement should form just at this moment is a good question. A partial answer is that a great number of people were moving from farms to cities, where no one would keep them from over-drinking. With no family members nearby to scold them, some people went to extremes. This, however, would not apply to married men, one of the chief targets of the temperance movements.

The other answer to why temperance movements became big at this moment is because the righteousness plus force strategy had been victorious. It had ended slavery. And so, energetically righteous people (of whom there were many in the United States, especially among northeastern descendents of Puritans) manipulated governments into fulfilling their desires.

Increasing numbers of people, typically religious, sought to pass laws enforcing righteous living upon the people of England and the United States. Temperance laws were passed in Maine by 1851, in eleven additional states within several years, and English activists attempted laws several times, beginning in 1854.

Interestingly, one cause that is often given for less progress in England was that the movement was split. There was a significant part that opposed hardliners and preferred moral persuasion to the force of law. The US-based groups did not split this way and remained committed to forcible prohibition. And not only that, but many temperance activists used vigilante violence to stop people from drinking. Righteousness plus force had become the new model, as well as a good way to become famous.

The temperance movement, of course, led to the 18th Amendment to the US constitution and the outlaw of alcohol sales in 1920. (Commonly called *Prohibition*.) In England similarly restrictive laws were passed, such as the *Defence of the Realm Act* (1914) that restricted pub hours and taxed beer. Some breweries were nationalized two years later, but with World War I raging, further temperance laws were pushed to the side.

Prohibition in America ended the temperance movement. To reverse a famous business dictum: they over-promised and under-delivered. The temperance movement had promised that Prohibition would be the solution to the nation's poverty, crime, violence, and other ills. On the eve of Prohibition the invitation to a church celebration in New York said this: *Let the church bells ring and let there be great rejoicing, for an enemy has been overthrown and victory crowns the forces of righteousness.*

A famous baseball player turned evangelist named Billy Sunday said:

The slums will soon be only a memory. We will turn
our prisons into factories and our jails into storehouses
and corncribs.[124]

The Women's Christian Temperance Union (WCTU) went so far as saying that after Prohibition passed, it would go onward and bring "the blessing of enforced abstinence" to the rest of the world. People committed to righteousness were now fully invested in using force to create blessings upon earth.

Prohibition, of course, failed to solve crime and created immensely profitable criminal enterprises. Once the results were clearly seen, the experiment was discredited and Prohibition was repealed. The strategy of *righteousness plus force*, however, did not end with it.

Part Three: Progressivism

> *The role of the public official, and in particular of the public school teacher... is to collect little plastic lumps of human dough from private households and shape them on the social kneadingboard.*
> – Edward A. Ross, *Social Control*, 1914

The quote above is from Theodore Roosevelt's favorite sociologist, during what is called the Progressive Era (roughly 1890 through 1920). You can see that Mr. Ross was fully committed to using compulsory schooling to shape children (the lumps of human dough) into the types of adults that he thought they should be. The Progressive Era is known for many things, but nearly all of them revolve around righteousness plus force. Under this model, people would not be persuaded, one by one, to do the right thing; they would, rather, be forced en masse. This was not only seen as righteous, it was seen as efficient as well.

Murray Rothbard, in his paper, *The Progressive Era and the Family*[125], traces the roots of the Progressive era back to the Pietist revival movement of the 1830s. Pietism broadly taught that the creeds of churches or sects did not matter, nor did obedience to rituals. What *did* matter, however, was being "born again," and establishing a direct relationship between the individual and God.

Pietists in the South tended to be self-contained, holding that the experience of individual regeneration, of being born again, was enough to ensure salvation. Pietists in the North, however, added that it was necessary to ensure the salvation of everyone else in society, at least as much as was

---

[124] A number of towns did actually sell their jails, only to buy them back or build new ones shortly thereafter.

[125] Available on the mises.org web pages.

humanly possible. A common goal was "to transform the world into the image of Christ."

In any event, Pietists in the North soon took it upon themselves to stamp out temptations and occasions for sin. Accordingly, many of these people were drawn into abolitionist and temperance movements.

The other large religious groups in the United States at this time were "liturgical" Christians, such as Lutherans and Roman Catholics, who were arriving in large numbers. Both of these groups relied upon their churches for salvation, rather than individual experiences.

It was the shock of immigration that brought the Progressive Era to full force. In particular, the ideals of Progressivism were applied to Catholic immigrant children in public schools. Teachers frequently lectured on the dangers of "Popery" (Roman Catholicism), the wickedness of alcohol consumption and so on. By 1901, for example, every US state required classroom instruction in temperance, which was *not* a Catholic doctrine. Roman Catholics felt that drinking to excess was a sin, but that drinking in moderation was acceptable.

Since most Catholic children went to state schools, many Catholics worked to rid the schools of Protestant requirements and ceremonies, and of anti-Catholic textbooks. Many battles ensued, including massive anti-immigrant efforts; again with the final decree of righteousness enforce by the state.

Progressivism was the third step in the evolution of righteousness plus force, and it expanded into many areas. Beside mandatory state schooling of all children, Progressives wished to regulate most aspects of economic and moral life, and even family life. They fervently pursued regulation upon businesses, wilderness use, and labor. In all these cases, the underlying motivations were to save America and the world via state force.

By about 1920, Progressivism began to change. New laws restricted immigration for the first time, and with the stock market making people rich, the previous desire to reign in corporations began to wane. But, far more importantly, Prohibition was failing dramatically, which discredited Progressivism's Christian base. Religious Progressives said that Prohibition would solve all ills, and it clearly did not. That line of Progressivism failed. In its place came several new ideals:

- Populism: That "the people" were the proper ones to direct power, and not politicians, business owners and "interests." In short, the people versus the elites.

- Social sciences: As former pietists replaced religion with intellectualism (their zeal remaining), they began using social science to direct force in the right directions.

- Collectivism: Social Gospel ideals, with their elevation of equality, had been circulating for some time, but the Bolshevik revolution in Russia gave great hope to many Progressives. Here was a vibrant new government, committed to scientifically and forcefully creating a righteous world. And since Progressive Christianity had embarrassed itself, Bolshevik atheism was hard to argue against.

The result of this, leading into modern times, was that the Progressive's feeling of active righteousness – and especially of zealotry – has been passed down consistently, but Christianity per se was removed[126]. *The rights of the working man*, *people power*, *social justice*, and similar ideas were enthroned in religion's place[127]. The various feminist, environmental, housing and other movements extending into our time share this base. The civil rights movements of the 1960s featured a temporary return to religion as an influence, but that has not lasted.

The religious aspect has returned, however, as "social conservatism." Here, again, we see religious people seeking to *enforce* proper living, rather than *convincing* individuals to live righteously. Regardless of political party, the motive force is the same.

The formula of "righteousness plus force" endures through all of these examples. For every end to be reached, the prescribed course of action was for a government to enforce it.

And Law Changed

Back in Chapter 6, we explained how John of Salisbury and others developed an ideology that put the ruler in subjection to the law. We quoted a key line from John's work: *It is established ... that the prince is subject to the law and to justice.*

The key point had been that the ruler was beneath the law. But as legislative bodies arose, such as a Parliament or Congress, legislation overtook law (as we noted earlier). The edicts of these groups slowly displaced the findings of judges as law; not because they were morally or practically superior, but because they were more directly backed by force, and because legislatures were often seen as more legitimize than judges.

Again, as we said previously, the seat and legitimization of sovereignty in Western society had been "the law." A king was a worthy ruler if he upheld the law, and unworthy if he did not. The law was above the ruler.

When law became legislation, however, this "rule of law" formula was ruined. Now, groups of rulers were not *subject* to the law – they *created* the

---

[126] The Scopes Monkey Trial seems to have cemented the removal of religion from the Progressive cause.

[127] Several strains of Progressivism after 1920 were financed, directly or indirectly, by the Soviet Union.

law. Worse, they could change the law however they saw fit. They were no longer beneath the law, they were above it. This was a re-conquest. From roughly 1200-1800, rulers in the west were subservient to the law. From roughly 1800 onward, groups of rulers made the law and were superior to it. "The law" became something wholly different than what it had been, and sovereignty was transferred.

During the 19th century, this change caused fairly little trouble, for two primary reasons: The first was that the common law remained and continued to be held in high esteem in both the United States and in Britain. Even though new and different laws could be passed, the common law remained as a reference. Secondly, legislation was a slow and difficult process. Lawmakers arrived at the state house on horseback and had to return home for long periods. Legislatures would meet for a few weeks at a time, and only a few times per year.

Since the beginning of the 20th century, however, legislators have spent extended periods in their various capitals and have begun measuring their effectiveness by the numbers of laws they passed. So, by the middle of the 20th century, the process was mostly complete and rulers were no longer subject to the law.

Six hundred years of kings in subjection to the law were over. The rulers had taken back their power and retained their legitimacy. So long as people believed in the democratic process, lawmakers were sovereign without challenge.

Size & Specialization Ruin Understanding

Industrial production, as it spread across the West in the 19th and 20th Centuries, required workers to be organized into huge factory operations and into specialized work. This was immensely productive, but it took a terrible toll on people's understanding of the world.

When working for a factory, the young man or woman never saw much of the entire operation, only their little part of it. Unless they were unusually well-informed, they saw only a system, which they didn't understand. The system was not creative so far as they could see; instead, it was a huge organization that demanded blind obedience and issued a paycheck in return. In most cases an individual never met or even saw the ultimate boss – he was probably several states away, seated in a tall office building.

All of this created immense distance between the goals of the worker and the goals of the business in general. The worker seldom understood why production mattered, aside from making distant people rich and for hanging on to his job. This made the worker ignorant.

Workers lost sight of economics. A shoemaker (*cobbler* in old terminology) understood the economic value of his profession: he purchased leather and other supplies from traders, he worked with customers to deliver the best value he could. He understood making compromises on products because the customer could afford no better and that something was better than nothing. The factory worker understood none of this, unless he or she went out of their way to understand it.

But as bad as economic ignorance was the fact that workers became ignorant of the world in general. They obtained a job through the help of a friend or relative, learned only that specialty, showed up to work every day, purchased a house, sent their children to the local school, imbibed mindless entertainment, and precious little else. They didn't know how the world worked, how humanity had arrived at its present state, or what the principles of civilization might be.

If they had some understanding of the whole, rather that one isolated piece, they would have been able to see the gaps in their knowledge and could have filled them. But size ruined their view; they became knowledgeable a small sliver of the whole and ignorant of the rest. This, of course, made them easy to manipulate: They had no way to tell if the manipulator was describing the world correctly or not.

Perhaps the worst part of this was the death of moral understanding. As we explained in Chapter 9, the human inability to hold more than about 150 identities required that de-personalized controls were involved. Rules were defined and enforced with no explanation attached. "The office says we have to do it this way," was an ever-so-common phrase in industrial production. People were told *what* to do, but they were not told *why* to do it. Having to explain was thought to reduce one's power, not to mention being a waste of time. Inside the factory, the higher levels dictated and the lower levels obeyed – understanding and reasons were discouraged, if not forbidden. The end result of this was that understanding wasn't sought. Things were "good" or "bad" because someone in a high position said so. Reasons were non-essential.

This was a massive change. As mentioned previously, commentaries on the common law were popular reading prior to the industrial revolution. People judged themselves competent to decide and to understand what was right or wrong, and to debate the reasons. After a generation or two of factory-style living, this pattern was broken. The phrase, "You're not qualified to think" may have been used in humor, but it was used often.

The effect of state schooling on this change can hardly be overestimated. Schools were specifically designed to eliminate questioning and to instill blind obedience to authority. This was death to critical reasoning. To illustrate, here is a comment from William Torrey Harris, US Commissioner of Education in 1906:

> Ninety-nine [students] out of a hundred are automata, careful
> to walk in prescribed paths, careful to follow the prescribed
> custom. This is not an accident but the result of substantial
> education, which, scientifically defined, is the subsumption
> of the individual.

The crucial aspect of compulsory education is that it forces children, at their most vulnerable stages, to endure psychological conditioning for the majority of their conscious time. This system dominates their minds and their development. It is a process designed to produce automatons, as was honestly expressed by the Commissioner of Education in 1906[128].

In brief, children in schools are taught to obey rather than to question, to repeat rather than to think[129]. Unless of exceptionally strong character, they fail to develop skills for judging; they seek the opinion of authority rather than reasoning.

Logic Fails

An important area of decline has been in critical thinking. This has been broadly noted and a few organizations have tried to address it, but the ability of the average person to reason carefully is considerably worse now than it was in 1900. A review of schoolbooks and newspapers from the mid-19th century usually illustrates the point quite well. The study of logic (non-contradiction) is completely absent from almost all state educational courses and shows up in college only as an elective. Self-contradictions are never noticed by most people.

When logic is gone, people tend to form opinions based upon emotion and identification with famous persons and groups. This is extremely dangerous. The worst actions of history have been performed by groups of people who chose not to think. This affects the West in myriad ways, making complex interaction between human minds more difficult, more problematic, and more frustrating.

A special danger is that a lack of logic removes restrictions upon political leaders, especially charismatic ones. As mentioned above, logic's absence leaves emotion to operate unsupervised. This is how dictators come into

---

[128] At some point in the future, people will look back at this with horror. Right now the majority avoids such thoughts, since almost all are guilty of feeding their children into the system or at least of praising it. But at some point this conspiracy of denial will break.

[129] Certainly there are a number of dedicated teachers within the state schooling system. Unfortunately, the system works against them, as they will generally admit. These teachers most certainly do some good, but not only are there many others who do not produce as well, but the system wears all of them down over time. Over and beyond this, the ambient curriculum is far more continuous than the occasional excellent teacher. This curriculum remains constant from kindergarten through high school (and beyond), punishing independent thought and rewarding obedience.

power and this is how a populace does things for which their grandchildren remain embarrassed a century later.

Surplus Production

In all successful civilizations, the production and use of surplus has been crucial. We have seen that as surplus remains in the hands of the people who created it, civilizations arise and grow in a more or less distributed fashion. We have also seen that when surplus is redirected to a central point, that civilization travels a downward path. This pattern held in Mesopotamia, Greece, Rome and in others.

In like manner, the crucial step in the decline of Western civilization was the forcible rerouting of surplus from the producers to centralized governments. Before World War I, surplus in the West generally remained in the hands of those who produced it. From a modern perspective, we would say it this way: *In the 19th century, it was normal for people to accumulate money.* After 1913 this changed very quickly and surplus was gathered and transferred to central governments all through the West. The primary instrument of this transfer, of course, was the income tax. There have been other direct taxes, but none comparable in scope.

Before the income tax, young men would go out to "get their fortune."[130] They would go to where money was being made, work hard, cooperate with similar young men, learn everything they could from the older men, save, invest, then return home as a prosperous adult[131]. This was certainly not a universal activity, but it was quite common, and very often expected of the young man by his own family and by young women.

In the modern world, everyone's fortune is taxed away as it is being formed, and very few of us are able to accumulate money. Prior to World War I, it was the opposite: surplus mostly remained in the hands of those who produced it.

The graph below shows how this affected people. It contrasts the amount of money a hard-working young man could save in 1890 with the savings of an identical young man in 2008. Notice the left-hand (vertical) scale: Years of living expenses retained. The horizontal scale shows merely the number of years[132].

---

[130] "Fortune" meant enough money in the bank to provide capital for the rest of your life.

[131] This healthy mating strategy was destroyed by the rerouting of surplus from the producer to the capital city. As the strategy failed in the 1920s and 30s, people busied themselves finding ways to criticize it, since they could no longer live up to it and didn't wish to be compared to people who had.

[132] The numbers were generated as follows: $725. per year is the income in 1890, based upon discussions with men who lived through the time. The 1890 figure of $325. for living expenses is taken from a New York Times article, dated 29 September, 1907. Assets were presumed to appreciate at 10% per year. For 2008 the annual income is $45,000 and monthly

174

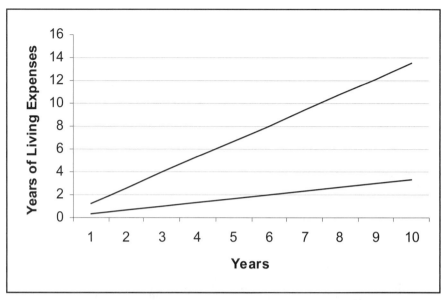

The top line is the young man of 1890, the bottom line is the young man of 2008.

But at the end of five years, the young man of 1890 has about seven years of living expenses saved, while his great-grandson of 2008 has less than two. After eight years, great-grandpa has eleven years of living expenses in the bank and his descendant has less than three years worth. This illustrates an important point regarding surplus: The income tax moved almost all surplus to central governments, and left precious little in the hands of producers. In fact, the withholding tax removed the surplus of every working man before he ever held it in his hands.

Consider the effects: The young man of 1890 had money in the bank. That taught him, first of all, that hard work paid off, also that he was capable of it. Secondly, he had security. Thirdly, he had money to invest in projects that he thought would be successful or that he thought were important. Contrast that with the factory worker who lives paycheck-to-paycheck and doesn't know how to do anything except one highly-specialized job that was of value to only a single employer. These are radically different positions in which to live. The first is healthy, the second is much less so.

The man of 1890 had a solid base, from which to act in the Western tradition and "take things upon himself." The factory worker of the industrial era had a fragile and broken base; one misstep and he was vulnerable. As a result, he took orders and not risks.

expenses were $2,000. This young man pays 30% income taxes and investment return is calculated at a reduced rate of 8.5% because of taxes upon interest. The young man of 1890 is investing $400./year against living expenses of $325. His 2008 descendent is investing $7500./year against living expenses of $24,000.

One notable area where this is shown: in the era when men kept their surplus, great museums were founded and financed by highly successful individuals. Museums of modern times are generally financed by giant corporate (most often financial) and government institutions.

This forcible removal of surplus was a crucial step, and one that is difficult to overstate: *It destroyed the expansion mechanism of Western civilization.*

By the mid-20th century, Western civilization no longer functioned in its traditional form. Many aspects of the culture continued, but its core economic principle had been replaced with an opposing principle.

It may seem overly dramatic to say that the income destroyed Western civilization, but the statement isn't far from the truth. Through the 19th century, surplus capital was gathered from productive enterprises and remained in the hands of those who had produced it. These people generally knew how to use it effectively. And, in fact, the great expansions of the 19th century attest to the fact[133]. Once income was taxed, however, surplus was removed to capital cities and spent wildly by politicians, and only after it was filtered through a rapidly growing bureaucracy.

From the time permanent income taxes were instituted (1914 in the US), a new surplus mechanism operated. The expansion mechanism of Western civilization had been supplanted. Without returning to it or replacing it with something better, Western civilization *will* end.

The Magic Money Mechanism

Prior to the First World War, money in the West was gold, silver or other metals that were inherently valuable. The various paper currencies which circulated were generally receipts for these metals. The few unbacked currencies that were tried became famous for their failures. After 1914, however, the West changed over to national currencies controlled by central banks.

The mechanics of the changeover, the reasons for it, and complexities of how money is created under the new system are the subject of other texts and are not central to this discussion, so we will pass over them, interesting and important though it may be. What is critical here are two facts:

1. Currency was partly (later fully) disconnected from actual value. The prestige of the state replaced the value of gold and silver.

---

[133] There are volumes to be added here regarding the common slanders against the 19th century and its economics, but I must leave most of them aside. One notable falsity should be mentioned and rebutted, however: It is often said that state financing is required for the largest ventures and that Laissez-Faire fails in this regard. The construction of the Great Northern Railway by James J. Hill displays the falsity of this claim, in that it was a trans-continental railway constructed with private funding.

2. Currency was not only controlled but created at will, by politically powerful bankers.

From 1914 onward, currency could be manipulated, and it was. Schools of economics[134] arose to examine how currency could be used in the new system where it was simply created by a central bank. This had limits because it was tied to gold, but in 1971 that tie was broken for the US dollar, and most currencies of the world became nothing but fiat currencies: they have value only because people think that they have value and because it is legally required to use them[135].

From 1971 onward, currency was available to legislatures upon demand. There was the problem of inflation to face on occasion[136], and the problem of massive national debts (still not faced as of this writing), but the ability to create currency became the great supercharger of the late 20th century and the early 21st, enabling politicians to spend money on a scale previously unimagined.

Capitalism Without Capital

> *This is a staggering thought. We are completely dependent upon the commercial banks. Someone has to borrow every dollar we have in circulation, cash or credit. If the banks create ample synthetic money, we are prosperous. If not, we starve. We are, absolutely, without a permanent money system. When one gets a complete grasp of the picture, the tragic absurdity of our hopeless position is almost incredible, but there it is.*
> – Robert H. Hemphill, Credit Manager, the Federal Reserve Bank of Atlanta.

This is a strange idea for those who have not studied it, but the quote above is true, and all modern money is debt. Properly, your dollar bills are debt (or credit) tokens. This has made no obvious difference in the lives of Westerners of the 20th and early 21st centuries (trading these debt tokens to the baker will still get you bread), but it matters in many subtle ways and will matter in overt ways at some point in the future.

Once surplus was removed from individuals, all investment capital was forced through institutions. Money was not saved and invested, it was obtained through banks. In this way, finance was centralized, and removed from the hands of individuals.

---

[134] Most notably that of John Maynard Keynes.

[135] By Legal Tender laws.

[136] Aside from the problems of rising prices following large increases of currency, inflation is a stealth tax, removing roughly 90% of the value of savings over a life-span.

Your local bank may not be a direct organ of your government, but it is chartered by a central government, overseen by a government and managed by government employees. They are not only subject to every new law, but their right to operate can be revoked at any time. Central governments, by the late 20th century, regulated very nearly all investment capital.

The effects of this were many, but large among them is the fact that it gave the state a monopoly on one of the primary tools of production, having removed it from the laboring man.

In the 19th century it was very common for a farmer or a mechanic to amass capital and to make loans to people he knew and trusted. Since these people lived in close proximity to each other, they knew who could use the capital well and who could not. This set of interactions was never perfect, but it was healthy in important ways, including economic efficiency and personal virtue. The removal of surplus capital into central institutions beggared the farmer and the mechanic. In the 20th century, their children would shuffle into banks and beg for loans. It was the centralization of surplus that did this to the working man.

Loss of Confidence

One of the more widespread characteristics of Western life at this moment is that most people in the West have no confidence in their culture. Schools and the mass media promote discussion of Western Civilization's flaws and are especially eager to imply crimes to it. Primitive civilizations are portrayed as better, more authentic, and far more noble.

The causes of this are important and so we'll itemize a few:

- The reactionary hatred of the modern and preference for the primitive caused by the Industrial Revolution. A primary transmission path for such ideas has been Rousseau's "myth of the noble savage," also championed and passed down by Margaret Meade and like-minded social scientists.

- The championing of equality as the primary virtue. If equality is *the* virtue, and if the West is richer than the rest of the world, then the West must have done something bad. If righteousness produces equality, the West is evil.

- Fear of envy. This is an ancient problem, running through hundreds of generations. These impulses still exist and still have effects, although dressed in modern clothing, so to speak.

But, for whichever reasons, the West lost its courage at approximately World War I. Sensitive commentators at the time (such as Virginia Wolfe) made note of it.

One interesting effect of lost courage regards the names of places. During the 19th century, places were commonly named after great men. Since the mid-20th century, they've been named after trees, birds, or geographic features. The West is embarrassed of its great men.

The New Temple of Righteousness

> *Increasingly, politics is not about "who gets what, when, how" but about values, each of them considered to be absolute. Politics is about "the right to life"...It is about the environment. It is about gaining equality for groups alleged to be oppressed...None of these issues is economic. All are fundamentally moral.*
> – Peter Drucker

We began this chapter by discussing the joining of righteousness and force. The end result of this has been the evolution of politics as the great forge of morality. As Peter Drucker says above, people see politics as the process that decides what is or is not moral. Political processes have become the temples of righteousness.

Numerous factors had led into this:

- The most active people have taken their moral fights exclusively into the realm of state force.

- Religion, the traditional place of moral teaching and debate, has generally receded in popularity.

- The central government became the lawgiver.

- The central government became the seat of financial power.

- Central power has been legitimized by democracy. Under Monarchy, there was less of a cloak for state actions; a king or prince bore responsibility for decisions that did not turn out well. Under democracy, decisions are made by hundreds of elected representatives; everyone is to blame and no one is to blame. Bad decisions are blamed on opposing parties, with no blame falling upon the state itself.

In short, the state has become the organization that decides upon morality and punishes or rewards it accordingly. It is no stretch to say that the state has taken over many of the attributes of a deity to its citizens. In Rome, the ruler became a god; in the 20th century the state attained the attributes of deity, but not the name. The differences are less in substance and more in form.

We may not say "Hail Caesar," but both our power and our virtue have been handed to a centralized state as much as that of the Romans. And in the end, our attempts at centralization will work no better than theirs did.

Summary

Several main points have been made in this chapter regarding the decline and inevitable dissolution of Western Civilization if it continues on this course:

- Surplus production, by the middle of the 20th century, was sent directly to the national capital, for redistribution. This removed it from the hands of the producers and mostly away from local governments. The working man had his strength and honor taken from him.

- A mechanism for creating currency at near-zero cost was established, replacing the actual value of metals with the honor of the state. Money is created with debt. This currency is manipulated by politicians and central bankers.

- Finance became centralized and run through a very few financial centers which were almost completely under the oversight of central governments.

- So long as standards of living rose, centralized control was accepted by most people, who had lost their ability to judge.

- Never in the history of the world has so much surplus been wasted in a more complete manner. The governments of the West have spent all the surplus they removed from their people and are massively in debt besides.

- Law, the seat of legitimacy, has been conquered by central governments. Law was previously independent of rulers and above them. Now, they create it.

- Under democracy, blame for failed policies was divided and muted, since there were always opposing parties to blame and because the policy makers were elected by the people. Esteem for the state reached what were probably the highest levels in history.

- Much of the populace has lost its initiative, which was the original kernel of Western Civilization. People have been scientifically conditioned to obey rather than to question, to repeat rather than think. Furthermore, the time that they might spend on learning is mostly spent upon empty entertainments. The old way of individual courage, virtue and initiative is routinely ridiculed, if not punished.

- The most active people in the West have adopted a strategy of enforcing their righteousness upon others. Morality was merged with state.

- The state greatly increased its share of involvement in daily life. Government regulations concern nearly every product bought or sold and nearly every area of daily life. It became difficult to exclude government from any area of one's life.

- The inescapable modernism of the Industrial Revolution led to many reactionary movements, some of which remain.

- The West has given up the philosophy of their founding. Christianity has been largely abandoned and the Christian philosophy that informed Western Civilization has not been replaced with equally useful concepts.

This situation cannot last. It will not last. Either the West changes or the West eventually fails. We will examine patterns of failure momentarily, but regardless of the specific dates and details, the West will either recover itself or it will be lost.

The Founders Are Now Criminals

> *It used to be the boast of free men that, so long as they kept within the bounds of the known law, there was no need to ask anybody's permission or to obey anybody's orders. It is doubtful whether any of us can make this claim today.*
> – Friedrich Hayek

Hayek, one of the leading thinkers of the 20th century, wrote this decades ago, and was entirely correct even then. "Taking it upon yourself" is now illegal. Consider:

- Peter Abelard would last on a modern university campus for as long as it took security to show up and remove him. Teaching students with no up-to-date certification? No tenure? They would, quite literally, eject him from the campus. If he persisted, criminal charges would be filed.

- The virtuous judges of the Vehm would be given enormous prison sentences. All forms of surveillance would be used against them and the public would be poisoned against them. There would be a tremendous outcry for them to be hunted, arrested and imprisoned.

- The Hansa would be indicted for smuggling, running criminal enterprises, tax evasion and money laundering. Plea bargains would be arranged to obtain incriminating facts. Every bit of their property would be confiscated. The states that imprisoned them would use the

Hansa's boats to patrol the coasts for any "immoral smugglers" that remained.

- The judges of the Law Merchant courts would be arrested for practicing law without a license, operating courts outside of the national legal systems and for breaking regulations. It is doubtful that they could last a month operating openly.

- Thomas Jefferson and John Hancock would have been arrested on July 5th.

It is clear that the values of the founders are no longer permissible in the West. The Romans, in an analogous time, complained that their people had lost their hardness, their courage and their virtues.

The decline of the West is in full force and will remain so until founders are no longer criminals. Such men are present in every age. In some times, they are grudgingly left alone to operate. In other times, such as ours, they are intimidated, chased away, or locked up.

11

A Chance For Renewal

*Freedom arises from within the individual: either you
are determined to be free, in which case you have
grasped the essential tool of your liberty, or not.
Nobody else can free you; you must free yourself, if
you mean to be free.*
– Jim Davidson

The people of the West have a chance to prevent the fall of their civilization, but it will require individual action. This was the original core of the West and it must be returned to if the West is to change course. Complaining about politicians and bureaucrats will not be sufficient. Either the people of the West get up and build something better or their civilization will fail.

This statement that the West will fail is not hyperbole; it is a simple conclusion to a simple pattern. When a civilization's method of expansion is changed, when centralization and complexity are imposed upon a populace, when the virtues and courage that started their civilization fade away, that civilization fails. The process is not fast, but it is consistent. It has happened many times before and it will happen this time as well, if the people of the West let it. That process is underway; it can be stopped, but stopping it will require effort, adaption, courage and risk. It will not happen by itself.

This cannot occur top-down, for the simple reason that the West was not formed that way[137]. There is no leader who will save the people of the West from their decline. That is an illusion, and often a cowardly one. Appeals to

---

[137] It is also true that rulers are empowered by the system as it is. They can be counted upon to favor more centralization and oppose renewal.

central power will not diminish central power. Either millions of individuals take it upon themselves to act or the decline will continue.

At one time people in the West believed strongly in their ideals, and in acting alone. They gained these lessons from the examples of Abraham, Moses, Jesus and other traditional heroes. The crucial question by which history will judge the current members of Western civilization may be this: *How many people remain capable of independent action?*

All that said, there has been progress made toward renewal, to which we now turn our attention.

Decentralizing Technologies

> *A new civilization is emerging in our lives, and*
> *blind men everywhere are trying to suppress it.*
> – Alvin Toffler, *The Third Wave*

The transistor and the integrated circuit have changed the world and continue to change the world, primarily by enabling information technologies. Because information can now be assembled and distributed in massive amounts and unlimited ways, centralization has ceased to be necessary. This does not mean that decentralization has gained in all areas of life – it is often forbidden by law – but where decentralization has not been forbidden, it has gained.

Primarily, decentralization has occurred in commercial settings, where economies of scale are slipping and where standardization and specialization are no longer essential. More information means that less people and things need to be present at the same places and times.

The greatest decentralizing technology, rather obviously, was the internet, which allowed hundreds of millions of people to communicate person-to-person, with no gatekeeper or central switch. The internet was decentralized by design and grew spontaneously. It was not planned by central governments; it was built by scattered enthusiasts who turned a decommissioned system into a world-wide communication tool without precedent.

In many ways, the internet became *the* technology of free thought, free communication, and progress. It reduced the lifespan of bad information, it disarmed mindless hatreds, it allowed world-wide friendships, and much more. And while the internet has been captured by governments and mega-corporations, new applications of the technology are within easy reach. *Elite capture* can be evaded, if and when individuals muster the courage to be more than passive.

One New Avenue of Escape After Another

We don't tell people what to think – we tell them what to think about.
– Michael Gartner, President of NBC News

Through the 1970s, a large majority of news stories in the United States found their origin within only two zip codes of New York City. The owners and operators of ABC, NBC, CBS, the New York Times and others shared the same small physical space and the same small worldview, with almost no variation. The American people asked few questions– they respected largeness and centralization.

In the early 1980s, however, cable television began to provide alternative sources. The draw of having twenty or thirty stations rather than only three or four was obvious and cable TV became financially successful. Soon there were hundreds of stations and the original national networks were facing difficulties; people had choices.

By the end of the 1980s, talk radio was springing up. Political discussion on these shows was far more in-depth than anything on the networks, who they usually opposed quite directly. Talk radio was more interesting as well.

While it was prone to flying off in odd directions from time to time, talk radio involved millions of people in thinking about current events and even about philosophies. Many of these people believed in self-responsibility, putting them more with those who built Western Civilization than those who are dismembering it.

Cable television, with its multiplied sources of information, has been adopted nearly worldwide. Talk radio, however, remains primarily an American phenomenon. Then came the internet, adding innumerable voices to the mix. The quality and distribution of new voices has been erratic, but the simple fact of their existence matters a great deal. By itself this isn't nearly enough to stem the downward move of Western Civilization (these are groups of people being talked to, not people acting), but it certainly helps.

Another American phenomenon that is spreading to other places is homeschooling. By teaching their children at home, parents not only remove their children from enforced conditioning, but they educate them better than state schools do[138]. According to published research, 1.7 million American children were homeschooled in 2012, although it is certain the actual number is substantially higher[139]. Even so, 1.7 million signifies that approximately

---

[138] Numerous studies have been undertaken, nearly all of which show home educated children out-performing children educated in state schools by a significant margin.

[139] A significant number of home school families avoid all reporting to governments. The Home School Legal Defense Association placed the number at 2.1 million in 2008 and it is doubtless higher now.

3% of American children are homeschooled. Figures on children homeschooled world-wide are hard to obtain, but it appears that the number of children homeschooled in other countries equals the number of those in the U.S.

In addition to homeschooling, state schools are being generally abandoned by those who are able to do so[140]. The educational establishment is in limited danger of cracking (its funding being extracted by force), but those people who are able very often avoid it. Almost no one believes that state schools are the best choice for their children.

With each family that chooses homeschooling, each parent that carefully involves himself or herself in their child's education, each parent who chooses to instill his or her personal ethics into their child rather than leaving it to the schools, uniform conditioning fades. With each drop in network TV ratings, with each percentage increase of people who get their news from internet sites[141], centralization and conformity decline. These are hopeful developments.

The Flynn Effect

The Flynn effect is the rise of average IQ scores over generations. This effect has observed in most parts of the world over the past few generations, although it does vary. James Flynn, a professor of Political Studies at the University of Otago in New Zealand, was the first to recognize and write about it.

IQ tests are re-normalized periodically, so that the average score always remains 100[142]. Revisions to these tests have surprisingly shown an average rate of rise of around three IQ points per decade. Numerous reasons and explanations have been proposed for this, especially among academics who seem troubled by it. One early explanation was that IQs were rising because "schools are so much better now." This has turned out to be false, since scores related to school content (vocabulary, arithmetic, general information) show small gains and frequent declines. The largest Flynn effects appear in general mental processing abilities.

It is likely that the Flynn effect can be attributed to improved nutrition allowing brains to develop better than in the past. But this too is uncertain and arguments are also made for adaptations to the modern world's more mentally demanding environment.

---

[140] "Those able to do so" are those who are able to pay double for their children's education. The state taxes them to pay for the government's educational system, whether they use it or not. Paying for a private school is to pay a second time: the first time involuntarily, the second willingly.

[141] Facebook cannot by considered one of these sites. Rather, it should be considered a new type of network.

[142] This process has been polluted in recent years by adjusting the results to school grades.

The importance of the Flynn effect is that faster thinking allows people to see through false arguments and manipulations more easily. This matters, for example, when a speaker moves quickly through unsupported statements, denying the listener enough time to consider anything deeper than the surface argument, a common method of manipulation.In most areas of life, the slower thinker can accomplish the same results as the faster thinker, albeit over a few extra seconds. When time limits are imposed, however, as in this example, speed matters. The fast thinker may be able to see through unsupported statements, while the slower thinker may not. The inability to analyze at speed, combined with intimidation, leads people to accept lies as truth. The general line of thinking is this: *The statements made some sense on the surface and other people nodded their heads in agreement, therefore I should accept them.*

To some unknown but probably significant extent, the Flynn effect makes manipulation harder. This can be overcome by restricting information and imposing extra intimidation, but it remains a positive development.

Legitimacy Is Cracking

Belief in rulers as ordained by God has vanished and rulership being respected for other reasons is cracking as well.[143] The "compliance inertia" of Westerners is slowly breaking.

For example, through the middle 1960s, people spoke of politicians with respect and even reverence. Now, throughout the world, people calling politicians liars and thieves are met with approval. This is a major change, and one that is having, and will have, profound effects.

Most people are still holding on to the idea that the state is somehow legitimate, even when the people who comprise it are crooks, but this is mostly due to compliance inertia, and it's fading as well.

New Philosophies

> *There are only two means by which men can deal with one another: Guns or logic. Force or persuasion.*
> – Ayn Rand

By the mid 20th century, a number of new philosophies began to develop. Because of the diversities among them, they are hard to categorize, except to call them pro-liberty. The earliest of these were people who wished to hold on to classical liberalism, the predominant philosophy of the 19th century, focused around laissez-faire capitalism and human liberty, and taken from the ideas of men such as John Stewart Mill, Adam Smith and John Locke. It was similar to modern libertarianism.

---

[143] See FMP #40.

A major point in the development of counter-philosophies to the centralization and uniformity of the 20th century was in 1943, when three women combined to give the modern liberty movement a set of foundations. In that year, Rose Wilder Lane published *The Discovery Of Freedom*, Isabel Patterson published *The God Of The Machine*, and Ayn Rand published *The Fountainhead*. All three are still in print more than seventy years later; one or all of which have influenced nearly every pro-liberty thinker since.

Following 1943, works promoting liberty and opposing what is now called *statism* continued. Economists like Frederich Hayek, Ludwig von Mises[144], Murray Rothbard and Milton Friedman produced a huge body of work, and many others contributed greatly in fields ranging from law to psychology. Many of the era's best science fiction works portrayed the future as embodying a pro-liberty philosophy of one sort or another.

At various times, movements have come out of this general freedom philosophy, often to fracture and fade. But the philosophy remains, and it routinely attracts many of the best human minds. What will develop from this is uncertain, but there is now a great body of information on the subject for anyone who seeks it.

New Nations, Cypherpunks & Cryptoanarchy

A surprising number of people, reading the literature mentioned above, have sought new territory in which to live their own way, leaving the state behind. If these people were living in the 17th century, they would have boarded boats to the New World. Stuck in the 20th and 21st centuries, however, with no open territory available, they dreamt of carving out new civilizations in creative ways. In fact, some of the more entertaining stories from the 20th century involved people who tried to buy, rent or steal territories from existing states and to start new nations. None have ultimately succeeded, but they tried quite hard.[145]

The failure of a long line of new nation projects did not, however, stop pro-liberty people from wanting a place to run away to. And at the end of the 20th century they found an opportunity, as the internet opened a new type of territory to them. Very quickly, groups known as *Cypherpunks* began building enclaves on the internet that were protected by encryption, much as city walls might have protected them several hundred years prior. In the course of time, the set of ideas that began with the Cypherpunks became a broader set of ideas called *Cryptoanarchy*.

---

[144] Mises was writing long before 1943, but his work was little known outside Austria at the time.

[145] This is a grand indictment of the world's states: people who are desperate to separate themselves and try a new thing are forbidden from doing so.

Cryptoanarchy is a way of separating one's life from outside interference, for at least as much of their lives as can be conducted over communication systems. Cryptoanarchists want to interact with no person, state or group watching or interfering. This can be accomplished reasonably well with cryptography and anonymity technologies. Both individuals and companies have been using these technologies for years, whether or not the name, Cryptoanarchy, is attached.

One important and unusual thing about Cryptoanarchy is that – unlike many other new ideas – it does not seek to change the state or become involved with politics; it rather attempts to leave them behind. These ideas and technologies are not reform movements, they are secession movements. They seek to build over and around the existing systems of the world; not to take them over and order them aright. This is a fundamental difference, and one that puts them squarely in line with the founders of Western Civilization.

The philosophy to come from this line of development is called *Voluntaryism*, which is the general theory that *all* coercion[146] is immoral, and that all men should be left alone unless they engage in force, fraud or similar forms of aggression. There are many variations of this philosophy, but all hold to a core moral concept: that of peaceful, voluntary conduct.

Voluntaryism makes no demands upon the future; is specifies no final condition for humanity; it merely focuses on what are moral or immoral actions. That said, most voluntaryists are working toward a decentralized human society.

Voluntaryism and similar philosophies[147] are clearly throwbacks to the beginning of Western Civilization, when people took responsibility upon themselves and built things they needed. People who want to start new nations and who want to build crypto-tools are taking responsibility upon themselves to create a better world. By doing this, they align themselves with people like Thomas Jefferson, John Adams and James Madison, the overly-studious men who laid the moral foundations of the American experiment.

The Fight for Honest Money

> *The study of money, above all other fields in economics, is one in which complexity is used to disguise truth or to evade truth, not to reveal it.*
> – John Kenneth Galbraith

Those few people who have studied money, currency and central banking are generally horrified by what they find... if, indeed, they are lucky enough or tenacious enough to uncover the facts. Once, however, they come to grips with what they have found, they tend to oppose central banking vehemently.

---

[146] Including that of the state.

[147] Such as anarcocapitalism, agorism (technically a tactic) and "anarchy without adjectives."

Many of these people have taken it upon themselves to either return to honest money, or to create honest money themselves. This, again, puts them back with founders of Western Civilization, and not with the operators of states and their fiat currencies.

Ever since unbacked currencies have existed, a few people have been complaining about them and demanding a return to gold or silver as money. These movements rise and fall from time to time, but always seem to continue. They showed surprising reach during the 2008 and 2012 Presidential candidacies of Ron Paul, when thousands of young people turned out to hear Dr. Paul lecture on the Federal Reserve and sound money.

Another group of honest money people are those who have been creating digital currencies. Provided that they are operated honestly, digital currencies have many the benefits of the old gold standard and few of the drawbacks. It is simply better money.

Predictably, digital currencies came currently under attack by the United States and other governments, but the idea refused to die and new operators moved to foreign jurisdictions rather than quitting or fighting the US government. This again is strongly in the Western tradition.

And Then Came Bitcoin

Bitcoin, an electronic currency designed to be decentralized, was released onto the internet in January of 2009. It became something of a phenomenon when its exchange rate rose from less than a dollar each to over one thousand dollars each in 2013.

As a result of the price spike (at this writing, Bitcoin exchanges for several thousand dollars each), it gained the attention of the financial industry. Nonetheless, it is crucial to understand that Bitcoin is not a typical financial instrument. Rather, Bitcoin is the creation of cypherpunks: confirmed outsiders seeking escape from the current ruling systems.[148]

As of 2017, Bitcoin faces technical challenges and adverse interest from central banks and governments. In this regard, it should be understood that if Bitcoin or others like it are successful enough, they will displace the currencies of central banks. Those banks are certain to fight.

Still, wherever history is recorded, it will be known that cryptocurrencies work very well, even in hostile conditions. The genie, as we say, is out of the bottle.

Furthermore, there are currently tens of thousands of scattered individuals working on Bitcoin and Bitcoin-related projects. There are decentralized marketplaces like Open Bazaar, automated contract currencies like Ethereum, non-state arbitration and mediation services, and many, many more. The

---

[148] See the FMP Bitcoin Report.

people working in these areas are building a decentralized future on a daily basis.

The Blueprint for Renewal

So, with all of these streams (and others) leading toward renewal, will renewal occur? And if so, how? While we will cover this in some depth in the next chapter, there's an important point to make first: *There is no blueprint for renewal.* And there will not be one.

A central plan is precisely what will *not* work. Renewal will occur – if it occurs – because millions of individuals decide that they are going to take actions that they don't have to, to do things that are not expected of them, to create unapproved but superior ways of living for themselves and their families. In whichever directions they *act* – not talk, not plan, not debate, but *act* – those will be the directions that renewal tends to take, and no others. And they will have to act on their own initiative, not following someone else's plans.

Again, this point hearkens back to Jesus, who says:

> *Whosoever heareth these sayings of mine, and doeth them, I will liken him unto a wise man, which built his house upon a rock: And the rain descended, and the floods came, and the winds blew, and beat upon that house; and it fell not: for it was founded upon a rock.*
>
> *And every one that heareth these sayings of mine, and doeth them not, shall be likened unto a foolish man, which built his house upon the sand: And the rain descended, and the floods came, and the winds blew, and beat upon that house; and it fell: and great was the fall of it.*

Talk is cheap; often less than worthless. Only individual action will save the West.

12

The Two Futures

Multitudes, multitudes in the valley of decision: for the day of the LORD is near in the valley of decision.
– Joel 3:14

Two futures stand in front of us. The world we stand in is halting between them, and this straddle may continue for some time. Ultimately, however, the West will go either one way or the other; information technology is making the divide sharper and the process faster than it would be otherwise. If people of the West choose to change their recent trajectory, the better of the two futures may still be obtained. If they do not wish to make a choice, one is made for them: continuing the decline.[149]

Timidity, stasis, and quiet acceptance of life as it is will bring the West into a steep decline and into a new dark age that will doom generations of their offspring to yet another long regrouping. In all likelihood, it will take our descendents centuries to drag themselves out of the pit their great-grandparents dug. It happened in Sumer, Greece and Rome and it can happen now. We are them; they were us.

Self-reliance, courage, innovation, initiative, and doing the right thing regardless of cost will secure another growth cycle for Western civilization. And if this growth is sufficient, mankind's continuing cycles of expansion and contraction, pained creation and mindless wasting, may in fact end.

So, the moment of truth is at hand, in this, the West's valley of decision. The choice – or the evasion of choice – sits directly in front of us.

---

[149] See FMP #18.

Seeing Beyond The Daily Explosions

Trying to determine what is going on in the world by reading newspapers is like trying to tell the time by watching the second hand of a clock.
– Ben Hecht

The overwhelming majority of information people receive about the world involves daily reports of the strange and the shocking. Most of these reports will be gone within hours, to be followed by the next cycle of the bloodiest events that can be presented on video. Developing a clear view of the world based upon these bits of information is impossible.[150]

Our interests here, however, are not daily outrages, or even wars, but the structures of rulership and changes within civilizations. Wars and borders come and go, but the necessities of rulership are more or less the same in all modern states.

For example: Passport treaties are signed by every nation, communist or capitalist alike, Christian and Muslim alike, and all for the same reason: Once travel was available to the masses, some method of containment was required, or else they could evade rulership. So, passports were mandated and every ruler agreed to force people entering their area of dominance to present travel documents, or else to forbid entry. It was a restriction created solely by the necessities of rulership.

Paper currencies are adopted by all, taxation and control systems are similar or identical, use of the media is the same, and elections are conducted in the same ways. They all endorse the same rules of war. They all run courts of law and prisons. Nearly all run some type of legislature. Groups of rulers fight for more and better territories, but the structures controlling life within those territories are strikingly similar.

So, subjects like "the balance of power" and "area of hegemony" are unimportant to this analysis. Who gets to enforce the law over any particular slice of geography is not our subject: We are interested in the structure of an overall civilization, not the minutia of border changes and which ruler's portrait hangs in government offices.

The Two Structures

Every chapter of this book has, in one way or another, highlighted a critical choice in the structure of civilizations: centralized or distributed.

It is neither a simplification nor an overstatement to say that *centralization is a framework suited to plunder*. Centralization, by its very nature, requires that goods must be taken away from the people that produce them and

---

[150] Broadcast fears, however, are wonderful tools for keeping humans frightened and manipulable.

transferred to a central point. This is *always* done by force or by a credible threat of force.

Likewise it is no stretch to say that *decentralization is a framework suited to production.* The most productive structures in the history of the world are free markets.[151] There is no legitimate argument to this statement; the only objections to it are tightly focused around the times and places when markets were not operated freely. A truly free market involves no involuntary transactions; whoever takes part does so willingly and cooperatively. All else are thieves; attackers of the market, not players within it.

Note that the plunder or cooperation mentioned above are not results of good or bad *intentions*, they are the result of the *structures*. This is a crucial point. When things go wrong, humans nearly always want to find a person to blame them on. In this case, that is simply wrong.

> The people operating a centralized structure may actually mean well, but their system will always produce plunder, that is the nature of a centralized system.

> The people operating a decentralized structure may be unkind, but their system will always produce cooperation, that is the nature of a decentralized system.

Certainly all systems are operated by real humans, and this means that things can and will go wrong under either type, but that only makes the processes sloppy, it does not change their natures.

It is a great and common human stupidity to find some fault with a new thing and to reject it based upon a single flaw – even when the old thing has many flaws. For example, when new systems of education are proposed, the operators of the old systems inevitably argue that something could go wrong with the new way. (Usually with a lot of emotion attached.) When doing this, they imply that this bad thing negates every virtue of the new system. Something could go wrong... it's dangerous... it must be rejected. But at the same time, horrible things are happening in their system, every day and in huge numbers.

The effort to find a flaw, to create ridicule and shame, and to reject the new thing... this is nothing but an effort to overpower reason with fear. It's a trick to paralyze human thought.

Decentralized structures, like centralized structures, will always contain a few bad people doing bad things; that's just the present nature of humanity. Real-life operations are not going to be pure. But rather than highlighting the weakness of decentralized systems, this actually highlights their greatest virtue: *Decentralized structures are inherently self-correcting[152]*.

---

[151] See FMP #29.

When something goes wrong within a decentralized structure, the first person that is injured may directly respond and communicate the problem to other members. The ability to react is present in every part of the structure. That means that the first response is immediate and tends to be proportional to the offense.

When something goes wrong within a centralized structure, the first person injured is forbidden from responding directly. The ability to react is present in only one specialized organ of the structure, and only after orders are received from the executive portions. That means that the first response is almost never immediate and tends to be overdone, since centralized structures rely upon overwhelming force.

Finally, centralization requires size. The surplus production of thousands or millions cannot be gathered to a center without a large number of specialized employees. And it cannot be justified without large groups of people upholding the honor of the centralized institutions. Because of this, the problems we saw with Dunbar's number related to factory work come into play. Rules are required to keep the system organized, and rules – by their very nature – forbid human judgment.

This is why governments (or other large systems) cannot treat people sensibly or compassionately, even when they try. The man or woman dealing with the individual citizen is forbidden from considering the citizen's personal circumstances by a long list of rules. And every time something goes wrong and embarrasses that institution, more rules are added to prevent it from happening again... which further restricts the possibility of human sympathy. It is a system that chokes itself to death over time.

The Reconquest

Western Civilization is currently declining and this process is clearly a reconquest of plunder over production.

When the Church entered the Middle Ages, after the failure of Rome's central authority, all it had was legitimacy. It did not have temporal power. In other words, it could not do what previous empires had done, simply overpowering what stood in front of them. The Church had to *convince* the scattered princes of Europe to cede power to them.

This is the same position the rulers of the West found themselves late in the 19th century. Up to that point, control had continually slipped away from them: Unapproved learning had taken root and they had to work to bring it back under control. Commerce and international trade found their footing, built their own systems, and even dealt with powerful states like England as equals. More importantly, law – at that time created and expanded in a distributed way – had been placed above the ruler. These were debilitating to

---

[152] The works of Frederich Hayek cover this.

the state. The rulers worked to get their power back, but new developments kept moving the goal further away: New continents opened up and allowed people to live and grow beyond their reach. New machines made unregulated production possible; people went ahead and prospered without seeking permission. Then came the steam engine which created overwhelmingly powerful commercial activities. The state was overmatched and couldn't catch up. *The state had lost control of production.*

But all was not lost to the rulers: they still had strengths, the primary of which were these:

> *The Great Trade.* As we have mentioned twice previously, humans are inherently conflicted beings, and seek to sublimate those conflicts into something larger than themselves. This became newly important at the end of the 19th century, since the legitimacy of the Church was failing badly. People sought something big to identify with – something that told them they were special for being joined to it. Markets, the structures of production, had no interest in providing this to people and lacked status for doing so. Only something large, impressive, and centralized would do. The state stood alone as a suitable actor for the role of "larger than man."

> *Military power.* Rulers couldn't make war directly against their subjects for fear of losing legitimacy, but military power became a great source of national pride. "Leader" personality types plus permanent armies is a recipe for war, which almost always focuses the minds of the people around foreign threats. And when people fear threats, they run to the state for protection. The saying is true: *War is the health of the state.*

> *Ceremonial legitimacy.* This is a part of the Great Trade. It can still be a highly emotional thing for people to receive awards from "important people" dressed in impressive garments. Think of college graduation ceremonies, where the proud parent sees his or her child receive a degree from an important official. The emotional impact is significant and long-lasting. Markets and rogue inventors don't provide this, but institutions major in it.

> *A central position in the attention and imaginations of men.* A ruler is different than the rest of us. That has always generated an immense amount of interest, particularly among people whose own lives are uneventful. The larger the ruler is in the minds of his subjects, the more power he has.

It was from this base that the state was able to resume its conquest. Soon enough, a few breaks went their way, primarily the following:

Legislatures. Legislative bodies gave people a feeling that they held a share of state power. Unbeknownst to them, and probably unplanned by the rulers, this changed the nature of law and put it back beneath the state. It further empowered central banking, and especially state debts: These were no longer tied to the royal who signed for them, but to every "citizen" in the nation, indebting them all.

Economies of scale. The state had no hope of controlling commerce when it consisted of thousands or millions of home-operated looms and family businesses, but small numbers of large industrial firms were controllable. Close down a two-man shop and the operators will move somewhere else and start over. General Motors, on the other hand, cannot. So, the state had power over large economic actors and in this way exerted great control over commerce in general.

Taking over money. As we have explained in some detail, money was historically silver and gold. This was certainly true in the 19th century. But in the early 20th century, people were willing to accept state ownership of money. The power of controlling a nation's currency is a far greater and more subtle than is commonly understood. As U.S. President James Garfield said, "Whoever controls the volume of money in any country is absolute master of all industry and commerce."

Truth comes from experts. This was another effect of the Industrial Revolution and its splintering of knowledge. People began to stray from the core of Western Civilization that *truth is revealed by a cooperative process* and so the shift was made to truth coming from experts. This made the individual feel unable to learn the truth through their own powers[153]; it had to be provided to them by experts. This transferred great power to the state, which put itself into the business of acknowledging experts.

Mass conditioning. Through state schooling, as we have mentioned. This has greatly affected the minds of the populace.

All of these avenues were paths of reconquest for the state, and by the middle of the 20th century, the state had been restored to tremendous power[154]. The greatest tool for conquest, however, is coming into the state's hands as the 21st century begins: Surveillance Technology.

---

[153] It is one thing to take input from specialists on complex subjects; it is quite another to simply adopt the conclusions of experts. In this second case, the individual's powers of analysis and judgment are bypassed.

[154] It is my opinion that the massive numbers of state-induced deaths at this time are directly related to massive state power. Rudolph Rummel showed that 262 million people died in one form of state action or another during the 20th century, far outpacing any previous disasters.

Worse Than You Think

> *I know why you did it; you were afraid. Who wouldn't
> be? War, terror and disease. There were a myriad of
> problems that conspired to corrupt your reason and
> rob you of your common sense. Fear got the best of
> you.*
> – V For Vendetta

Odd though it may seem, the first surveillance state was the empire of ancient Sumer. As we explained in Chapter 2, the basic organizational units of Sumer were small cities, each with a temple and government buildings, and there were so many of these units that they were nearly within sight of each other.[155] The rulers and a state-associated class of scribes spent tremendous amounts of time cataloging almost every sort of financial transaction. Sales of land, wheat, seed, gold, silver, oil, beer, and almost everything else were recorded and stored in record-houses. And the cities being small meant that everything was seen.

During all the intervening years, staying away from the state was possible to a greater or lesser extent. The rulers did try to see and record everything, especially if it involved collecting taxes. One of the last Roman Emperors, Valentinian III, instituted a $1/24^{th}$ sales tax in 444, requiring all sales to be conducted in the presence of a tax collector. These measures, however, were of limited effectiveness. Taxing land has always worked well, since it couldn't be moved and was easy to seize, but mobile wealth has continually remained a problem... until now.

The disaster of September 11th, 2001 was to Western states what The Donation of Constantine was to the Church: a path to power. The people of the West were terrified, and ran to the state to protect them. The state, of course, was eager to oblige. In effect, a new role for the state was found: *The Great Protector.* Massive new agencies were placed over and around existing agencies and new systems of control were instituted. Chief among these was surveillance: interception and storage of telephone calls, emails, money transfers, internet use, cell phone trails, traffic cameras, and much more.

Crucial to all of this, however, was some way of sorting through all of the data that is gathered. In 2001 technology to manipulate all that data was lagging, but not anymore. One of the advantages of computer technology is that its capacities increase rapidly and continuously.

There are observers who complain about the failure of character in the West, and they do have points to make, much as Romans who complained about the death of their virtues. What most of them fail to understand, however, is

---

[155] See FMP #24.

that a surveillance state makes the process much, much worse. If it continues, there may be no reverse of the decline.

Surveillance is a subject worthy of its own book[156], and we will not take much space on it here, but it is crucial, not only for its direct effects, but for its indirect effects: It returns men to serfdom. The state has everything you do in their files: All the emails you sent when you were depressed, every porn site you've surfed, every phone call you've made, every dollar you've ever spent. This is not overly-dramatized hyperbole. States can do this right now, and they have no reason to step back from it: The people are in fear and want to believe the state will protect them.

Even this, sadly, is not the end of the decline. A new method of data analysis called Big Data is making this much, much worse. Briefly, these systems are able to review oceans of data and learn from it what you will and will not respond to. With that information, the content you see on the internet is changed for the specific purpose of manipulating you. And please understand that this is *already* being done, and by the biggest internet corporations, not to mention intelligence agencies.[157]

At the end of this process, demoralized human beings are "lived" by the system, still thinking that they run their own lives. Things most certainly *can* get worse, and if this process continues, they will.

Sumer was not conquered because their opponents had any natural advantage, but because they had closed themselves in and rotted. The empires of 1200 B.C. fell because they failed to adapt military strategies; something that was clearly within their power to do. The armies of Church-aligned princes failed to defeat much smaller armies of Protestants, simply because they did not adapt.

In all of these cases, and in many others, it was a failure to adapt that made a civilization vulnerable. In simplistic terms, ruling systems hardened and the subjects became tuned to obedience. They sought status inside the system and didn't look beyond it.

Once again, the Christian creed of the foundational moment runs contrary to events during a decline: The man Jesus wants is one who takes things upon himself and produces[158]. The obedience model chokes this process. Always and forever it heralds the death of a civilization.

The Future

This brings us more or less up to date in our coverage of the state's reconquest of production. We will now look ahead. Bear in mind that no one

---

[156] See *The New Age of Intelligence*, by myself and Jonathan Logan.

[157] See FMP#59. You will also find this dramatized and detailed in *The Breaking Dawn*.

[158] The parable of Matthew 25:14-30 is especially clear on this point.

knows enough to say which trend will be more or less powerful than another or when and where each will have more effect. What follows are simple conclusions, based upon the concept that large things in motion will tend to remain in motion.

We don't know how these things might deviate from their present course, but we do know in which directions they are moving, and we do know something of their overall mass and speed.

The Fruits Of Complexity

In his book *The Collapse Of Complex Societies,* Joseph Tainter describes how the state's desire to be source and savior leads to the collapse of a society. He describes a process that runs like this:

1. You intervene to make society work for a goal that people don't want to provide for themselves. (Defense, for example.)

2. This produces side-effects that cause new problems.

3. Then you intervene to mitigate these side-effects from your first intervention.

4. Then you intervene to mitigate the side-effects of your second intervention.

5. Then you intervene to mitigate the side-effects of your third intervention, and so on...

Tainter describes how this process ruined the Romans, the Maya and others. In our time, it is playing out in these general directions:

1. Citizens have their rights voided in the name of being protected.

2. The government becomes unable to provide full protection.

3. Government spends more money on protection, restricting the abilities of individuals to produce.

4. Government debt (with its many complications) rises.

5. Economic progress stalls and distractions must be found. The state's guns turn inward toward the citizenry.

6. Ever-increasing laws and taxes mean that almost everyone is a lawbreaker. The citizen stays out of jail only due to prosecutorial discretion. Rebellions brew.

By this process one bureaucracy is placed upon another, rules multiply, reform efforts proliferate, and overseers are added. Any progress is temporary: New bursts of new energy are dissipated in the structure, which continues unabated. In the end, this process chokes the society to death.

Complexity is expensive. This is what happened in Rome. By the end of their empire people were desperate to avoid the state. Serious numbers of them (sometimes called *Begaude*) ran away to live with the barbarians. Historian R.M. Adams described the situation this way: *By the 5th Century, men were ready to abandon civilization itself to escape the fearful load of taxes.*

Small Business Ruined

Commerce is always choked by multiplying regulations, for the simple reason that regulation forbids adaptation... and small business is based upon rapid adaptation. New regulations prevent small businesses from adapting. Or, more likely, they prevent them from ever opening. (This is why black markets always flourish in oppressed economies: small operators cannot keep the rules and are forced to go around them.)

As a nation turns into a regulatory state, only the very largest and best-connected entities are able to get their concerns dealt with. Small firms are immensely vulnerable in such conditions, and they tend to merge with larger entities for survival's sake. This results in fewer but larger firms, each with as many ties to the state as they can obtain. It approximates the fascist model, minus the dictator.

Centralized systems address only the largest issues, pushing all others to the side. Again, this is a result of the system's structure, whether or not ill-intent is present.

The State Overtakes Society

Large central structures remove information, initiative, adaptation, and virtuous traditions from individual men and women, forcing them into a fixed structure. The crucial factor is that when regulation is *within* the individual, complex and beneficial interactions thrive. When regulation is *outside* the individual, personal virtues fail.

> When civilization is *within* people, they tend to cooperate and to develop themselves positively.

> When civilization is *imposed* upon people, they degenerate.

This damage is structural: Rather than referring to their own information and their own analysis, they defer to the judgment of the greater power, and lose themselves in the process. The result of this is denuded individuals and non-adaptive structures.

Do not assume that this cannot happen in the West. If you can, think back to equally human individuals in North Korea at the death of Kim Il Sung in 1994. Video from the time shows this in horrifying images. Millions of human beings, denuded just as mentioned above, were brought to such a state of dependence that some literally cried themselves to death following the death of their "great leader." At Kim's funeral, a radio announcer went so far as to implore the dead ruler to raise himself back to life:

> All the people have finally come forward to bid farewell to the soul of our Great Leader. Children, adults, young and old, all are crying out for our father, the Great Leader, and we all yearn for you to just open your eyes, at least once. Great Leader, who has been able to fulfill all the people's desires and dreams, our great father, can you not grant us this final wish?

These Koreans are not a subspecies of human beings; they are the same as us, and if we allow ourselves to travel the same road, what happened to them can happen to us. This is not a comforting thought, but it's true nonetheless.

The Intel State

The post-9/11 Protector State of the West has promoted intelligence agencies to special status. But intelligence operatives have never been benign beings. Their daily work involves forcing people to do things they'd rather not. That's what an "asset" usually is. This work corrupts the people involved. Their job is to steal information, hide it, lie about it, mislead people, blackmail people, and worse. People who do these things are not made better by them.

The people who work in these operations are the wrong people to entrust with power for other reasons as well. Intelligence agents have their views of the world formed by traumatic experiences. That leads them to bad conclusions.

And, of course, the results provided by these agencies have been far from stellar. Each new terrorist attack is another intelligence failure, although most people – their minds fixed to terror delivery systems[159] – are unprepared to consider it.

It is also worth noting that Intel agencies have a long and uninterrupted history of fighting each other. This is likely to get worse, not better. They will manipulate events (ignoring the lost lives) to position themselves above their competitors. The competitors, of course, will manipulate back. This makes for a lot of damage.

Still, people want to believe in Hollywood fantasies and we already have partial Intel states, resting on a foundation of mass fear. That makes it necessary for them to create more fear.

The Intel/Protector state has been working on the Big Data system noted above. It is, for them, an irresistible tool. They'll do anything they have to, to complete it and keep it.

---

[159] News networks.

Hollow States

The term "failed state" has been popular, but "hollow state" is a better term. A hollow state is one that exists in all outward ways, but that is "hollowed-out" and used by a criminal organization for cover.

Criminal organizations need safe havens, and hollow states provide them. These organizations make massive amounts of money from data theft operations, product piracy, traffic in illegal drugs, and in any number of additional operations. They can afford to create and support corrupt states, and so they do.

The hollow state is a perfect protection from other states. The system of Sovereign States is held with religious fervor by their operators and criminal organizations take advantage of this fact.

Western nations might want to stop criminal organizations that are stealing their data, but they aren't going to bomb another sovereign nation that has committed no aggression against it[160]. The non-state criminal group may have paid a dozen officials to obtain virtual control over territory and free operating rights, but they are not formal rulers. Rather, they rent the state's infrastructure.

Renting France, for example, would not be possible. But a war-torn African nation can be obtained. The ideal hollow state is one with clear international standing, but with massive internal problems. So long as a titular government remains in place, there is no requirement to provide social services. The state can be held responsible for any failure in this regard.

This is now the sensible strategy for all sorts of non-state groups. The West is adapting slowly to this[161] because they have difficulty compromising on the issue of national sovereignty.

"Smart" Centralization Programs

At some point, it is highly likely that a leader in the West will begin tearing down his or her bureaucracies and replacing them with technology. Because of the massive political forces involved (especially government employee unions) this will probably require one or more crises, but it's the sensible move and will probably be done at some point.

For example, it would be far, far cheaper for all Western states to eliminate their welfare structures and simply issue minimal credits to everyone.

Research programs, also, could be nationalized and better managed. They could go so far as to hire people for 4-year terms. If they solve their problem, they get a bonus, if not, they lose their job. The one area where this is most

---

[160] Except, sadly to say, for the United States.

[161] Usually by endorsing some type of trans-national war.

likely to happen is in medical research, because states have promised free medicine to their people and because it's so very expensive.

This technique might work for the first several years, but even with exceptional success, the process would soon stagnate. The steps might run like this:

1. Researchers cure Alzheimer's Disease.

2. The public cheers and the programs are greatly expanded.

3. The players figure out how to manipulate the programs.

4. Complex rules are made, then more rules to fix the gaps of the previous rules, and so on.

5. Complexity grinds everything to a halt.

None of this should be interpreted as implying that such reforms would be improvements. Centralization in these areas is just as bad as it is in others. But the initial impacts of these changes could be positive, and politicians seldom consider more than the initial impact.

Removing Troublemakers

States have never been benevolent organizations and they are not likely to become benevolent at any point in the future. That means that they will, in one way or another, move to get rid of people who make trouble for them[162]. All the elements of the police state are already present in the West; the only issue is who they are directed toward. This may seem like an overly dramatic statement, so an example is in order:

> A SWAT team charges out of their black van in the middle of the night and breaks down someone's door; they charge in with shields and automatic rifles. They drag out a bound man and drive away. If this person was a drug dealer, people are calm and satisfied. But what if a Jew or a homosexual were dragged out instead? The only difference lies in the victim – the mechanics are identical, and they are already in place.

It is crucial to understand that the people of Nazi Germany thought they were living in conditions of law and order. The Jews being dragged away were, in their minds, bad. Before states can remove troublemakers, they have to convince their masses that these people are threats. It may seem that this could not happen in the modern West, but it happened to the highly cultured people of Germany only two generations ago. These people were not a different species than the rest of us. What happened there can happen

---

[162] This is not referring to one party arresting their opposing party members. This refers to states removing people that oppose the state itself. Parties fighting parties is no real threat.

elsewhere. It's right to say "I won't let that happen," but it's wrong to say "it can't happen."

In general, states will be careful to avoid large actions that make them look bad, but there will be exceptions. These will probably be conducted via the "two steps forward, one step back" method.

Another method of removing troublemakers is to leak damaging stories to news organizations, then to create a criminal case against them. (Reporters make their careers with leaked information.) With public opinion against the troublemaking person or group, everyone expects them to be indicted and almost no one cares when they are. Furthermore, no one wants to step forward and say, "the state framed them," because only crazy people are believed to say such things.

Diversions

The Roman Empire kept its people happy with free food and massive entertainments – the proverbial "bread and circuses." The nations of the West are doing the same and will need to do more of the same. But the balance may have to shift toward more circuses and less bread, simply because they cannot afford endless handouts, especially now that those handouts include doctors, medicine and retirement income. There is simply a limit as to what the state can afford, especially with oceans of existing debt.

It will be increasingly in the state's interest to have entertainments that uphold its legitimacy, or at least to distract people from acting against their interests. Aside from influencing entertainment, the logical methods for the state to take would be along these lines:

- Elections are staggered so that at least one major vote is held every month, to keep people involved. Votes are cast online and may be changed until the last moment.

- Referenda are held on all matters of moral judgment. The majority rules.

- Trials are broadcast and the public votes to decide guilt or innocence. Juries are eliminated.

Laws regarding proper treatment of animals, loud music at night and a hundred other things can be shifted from the legislatures to the voting kiosks. News broadcasts would end with: *Have you voted this week? There are important cases to be decided and your vote counts! Full coverage here immediately after the polls close.*

A related area is the dissipation of instincts and energies that could be used against the state. This usually involves living vicariously through entertainment or sporting events, with active impulses drained away. Video games already play a role in this, and that role may increase. Not much is certain here, except that it is strongly in the state's interest to make this happen.

One final and obvious way of dissipating rebellious energies is by the use of drugs. Psychoactive drugs are already administered to children in schools. It will be easy for desperate states to build on this model. At some point in the future, if the current line of decline continues, drugs will be used. It's obvious, effective, and people are already used to the idea. It just has to be done carefully.

Harmless Ideologies

States since Rome (and probably earlier) have encouraged ideologies that they found harmless to their interests, and removed ideas that were against their interests. As always, large organizations tend to act amorally toward their own power.

As the West declines, states will have to discourage Christianity – it is simply not in their interest.[163] This has nothing to do with the truth of falsity of Christianity's tenets; it is due to the fact that Judaism and Christianity are bad ideologies for rulership.

Judeo-Christian beliefs are inherently subversive, even though many of their adherents are afraid to face that fact. Saving an endangered species, on the other hand, is anything *but* subversive. Environmental activists *need* a powerful state; in fact, they'd be best served by a dictator who was on their side.

Political activism is righteousness plus force. Politicians and institutions alike encourage and praise these activities. The more energy is spent in these ways, the more it's kept away from dangerous activities. Typical modes of activism are harmless to the state.

The Frame

One of the most crucial things for modern states to do – if they continue on the path of centralization and decline – will be to build a comprehensive mental framework through which its subjects view the world. The states that embraced "scientific socialism" tried long and hard to construct such frameworks and had some success doing so, but modern technology plus scientific manipulation techniques will make such systems far more effective and at less expense.

For simplicity's sake, we will simply call this unified mental and emotional framework "the frame." The key elements of constructing and maintaining the frame are the ability to inject clear messages into all significant public information sources, the manipulation of basic human instincts, public

---

[163] Huge numbers of American Evangelicals have formed a partnership of sorts with the US military complex, but that is contrary to the nature of Christianity and may not hold.

shaming and simple fear. At some point, escape from the frame becomes nearly impossible; like North Korea, only worse.

Within a frame, there are specific limits, within which everyone knows their thinking is safe. If you leave that box you first become "strange," then "an extremist," and finally "dangerous."

A crucial element of the frame is that a man is seen to exist only as part of a community. (This is popular already.) Next, this community-man is led to identify himself with one or more people who define the frame. These will typically be the experts seen on television[164]. To challenge the frame is to declare yourself less than human.

In effect, the public framers create a firm tribe/not tribe line. This is not done with fiery claims, but with endless, mundane repetition.

Another element of the frame that already exists is this: many people perceive that if something is important, it will be televised. What's on TV, then, becomes the central reality.

Another necessary element of this is the belief that thinking is for experts. Obviously this is silly; even an average intellect is very powerful, and thinking is for all humans, save the very few who are seriously damaged. Soon enough, a non-thinking person becomes a neutered person.

A generalized view of a fully framed world follows. Many elements of this are already in place:

1. Professionals engage in endless manipulations of the minds of the populace.

2. All public intellectuals are sycophants.

3. Rulers are not judged by their actions, but by their stated intent.

4. Entertainment continually reinforces the nobility and power of the state.

5. Education is mandatory, systematic conditioning.

6. Private learning is replaced with nonstop entertainment.

7. Sentences for crimes are astronomical, forcing you to confess or face life in prison.

8. All money is tracked and controlled. Everything is accounted for, nothing is beyond punishment.

9. All of your life is open to the rulers; they can get you no matter where you hide.

---

[164] These experts will not need to be unified; in fact it is far better for them to have certain conflicting opinions. They would always, however, support the state and remain within the borders of the Frame.

10. Everything is recorded.

11. All remain free at the mercy of the state.

12. Police can break and enter at any time.

13. Warrants are no longer required.

14. Anyone who tells you about a forthcoming law enforcement action against you will go to jail.

15. Anyone attempting independent thought threatens the self-esteem of everyone else. Think differently and you insult them all. Act differently and you will be attacked by all.

16. Harmless activities abound.

Denial

Most people don't want to believe a decline is possible, and if the elements of the decline listed here do happen, a huge number of people will go far out of their way to find plausible explanations for them; anything except facing the fact that bad things are happening. The alternative would demand too much of them – better to blank it out.

And this denial does *not* have to break at any point. It will be stable enough for a generation through fear and manipulation; after that it becomes self-enforcing.

The Great Default

The ability to create currency upon demand gave states in the 20th century a way to promise lifelong security to their citizens, and to deliver on them… at least for a generation or two. This process, however, cannot continue forever. As of 2017, the point where the national debt of most Western states could be paid has long been passed. The two obvious solutions, increased taxes and printing more currency, are no longer possible. The military, the embedded entitlements and the interest due are now more than tax receipts, so paying the debt down with current taxes is mathematically impossible. Even if the state were to create more debt-currency, the amount of interest that would be due upon it would be beyond payment.

Default will occur, in one way or another. How much of a shock to the world this may be is unknowable, but it could be very large.

The Reverse Economy

The money problems of the 21st century have a strange but obvious solution, which is something we might call a reverse economy. What follows here is speculation, but some system of this type will probably be instituted, merely because of necessity.

In a reverse economy:

- The traditional role of currency is replaced with the right to goods and services. These may or may not be denominated in currency names ("20 dollars for a toaster"), but the purchaser never has real currency, only a right to a certain amount of stuff.

- All credits are distributed by the state. A typical notice might say, *You have credit toward four meals worth of groceries.* With that, you could go to a store and choose ground beef, vegetables, fruit, bread, or similar items, but not gasoline.

- By doing approved work, you could obtain additional credit, which could be used for a wide variety of products or services, but the limits to these would be set by the state.

- The rates of "pay" for the work mentioned above would be set by the state and changed as required to control production – paying more or less for things that they presume are needed or that are in surplus.

- A basic level of sustenance will be promised to all. Government simply credits everyone for basic groceries and a cheap apartment. The welfare bureaus are eliminated, reducing the state's burden. (This will be very popular.)

- If you don't collect the goods credited to you within a specified time, those credits disappear.

- Super-strong biometric identification systems will be required. Realistically, all humans will have to be fitted with some type of non-removable ID device.

- Powerful computer programs will mimic market interactions in virtual space, and then distribute credits accordingly. In other words, a virtual free market will exist as an advanced computer model. This will be the *only* free market that will exist. The results from this model will decide how credits are distributed in the real world.

- Such a system requires that there be no possible escape. If there were, the system would fail. This is the lesson that the Soviets learned in Germany, requiring the Berlin Wall. This applies both to individuals and to "rogue nations." Violence will be used to keep everyone in the system.

Every element of this can be justified in one or more ways. For example, limiting the choices for your personal credits can be advertised as preventing non-farmers from obtaining fertilizer for bomb-making.

At some point, this will be the way states have to go[165]. It will probably be the only path left to them. One question is how many Christians will take action against it. The system described above bears a great resemblance to the ominous predictions of Revelation 13:17 – *That no man might buy or sell, save he that had the mark, or the name of the beast, or the number of his name.* But, as long as the ID devices cannot be described as "marks," many Christians will acquiesce.

Such a system, however, would require a perfect virtual market model, accounting for weather, social influences,and more. Thsee predictions would have to reach years into the future for many goods. Were the program to fail, plagues, mass starvation and associated horrors could be the result.

The Great Entropy

The Great Entropy is what happens if the advocates of "global governance" get their wish, and it is the worst possible outcome.

What if all the world's states cooperate together, and all decline together? How does that end? Or does it?

The horrifying thing about this scenario is that the normal breakdown leading to a dark age is avoided. This means that humanity, as a species, descends past their usual reset point. Normally, that cannot be done, but with the Big Data manipulation system we described earlier, such a reset point could be passed without difficulty. This would create a permanent decline, broken only by some kind of natural disaster.

The examples we have of people being held within conditions of permanent decline are war zones, housing projects and the worst prisons… which are not comforting thoughts. Humanity *can* decline horribly, and such conditions do not have an inherent endpoint. If states can hold together, humanity can be degraded far beyond the normal dark ages reset. What this means for the species is hard to gauge.

In conditions of global governance and universal manipulation, the whole operation withers together, lifestyles steadily degrade, and starvation returns, even if news of it is suppressed. States covertly promote drug use and activities that cause early deaths, simply to reduce medical outlays. They would probably need to align with religion at some point, that so much death can be addressed with theologies of suffering.

By remaining interlocked, states would be able to stave off collapse from outside forces, but will require,

- More distraction.

- Lower standards of living.

---

[165] The current (2017) push for banning cash and instituting negative interest rates would lay a foundation for such a system.

- More surveillance, control and regulation.

- Substitutes for escape. Drugs, movies, etc.

- More legitimization. Worship of great men, terrorist events (real or staged), wars, invaders.

- Ideologies of suffering.

Wars might be avoided by the use of inanimate threats, such as Global Warming. This would make things easier for the states, since publicity is far cheaper than actual war.

In real life, such a system might not hold together terribly well. People seeking power will always seek more of it, which could cause the system to crack. Nonetheless, such systems can certainly form and hold partially. This would probably include a number of hollow states and large, "soft totalitarian" states. It is possible (but probably unlikely) that a few "less ruled" states would be tolerated. These would have to be well-separated from the biggest states and able to survive without international trade.

At some point even this type of system would fail. The likely scenario would be a natural disaster or plague. Inter-ruler battles, possibly including nuclear weapons, are also possible. There seems to be no inherent time limit to this process; it could preserve conditions of deep suffering and depravity for centuries. But aside from prison camps (where, in the extreme, people simply lay down and die), we have no good examples to base guesses upon.

The Declining Mind

This line of projection seems like a dark fantasy but much of it is already happening and all of it has happened before in one place or another. Dark, yes; fantasy, no.

Again: denial is a very strong thing. To face these things openly will be horrifying and demanding; most people will prefer to escape it at any cost. So, the first characteristic of the mind of a human sitting in the midst of such a decline is simple denial: "It's okay, I still have my puppy," "things will turn back around," "it's not so bad," and so on.

Associated with this is another characteristic: Failure to internalize experiences. By this, we mean that people don't take experiences within themselves; they keep them outside. People read books, not to internalize their lessons, but to pass a test or to impress someone. The self never changes. A Catholic of this type can attending a service at the Vatican and see only "the Pope show," not being affected internally. She will tell her friends about it, but she will talk about what she *saw*, not what it did for her. Life is an external thing and one's self can always be avoided by plugging in to some form of entertainment.

With no internal references (because of denial, lack of internalization, drugs and other factors), the only things that end up mattering are local references. If such people maintain their relative position versus the people they see every day, they will accept conditions of decline passively. People will care that they keep their balcony garden more than they care about their privacy and their liberty. So long as they have the little, external, daily things (excuses to say all things remain as they always have been), they will ride the tide downward; they may complain, but they will never act to change things.

Again, this *has* happened in the past and it most definitely *can* happen again. Actually, it is happening in smaller ways continually; the chief issues are the percentage of people who operate this way and how many are willing to do more than complain.

The De-Conquest

Having taken a look at the process of decline, we will turn around and examine the reverse: A De-Conquest.

As we mentioned in Chapter Eleven, decentralized ways of life have not only formed, but have been soundly established. In fact, the more intelligent and well-read a person may become, the more likely he or she is to hold to some form of pro-liberty philosophy.

Some essential elements of a less-ruled or un-ruled world are these:

1. Free human action.
2. Unregulated trade.
3. Individual or distributed defense.
4. The frustration of talent is a cardinal offense.
5. Unobstructed transportation.
6. Decentralized communications.
7. Ad hoc grouping and temporary hierarchies.
8. Market above state.
9. Self-regulation rather than legislated regulation.
10. Temporary Autonomous Zones.
11. Distributed justice and enforcement on the common law model.
12. Breakup of states into multiple jurisdictions.
13. Creativity overtakes Scarcity.

The process of going from the current world of massive, controlling states to a freer world will involve many small steps and can take multiple directions.

It is impossible to define them all now, but some of the more obvious ones are the following:

Federations Of Mini-States

The basic model for this is Switzerland, although the new federations may deviate from a pure Swiss model.

In all likelihood, the right to vote within these mini-states would go only to residents who had earned it. That would probably be done in the following ways:

- Property ownership above a minimal level
- Successful military training and continued readiness
- Passing a difficult test on the operation and philosophy of governance

Such states would have small, adaptive military units, featuring adaptive intelligence at the point of enemy contact. In other words, the brains at the tip of the spear. Orders would be *what*, not *how*.

Non-compliance

Through the 20th century, the governments of the West thrived on nearly 100% compliance. Accordingly, they have built that assumption into their operations and now rely upon it. Automatic obedience, however, is not a historic norm and ruling systems have become brittle in this way.

If and when the people of the West stop complying automatically, the governments of the West may find themselves in a difficult situation. Either they will take it quietly, allowing non-compliance to succeed and spread; or they can crush non-compliance with violence, thus damaging their legitimacy.

With a disobedience level of just 10% of the general populace, the governments of the West would be in serious trouble. If 20% stopped complying, those governments would fall apart.

Furthermore, any system that might be rebuilt in the ashes of the current Western governments would be very different.

Anti-State Money

Anonymous, digital cash has a number of benefits, one of them being that it solves the problem of identity theft. With no identity tied to money, there's nothing to steal. Nonetheless, governments world-over oppose digital currencies. The reason is two-fold:

1. The control of currency is of immense effect.
2. Widespread use of digital cash with encryption would mean that governments could never know who paid whom, and in what

amount. Tax compliance would slide toward the voluntary... and if it were voluntary, they'd collect next to nothing.

Anonymous currency – from silver coins to anonymized Bitcoin – is anti-state money. But this issue is much deeper than just that:

> If and when anti-state money comes into widespread use, the expansion method of Western civilization will be restored.

Untraceable income would put surplus back into the hands of the people who created it. Individuals would be able finance projects without bankers. Money games would be played only by confirmed crooks. Investments would once again chase yield, not trading price. If a de-conquest occurs, this will be a major component.

It is worth adding that commerce plus anonymity equals the impossibility of totalitarianism; even of discrimination.

Territorial Pullback

Given that the governments of the West are buried in debt, there very well may come a moment when they are simply unable to provide everything they've promised. And if that happens, they'll have to pull back in one way or another.

The most likely pullback is to their core cities, the major urban centers. And pulling back means cutting services to outlying areas. In some urban centers such plans are already in place.

The result of such a pullback would be highly controlled major cities, abandoned rural areas, and middle zones where both services and taxes are in a middle range. In this case, governments would try to maintain control in the abandoned and middle zones with inexpensive technologies like drones, but they'd be kept from overstepping by the fact that they need cooperation from those outer zones. Highways and railroad tracks must be kept clean, food shipments must be permitted, and so on.

The promising part about abandoned areas is that they'd be left to evolve without state control, and they would likely return to a proper Western model.

A New Safety Model

The old safety model was central control and central power. This model was not instituted because it provided the best safety, but because it was the model of the empire.

The new model is distributed power. Safety applications of this model could be many, such as:

- Every responsible adult plays some role.

- More responsible and better-paid policemen.
- An explicit preference for Peace Officers rather than Law Enforcers.
- Cell phones used as distributed justice tools.
- A Swiss model of territorial defense.

With each person involved in the process, evidence is gathered by anyone in the area. Non-specialists are almost always much closer to the scene of any crime anyway. Instead of 911, we can have a simple snapshot and text message upload to 555 for immediate local distribution.

This system would also be a powerful impediment to bad policemen. With thousands of camera cell phones surrounding him, the bad cop getting away with his crime becomes a remote possibility.

The obvious result of such a system is that more crooks get caught, more streets stay safer, cops become respectable, and the cost of safety plummets. But more importantly, everyone feels like they have a stake in the game and they begin to tend to their own world, rather than leaving it to central systems.

A fascinating passage is found in Alexis de Tocqueville's *Democracy in America*, written in 1835. In it, you can see the conditions that naturally develop in less-ruled and un-ruled places:

> In America, the means available to the authorities to uncover crime and to arrest criminals are small in number... However, I doubt whether crime evades punishment less often in any other country...Everyone feels involved in providing evidence of the offense and in apprehending the offender... I saw inhabitants of a county where a major crime had been perpetrated spontaneously form committees with the aim of arresting the guilty man and handing him over to the courts. In Europe, the criminal is a luckless fellow, fighting to save his life from the authorities; the population, to a degree, watches as he struggles. In America, he is an enemy of the human race and has everyone entirely against him.

Once systems such as these are in place, justice can re-form along distributed lines, with competitive agencies providing services that are a cross between insurance, law, police work and bounty hunting. Once again, a long document would be required to describe such services sufficiently, so we will abstain.

Resilient Communities

As states break down and a mix of free and unfree locations exist (and probably struggle), it may make sense to form strong, autonomous communities. These will be towns where the residents form strong bonds to assist and defend each other.

Such resilient communities form naturally in un-ruled frontier areas, but since there has been no frontier for generations, this is now a novel idea. However, people are already working on resilient communities and aside from the usual difficulties of human life, such communities will be formed with little trouble.

It is also almost certain that such resilient communities will form links[166] with one another and assist one another. They may also compete for the most talented people.

Private Charity Returns

Once people hold their own surplus in their own hands, private charity will almost certainly return with vigor[167]. Self-reliance and charity have always gone together... at least while people controlled their surplus production. When people keep their surplus, actual care for one's fellows tends to return, along with self-regard from it.

It is important to consider that *obligation is the enemy of compassion*. When we are forced to give charity, we get no internal benefit from the exercise. In fact, we usually get just the opposite. But when we give willingly – to people we think are suffering unjustly – we honor our own sense of goodness. We feel good about ourselves, we feel compassion for others, we are proud to be making the world a better place. That the state stole this from productive men is one of the greatest indictments that can be made against it.

In Virtus, Libertas

In virtus, libertas is Latin for, *In righteousness, freedom*, and this is a great truth of life. Without virtues such as courage, integrity, honesty and compassion, liberty can never be retained. Liberty is only for evolved humans, containing civilization within themselves and able both to produce and to defend. Only these are suited to post-institutional life. Others must be excluded to one level or another, in one way or another. Accomplishing this will give outward form to the new society of humans.

---

[166] I use the word "links" rather than "bonds" carefully here. Links are voluntary, while the idea of a bond implies permanence and rigidity. I think links, sustained by natural commonalities and interests, will be the better model.

[167] Private charities do certainly exist under the rule of states, but at an understandably low level. The average man's extra money is removed before he ever sees it, leaving him with only scraps to give the needy.

People who seek to put their responsibilities off on others, who seek to avoid work, who wish to intimidate others, are suited only to the lives of slaves or masters. Such people are not compatible with actual liberty. Certainly children[168], who have yet to develop these characteristics, can find places in a truly free society, but when they are grown, they will either hold these basic qualities or they will tend to tear down their free society. There is no other choice, only more or less willingness to face the fact.

This has always been true in every chapter of human history. In virtus, libertas. All other paths lead eventually to ruin.

The Demise Of Plato's Magic And The Great Trade

As states unwind, both Plato's magic idealism and the Great Trade sublimating human conflicts will unwind with them. This will require adjustment.

Individuals will have to get over the idea of getting more than they've earned, then roll up their sleeves and create for themselves. They will also have to accept the fact that they are conflicted beings and get serious about making peace with themselves.

In time it will be seen that these emotional tricks were never really necessary. Plato's deal, in particular, will be considered something akin to the story of Eden written in Greek letters, wherein Plato offers men a shortcut to the power of the gods, men accept the deal, then suffer for ages.

Privatization

The continual privatization of state services would be the smoothest path to de-conquest. (No route will be especially smooth, since the people who seek high office are not types who will relinquish power easily.) That said, privatization no longer remains a serious possibility. Before 9/11 it was. Now, with massive controlling states, the chances of a smooth passage have diminished.

Nonetheless, if and where privatization can be arranged, it makes for a smooth, manageable transition. All of the "scary" issues, such as firemen, roads and policemen are easy to solve, once people stop panicking over them. Even the most ridiculous, complex systems are streamlined and made efficient once people make or lose money on them.

New Spiritualities

New theologies will certainly develop during the process of de-conquest. To a far greater extent than most people have realized (even theologians), millennia of state rule have deeply affected theology.

---

[168] The same, of course, applies to mentally damaged people and other victims of cruel chance. Fortunately, they are few in number.

Abraham was no statist, nor was Moses. Jesus certainly was not. Regardless, the religions based upon them have taken on the assumption that states are ordained of God.

As states fail, the statist assumptions of theology will change, and the beliefs that emerge from this change will be far closer to the true intents of their non-statist founders.

Defending Virtue And Merit

The smartest child in school suffers for his abilities. The superior man suffers for his virtues. Envy reigns and even children learn to degrade themselves in order to escape its sting.

This situation will not survive a process of de-conquest. The smart child will not be placed in a situation where he or she is forced to deny the best parts of themself in order to escape torment. The innovator, who was previously an insult to the prestige of the state, will be freely rewarded for his work by an unregulated market.

Those Who Act Create The Future Their Own Way

No single individual, under the rule of states, can honestly think he or she will change the course of the world. States direct the course of mankind; young men dying on battlefields determine whether changes are successful or not.

In an un-ruled world, however, any individual who cares enough, expends enough effort, and who learns from his mistakes can chart a new course for the world.

Consider: There remain some people in the West who are willing to sacrifice for their beliefs. Among them are people of these types[169]:

- Homeschoolers.
- Some private school parents.
- Bitcoiners.
- Human rights advocates.
- Bio-hackers.
- Some journalists.
- People who emigrate for economic improvement.
- Parts of the encryption industry.
- Many missionaries

---

[169] At one time, openly gay people had to sacrifice to live their own way, but that is seldom required any more. A couple of generations ago, civil rights activists sacrificed, but most of those involved have now passed.

- Messianic Jews.
- Ex-Muslims.
- Some religious groups.
- Some Whistle-Blowers.

Through all of our lifetimes, most of these people have fought not only to move forward, but to avoid problems with states or state-aligned institutions. How much further might they have progressed if they didn't have to fight two adversaries at once?

In an un-ruled world, or even in a less-ruled world, these individuals *can* change history. In those conditions, the first man or woman to take up an important new job sets the course for all who follow. They *do* change the world.

And Then...

No one knows how far and in which directions humanity is able to progress. What will we discover once we have private space travel? What can nanotechnology do for us? What happens when genetic engineering allows us to control our own evolution? What faces us if we learn to conquer aging?

No one knows the answer to these questions, and only one of the two choices now facing the West gives us any hope of finding out.

Back To The Beginning

> *The evil of the world is made possible by nothing but*
> *the sanction you give it.*
> – Ayn Rand

Think back to the beginning of this book and to the first group of stationary farmers in the Tigris-Euphrates valley. What would they have been like if they hadn't been overrun by nomads and herded into mini-states, like sheep into pens? Where might humanity be now?

Do you think the organization of humanity into groups of *rulers* and *ruled* has been helpful toward progress? Would our pre-Sumerian farmers have chosen it willingly?

Was living as *the ruled* beneficial to the first society of farmers? They began as free and prosperous people. Their religion may seem strange to us, but we can certainly understand their love of production and their joy in discovering music and art and metallurgy and fabric and a hundred other important things that had never been before. After existing under state rule for a long time, this same group of people sunk to a tragic view of their lives: *Created for one purpose only: to serve.*

Now, consider this: The process that did this to the first society has never completely stopped; only a few temporary escapes have been made. This is a dangerous thought, but it is very definitely true.

The Denial section above was important. We said that the denial of a decline does not have to break. And, in actuality, *it has not*... for some eight thousand years.

Humanity is not a race that should be herded, reaped and used like sheep, yet that is precisely what has happened to us since 6000 B.C. Nonetheless, most of us remain in a denial that says, "it's not so bad; it'll be okay." We exist in this condition without even realizing it; it seems completely normal to us and probably has since the third or fourth generations.

We give our sanction to rulership because anything else would be far too strange. It would call too much into question. All the world knows that people are supposed to be treated like sheep and that rulers are the order of the universe. Rulership is that which was, and is, and ever shall be.

There is no sensible reason why humans should be grouped, ordered around and abused as they are, and it is nothing but their mass acquiescence that permits it to continue.